Prerog Wills - Geneol Office (15)

HANDBOOK ON IRISH GENEALOGY

The Great Famine : Hardship in Ireland caused by the failure of the potatoe crop in Black '47.

HANDBOOK ON IRISH GENEALOGY

How to trace your ancestors and relatives in Ireland

HERALDIC ARTISTS LTD.

Heraldic Artists Ltd., Trinity Street, Dublin.

First Impression	1970
Second Impression	1973
Third Impression (Enlarged Edition)	1976

Copyright — Heraldic Artists Ltd.

© 1976

I.S.B.N.   0   9502455   4   2

Library of Congress Washington
Copyright Certificate No. A F 37020

Printed in Ireland by Lithographic Universal Ltd., Bray, Co. Wicklow.

CONTENTS

A Blessing for Departing Emigrants.

INTRODUCTION

This book is intended for those with an interest in their Irish ancestry. Its purpose is to give them as briefly as possible the facts about genealogical research in Ireland. Today a growing number of people feel the need to seek out their family origins however humble these may have been. Why this should be so at the present time need not concern us here. In any case nothing could be more natural than for civilised man to take an interest in his ancestors. For each of us this interest has a personal origin. Man is an inheritor as well as a transmitter and people are curiously actuated to know what kind of people their forebears were — how and where and when they lived and what they did. For this is the kind of knowledge that enables them to understand themselves — and others — all the better and instils in them a deeper appreciation of the land of their forebears.

In ancestry research as in other types of research a proper approach is essential if worthwhile results are to be achieved. Much of course will depend on the amount of information already known about an ancestor. As a general rule it is advisable to check first records at central level before moving on to local sources.

Various avenues of approach appropriate to what is already known about an ancestor are suggested in the course of this book. There are sections on record offices, shipping lists, wills, land records, parish church registers and gravestone inscriptions. Included also is a map section containing thirty two maps — one for each county — reproduced from Samuel Lewis's Atlas of Ireland, 1837. These maps highlight state parishes and baronies into which counties were formerly divided. It is essential for the family chronicler to appreciate the importance of such bygone administrative divisions since they formed the basis for such vital government records as tithe, valuation, voter and census listings.

This guide is specifically designed to enable people of Irish descent to undertake on their own the work of tracing their ancestors so that by personal involvement in their own research they can experience the joy of exploration and the thrill of discovery as they journey back in time to make their acquaintance with quaint and lovable characters that only Ireland would have produced in a day that has been.

HERALDIC ARTISTS LTD. Trinity Street Dublin 1976

How to trace your Ancestors and

Relatives in Ireland

ORIGIN OF ANCESTOR

If you have Irish blood in you, you will almost certainly be proud of the fact. Indeed you may wish to add to the pleasure of your holiday in Ireland by indulging in a spot of ancestor hunting in the land of your forebears.

Let's say, for example sake, your grandfather Patrick Ryan left Boggaun, Co. Tipperary for America in the year 1847. Before coming to Ireland you had the good sense to inspect his gravestone in Calvary Cemetery in New York which shows that he died on February 7, 1888 aged 61 years. It is clear therefore that he was born in 1827 and was 20 years of age when he landed in New York.

The first important step is to determine the exact location of Boggaun. From *The Alphabetical Index to the Townlands and Towns of Ireland,* a copy of which any good library will have, we learn that Boggaun is the name of a townland in the County Tipperary, barony of Ikerrin, civil parish of Killavinoge and Poor Law Union of Roscrea. A word of explanation on Irish topographical divisions may be helpful at this point. A townland is the smallest administrative division of land in Ireland, with an average area of three hundred and fifty acres.

Parishes are of two kinds, civil and ecclesiastical. The civil parish, as the name implies, is a state unit of territorial divison for census and valuation purposes. The ecclesiastical parish is the normal unit of local Church administration and generally embraces a number of civil parishes.

The baronies, over three hundred in all, represent divisions of great antiquity based on the Gaelic clan and family holdings.

9

No. of Sheet of the Ordnance Survey Maps.	Townlands and Towns.	Area in Statute Acres.			County.	Barony.	Parish.	Poor Law Union in 1857.
		A.	R.	P.				
32	Boceshil . . .	80	2	2	Leitrim . . .	Mohill . . .	Mohill . . .	Mohill .
87	Bofara . . .	132	1	28	Mayo . . .	Murrisk . . .	Aghagower .	Westport .
9, 10	Bofealan . . .	78	1	28	Cavan . . .	Tullyhaw . . .	Templeport .	Bawnboy .
47, 59	Bofeenaun . .	659	0	10a	Mayo . .	Tirawley . . .	Addergoole .	Castlebar .
101, 102	Bofickil . . .	420	2	12	Cork, W.R. .	Bear . . .	Kilcatherine .	Castletown
25	Bog . . .	190	0	36	Waterford .	Decies without Drum	Kilbarrymeaden .	Kilmacthomas .
70	Bogagh . . .	214	0	31	Donegal .	Raphoe . . .	Raphoe . . .	Strabane .
21	Bogagh . . .	168	1	24	Londonderry .	Tirkeeran . .	Clondermot .	Londonderry .
90	Bogagh Glebe .	596	1	15	Donegal .	Banagh . . .	Kilcar . .	Glenties .
91	Bogare . . .	687	1	5	Kerry . .	Dunkerron South .	Kilcrohane .	Kenmare . .
53	Bogay . . .	91	2	7	Donegal .	Kilmacrenan . .	Aghanunshin .	Letterkenny .
47, 55	Bogay Glebe .	156	1	29	Donegal .	Raphoe . . .	Allsaints . .	Londonderry .
55	Bogbane . .	148	3	28	Tyrone .	Dungannon Middle .	Killyman . .	Dungannon .
26	Bog Commons	93	1	32	Kilkenny .	Kells . . .	Coolaghmore .	Callan . .
35	Bogderries .	412	0	14	King's Co. .	Eglish . . .	Eglish . .	Parsonstown .
47	Bog East . .	105	3	25	Wexford . .	Forth . . .	Mayglass . .	Wexford . .
27, 33	Bogesky . . .	305	1	31	Cavan .	Upper Loughtee .	Lavey . . .	Cavan . .
12, 21	Boggagh . .	139	1	2	Waterford .	Coshmore & Coshbride	Lismore & Mocollop	Lismore . .
11, 12	Boggaghbaun .	626	1	29	Waterford .	Coshmore & Coshbride	Lismore & Mocollop	Lismore .
30	Boggagh (Conran) .	150	1	26	Westmeath .	Clonlonan . .	Kilcleagh . .	Athlone . .
11, 12	Boggaghduff .	453	1	9	Waterford .	Coshmore & Coshbride	Lismore & Mocollop	Lismore .
36	Boggagh Eighter	234	3	24	Westmeath .	Clonlonan . .	Kilcleagh . .	Athlone .
36	Boggagh (Fury) .	106	1	12	Westmeath .	Clonlonan . .	Kilcleagh . .	Athlone .
36	Boggagh (Malone) .	89	2	39	Westmeath .	Clonlonan . .	Kilcleagh . .	Athlone .
13, 17	Boggan . . .	267	1	16	Carlow .	Forth . . .	Ballon . .	Carlow .
17	Boggan . .	230	3	39	Carlow .	Forth . . .	Barragh . .	Carlow .
17	Boggan . .	460	2	24	Kilkenny .	Crannagh . .	Tullaroan . .	Kilkenny . .
5	Boggan . .	119	2	22	Meath . .	Lower Kells . .	Moybolgue .	Kells . .
40, 42	Bogganfin . .	163	1	31	Roscommon .	Athlone . .	Kilmeane . .	Roscommon .
49, 52	Bogganfin . .	292	2	4	Roscommon .	Athlone . .	Kiltoom . .	Athlone .
49, 52	Bogganfin . .	105	3	15	Roscommon .	Athlone . .	St. Peter's .	Athlone . .
52	BOGGANFIN T.	—			Roscommon .	Athlone . .	St. Peter's .	Athlone .
50, 53	Bogganstown .	211	0	15	Meath . .	Dunboyne . .	Dunboyne . .	Dunshaughlin .
43, 44	Bogganstown .	395	3	31	Meath . .	Upper Deece .	Culmullin . .	Dunshaughlin .
42, 43	Bogganstown Lower	37	2	8	Wexford . .	Forth . . .	Drinagh . .	Wexford . .
42	Bogganstown Upper	26	1	35	Wexford . .	Forth . . .	Drinagh . .	Wexford . .
105, 115	Boggaun . . .	98	1	31	Galway .	Loughrea . .	Kilchreest . .	Loughrea . .
21	Boggaun . . .	108	3	18	Leitrim .	Carrigallen . .	Oughteragh .	Bawnboy .
11	Boggaun . . .	984	1	30	Leitrim . .	Drumahaire . .	Cloonlogher .	Manorhamilton .
23	Boggaun . . .	102	1	39	Tipperary, N.R. .	Ikerrin . . .	Killavinoge .	Roscrea .
30	Boggaunreagh .	86	0	3	King's Co. .	Garrycastle . .	Reynagh . .	Parsonstown .
32	Boggauns . .	416	0	26	Galway .	Ballymoe . .	Kilbegnet . .	Glennamaddy .
32	Boggauns . .	420	0	3	Galway . .	Killian . . .	Killian . .	Mountbellew .
95	Boggra . . .	184	1	14	Cork, W.R. .	Kinalmeaky . .	Templemartin .	Bandon . .
59	Boggy . . .	678	1	28	Mayo . .	Tirawley . . .	Addergoole .	Castlebar .
11	Boggyheary . .	90	2	2	Dublin .	Nethercross . .	Killossery . .	Balrothery .
46, 47, 59	Boghadoon . .	1,197	0	0	Mayo . .	Tirawley . . .	Addergoole .	Castlebar .
27, 31	Boghall . . .	344	0	11	Kildare .	Offaly West . .	Harristown .	Athy .
8, 9	Boghil . . .	371	1	23	Clare .	Corcomroe . .	Kilfenora . .	Ennistymon .
18, 19	Boghilboy . .	228	1	1	Londonderry .	Coleraine . .	Desertoghill .	Coleraine .
3, 7	Boghill . . .	341	2	39	Londonderry .	North East Liberties of Coleraine . .	Coleraine . .	Coleraine . .
68, 69	Boghilmore Island .	8	0	1	Galway . .	Moycullen . .	Moycullen . .	Galway . .
12, 13	Boghlone . .	306	3	31	Queen's Co. .	Maryborough East .	Clonenagh & Clonagheen	Mountmellick .
16	Boghouse . .	77	2	36	Carlow .	Idrone East . .	Fennagh . .	Carlow .
63,64,73,74	Boghtaduff .	931	3	4	Mayo . .	Costello . . .	Castlemore .	Castlereagh .
45	Bogland . . .	109	3	34	Wicklow .	Arklow . . .	Arklow . .	Rathdrum .
99	Bogpark . . .	138	0	4	Galway . .	Clonmacnowen .	Clontuskert .	Ballinasloe .
98	Bogside . . .	35	2	0	Donegal .	Banagh . . .	Killaghtee .	Donegal .

Facsimile copy of page 157 indicating exact location of Boggaun, Co. Tipperary.

The Poor Law Unions were constituted under the Poor Law Act of 1838 when the country was divided into districts or unions in which the local rateable people were financially responsible for the upkeep of the poor in each area. The Unions comprised multiples of townlands within an average radius of ten miles, usually with a large market town as centre in which the 'Poor House' was located. Many of these 'Poor Houses' may still be seen and many are still in use for other purposes of course.

Should it become necessary to do some map reading in the course of your research, it is useful to know that the Large Sheet Ordnance Survey maps on a scale of six inches to one mile show in great detail all the features of a given area. The maps are available from the Government Publications Sales Office, G.P.O. Arcade, Dublin, price £1 per sheet.

If despite your best efforts a particular place-name defies all attempts at identification the Place names Commission in the Phoenix Park will be glad to assist you.

Having established that Boggaun occurs in the civil parish of Killavinoge, we now turn to *A Topographical Dictionary of Ireland* by Samuel Lewis in order to learn a little about the area from which Patrick Ryan came. Lewis' article reads as follows — 'Killavinoge or Clonmore, — a parish, in the union of Roscrea, barony of Ikerrin, county of Tipperary, and province of Munster, 4 miles (N.E.) from Templemore, on the road from that place to Rathdowney; containing 3557 inhabitants. It comprises 8160 statute acres, including a considerable quantity of bog; and contains the residence of Dromard. It is a rectory and vicarage, in the diocese of Cashel, forming part of the union of Templemore; the tithe rent-charge is £277/18/6, and there is a glebe of 36 acres. In the Roman Catholic divisions the parish forms part of the district of Templemore, and contains a chapel.'

CIVIL RECORDS

Our search now leads us to an examination of the great property valuations of the last century with a view to tracing the family holding of Patrick Ryan.

PRIMARY VALUATION OF TENEMENTS.

PARISH OF KILLAVINOGE.

No. and Letters of Reference to Map.		Names. Townlands and Occupiers.	Immediate Lessors.	Description of Tenement.	Area. A. R. P.	Net Annual Value. Land. £ s. d.	Buildings. £ s. d.	Total. £ s. d.
		BALLYSORRELL, BIG. *(Ord. Ss. 29 & 30.)*						
1		John Maher,	Frederick Lidwell, Esq.	Moory pasture,	11 1 26	4 15 0	—	4 15 0
2		John Maher,	Frederick Lidwell, Esq.	Land,	94 0 2	59 5 0	—	59 5 0
—	a	Michael Trehy,	John Maher,	House, offices, & garden,	0 2 24	0 10 0	1 0 0	1 10 0
3	A a	Thomas Bennett,	Frederick Lidwell, Esq.	House, offices, and land,	20 1 27	11 10 0	1 15 0	13 5 0
—	B	Thomas Bennett,	Frederick Lidwell, Esq.	Land,	32 1 33	8 10 0	—	8 10 0
—	A b	John Cormack,	Thomas Bennett,	House,		—	0 15 0	0 15 0
—	c	Margaret Russell,	Thomas Bennett,	House and garden,	0 0 18	0 1 0	0 14 0	0 15 0
4		Frederick Lidwell, Esq.	In fee,	Land,	37 2 5	13 15 0	—	13 15 0
—	a	Margaret Henley,	Frederick Lidwell, Esq.	House,		—	0 10 0	0 10 0
—	b	Margaret Ahern,	Frederick Lidwell, Esq.	House,		—	0 5 0	0 5 0
—	c	Catherine Fogarty,	Frederick Lidwell, Esq.	House and garden,	0 1 31	0 5 0	0 10 0	0 15 0
5		Martin Carroll,	Frederick Lidwell, Esq.	Land,	62 1 30	30 15 0	—	30 15 0
—	a	Vacant,	Martin Carroll,	House and offices,		—	1 0 0	1 0 0
6	{ a	Michael Kerin,	Fredk. Lidwell, Esq. {	House, offices, & land,	31 3 13	{ 6 10 0	1 0 0	7 10 0
	{ b	Patrick Carey,		House and land,		{ 6 10 0	0 10 0	7 0 0
7		William Ryan,	Frederick Lidwell, Esq.	House and land,	20 2 27	11 10 0	0 15 0	12 5 0
8	{ a	Patrick Healy,	Frederick Lidwell, Esq.	House, offices, & land,		{ 15 0 0	1 0 0	16 0 0
	{ b	Daniel Lahy,	Frederick Lidwell, Esq.	House and land,	79 1 27	{ 3 15 0	0 5 0	4 0 0
	{ c	Michael Maher,	Frederick Lidwell, Esq.	House and land,		{ 3 15 0	0 10 0	4 5 0
	{	Fredk. Lidwell, Esq.	In fee,	Land,		{ 7 10 0	—	7 10 0
—		Patrick Healy & parts.	Frederick Lidwell, Esq.	Bog,	122 0 38	0 10 0	—	0 10 0
—	d	Thomas Carroll,	Frederick Lidwell, Esq.	House and garden,	0 0 12	0 1 0	0 14 0	0 15 0
9		Gt. S. & W. Railway Co.	In fee,	Land and railway,	9 2 3	6 5 0	—	6 5 0
				Total,	523 0 36	190 12 0	11 3 0	201 15 0
		BALLYSORRELL, LITTLE. *(Ord. Ss. 23, 24, 29, & 30.)*						
1		William Bennett,	Dudley Byrne, Esq.	House and land,	1 0 0	0 10 0	0 15 0	1 5 0
2	A a	Dudley Byrne, Esq.	Philip Gowan, Esq.	House, offices, and land,	133 0 19	70 5 0	16 10 0	86 15 0
—	B	Dudley Byrne, Esq.	Philip Gowan, Esq.	Land,	113 3 26	52 5 0	—	52 5 0
		Dudley Byrne, Esq.	Philip Gowan, Esq.	Bog,	107 3 20	0 10 0	—	0 10 0
—	A b	William Kirwan,	Dudley Byrne, Esq.	House and garden,	0 0 30	0 2 0	0 5 0	0 7 0
3		Daniel Dwyer,	Dudley Byrne, Esq.	House and land,	7 2 24	3 10 0	0 5 0	3 15 0
4		Gt. S. & W. Railway Co.	In fee,	Railway,	5 1 24	4 0 0	—	4 0 0
				Total,	369 0 23	131 2 0	17 15 0	148 17 0
		BOGGAUN. *(Ord. S. 23).*						
1		James Ryan,	George Goold, Esq.	Land,	29 0 7	15 10 0	—	15 10 0
2		Jeremiah Commerford,	George Goold, Esq.	House and land,	38 1 27	18 0 0	0 15 0	18 15 0
3		Michael Quinlan,	George Goold, Esq	Land,	12 3 29	5 15 0	—	5 15 0
—		Michael Quinlan,	George Goold, Esq.	Bog,	4 0 12	0 1 0	—	0 1 0
4		George Redding,	George Goold, Esq.	House and land,	18 0 4	7 15 0	0 15 0	8 10 0
				Total,	102 1 39	47 1 0	1 10 0	48 11 0
		CLONBUOGH. *(Ord. Ss. 24 & 30.)*						
1		Earl of Carrick,	In fee,	Bog,	88 3 10	0 10 0	—	0 10 0
2	A a	William Rorke,	Earl of Carrick,	House, offices, and land,	70 1 29	31 10 0	4 10 0	36 0 0
—	B	William Rorke,	Earl of Carrick,	Land,	41 2 1	31 10 0	—	31 10 0
—	A b	Vacant,	William Rorke,	House and offices,		—	2 0 0	2 0 0
—	A c	Mary Flynn,	William Rorke,	House,		—	0 10 0	0 10 0
—	B a	Mary Flynn,	William Rorke,	House,		—	0 5 0	0 5 0
—	b	Edward Long,	William Rorke,	House and garden,	0 1 33	0 5 0	0 5 0	0 10 0
—	c	Catherine Neale,	William Rorke,	House and garden,	0 1 16	0 5 0	0 5 0	0 10 0
3	A	William Rorke,	Earl of Carrick,	Land,	24 3 34	11 10 0	—	11 10 0
—	B	William Rorke,	Earl of Carrick,	Land,	6 3 35	3 5 0	—	3 5 0
—	A a	Patrick Burke,	William Rorke,	House,		—	0 5 0	0 5 0
—	A b	Henry Doyle,	William Rorke,	House,		—	0 5 0	0 5 0
4		Patrick Cahill,	Earl of Carrick,	Land,	6 2 14	3 10 0	—	3 10 0
5		Patrick Doolan,	Earl of Carrick,	House and land,	1 3 34	1 5 0	0 5 0	1 10 0
6		Patrick Brennan,	Earl of Carrick,	Land,	3 3 7	2 5 0	—	2 5 0

Extract from Sir Richard Griffith's Valuation of Ireland, Co. Tipperary c. 1850, showing details of holding of James Ryan.

The most important of these was Sir Richard Griffith's Primary Valuation of Tenements 1848-1864 undertaken by Government order after the Act of 1838 to determine the amount of tax each tenant should pay towards the support of the poor and destitute within his Poor Law Union. The Valuation which forms the basis of the present-day rating system in Ireland, was printed as a Government project running to over two hundred volumes. Only the major libraries such as the National Library of Ireland, Kildare Street, the Public Record Office, Four Courts Building, and the Genealogical Office, Dublin Castle would have anything approaching complete sets.

In the almost total lack of census records due to the destruction of the Public Record Office in 1922, the Valuation provides an invaluable source for the tracing of families resident in Ireland about the middle of the last century. In addition to giving the name of each occupier or tenant, it gives the name of his townland or city location, the area of his holding and of course the valuation assessment of the latter.

Significantly from the point of view of our search for the family holding of Patrick Ryan, the valuation returns for the townland of Boggaun list one James Ryan, in all probability the father of Patrick, who named his first born in the New World James, doubtlessly following the time honoured Irish custom of naming the eldest son after his paternal grandfather and the second son after his maternal grandfather. The eldest and second daughters were similarly named after the paternal and maternal grandmothers. James occupied Lot 1 amounting to slightly over twenty nine acres with a valuation of £15/10/0. Since the initial rate of tax struck was six pence per £1 valuation, his yearly contribution to the Union Exchequer was between seven and eight shillings. By reference to the records of the Irish Valuation Office, Ely Place, by St. Stephen's Green, it is possible to trace the name of the present day owner of the plot once held by James Ryan.

An earlier record of the Ryan family holding will be found in the Tithe Composition Applotment Book for the parish of Killavinogue dated 1827. Under the Tithe Composition Acts of 1823 and preceding years provision was made for the payment of tithes to the clergy of each parish in money

Towns-Lands		Occupiers Names	Quantity of Land A	R	P	Rate per acre S	D	amount £	S	D
Graffin		Brought forward	221	2	19			27	16	7½
	68	John Lahy &	7	1	"	3	4	1	4	2
	9	Thos. Darmody	1	2	"	3	4	"	5	"
	70	Wm. Maher & Michl. Cormick	10	2	5	3	4	1	15	1
	1	Andrew Kennedy	4	1	5	1	11	"	8	2½
	2	James Guilfoyle	4	2	5	2	7	"	11	8½
	3	Wm. Meara	4	2	25	3	4	"	15	6
	4	Timy. Ryan	4	"	20	3	4	"	13	9
	5	Wid. Kennedy & Wid. Lahy	3	1	30	2	7	"	8	10½
	6	John & Michl. Guider ½	11	"	"	2	7	1	8	5
	7	Pat. ⅔ & Wm. ⅓ Brien	15	3	4	2	7	2	"	9½
	8	James Dooley	1	"	"	3	4	"	3	4
	9	Patk. Kilmartin	3	"	"	2	7	"	7	9
	80	Widow Whelan	2	2	20	1	11	"	5	"
	1	⅙ Widow Key ⅙ Wm. Dulahunty ⅙ John Tracy ⅓ Roger & Pat. Tracy ⅙ Edmond Tracy	53	"	20	1	11	5	1	10
	2	Brien Fitzpatrick	10	2	"	1	11	1	"	1½
	3	Edward Mackey	4	1	"	1	4	"	5	8
	4	John & Widow Whelan	28	1	10	1	11	2	14	3
	5	James Whelan	7	"	10	1	4	"	9	5
	6	Dennis Whelan	13	"	"	2	7	1	13	7
	7	John Strahan	3	3	30	1	11	"	7	7
	8	John Whelan	12	"	"	"	7	"	7	"
			427	2	3			£50	3	8
Buggawn	9	John Howley	6	"	"	1	11	"	11	6
	90	James Monaghan	4	"	"	1	11	"	7	8
	1	Frank Lewis	2	"	"	1	11	"	3	10
	2	Frank Lewis & John Reddan	3	"	"	1	11	"	5	9
	3	John Reddan	4	"	"	1	11	"	7	8
	4	John & Michl. Tracy	12	1	12	3	4	2	1	3½
	5	Michl. Dulahunty	12	1	12	2	7	1	11	[illegible]
	6	Benjn. Rawlins & J. Tracy	10	2	22	1	11	£1	"	
			54	1	6			£6	9	[illegible]

Extract from Tithe Composition Applotment Book, parish of Killavinogue, Co. Tipperary, 1827 showing details of Ryan family holding.

rather than in kind. Consequent valuation surveys ranging in date from 1823 to 1837 were undertaken in all parishes with the exception of towns and cities. The records for each parish contain a list of land tenants all of whom were liable for the payment of tithes to the Established Protestant Church regardless of their religion. Beside the tenant's name was entered the name of his townland, the acreage of his farm, its valuation and the yearly tithe for which he was liable.

The Applotment records ran into thousands of manuscripts and are in the Public Record Office, Four Courts Building, Dublin with the exception of those for Counties Derry, Armagh, Antrim, Down, Fermanagh and Tyrone which are in the Public Record Office of Northern Ireland, May Street, Belfast.

Surname compilations for each of the thirty two counties based on the returns of the two valuations referred to above are now available in the major libraries and if you know the name of the particular county from which your forebears came you will be able by consulting the relevant *County Index,* to determine with reasonable accuracy the part of that county in which your people formerly resided.

If perchance your people happened to reside in one of the numerous small towns throughout the country then a good source to consult is *Slator's Directory of Ireland 1846.*

To help you visualise the interplay of placename and surname over the centuries in Ireland, *A Genealogical and Historical Map of Ireland*, widely available, shows among other things, the distribution and location of Irish family names barony by barony.

LOCAL VISIT

We now come to look for a record of the birth of Patrick Ryan. By Government order under the Compulsory Registration Act 1863 General Civil Registration of births, marriages and deaths became effective on 1st January, 1864. The Registrar-General was and still is charged with the custody of vital statistics in Ireland. Stand on Dublin's O'Connell Bridge and you can read the time on Gandon's stately waterside building popularly called the Custom House and now the Office of the Registrar-General. But since the subject of our search Patrick Ryan was born about 1827, the civil records are clearly far too late in time to be of any assistance in determining his exact date of birth. In this event we must now direct our attention to the local parish Church in which Patrick Ryan was baptised.

For most people a visit to the actual place or places associated with one's ancestors is normally a matter of great curiosity and interest. Living tradition is a powerfully potential source of information in the Irish countryside and the older inhabitants in the locality should be consulted. So too should the electoral lists publically displayed in all Post Offices containing as they do the names of all persons over twenty one normally resident in the locality. The lists are compiled according to townlands and special attention should be paid to the townland associated with one's ancestors since occurrence there today of the family name sought is a strong pointer to the existence of living relatives.

Where a visit to Ireland is not possible remember that a letter seeking family connections in the Emerald Isle is always a good news item for the editor of a local provincial newspaper. One could also of course consider placing a suitable announcement costing as little as fifteen shillings in the appropriate paper covering the area from which one's ancestor came. A list of such newspapers covering all Irish counties together with the name of the town in which each is published will be found elsewhere in this book.

On the occasion of a local visit every effort should be made to find the family gravestone in the local cemetery since many of these stones are Genealogical tablets in themselves containing as many as four generations of the same family.

Church registers are normally in the custody of the parish priest of each parish (Catholic) and the Rector (Protestant and Church of Ireland). Clearly it is necessary to know the religion of the subject of a search in order to avoid having to inspect a double set of records.

FAMILY TREE

Assuming we are successful in locating the baptism entry of Patrick Ryan in the records of Templemore Parish we are now in a position to begin to construct a modest family tree. The pedigree or tree shown below is almost self-explanatory. It shows three generations of the Ryan family with dates of birth, marriage and death where the facts have been ascertained. Genealogical information so tabulated is more readily understood and as further pertinent facts come to light the tree can be extended laterally and in depth.

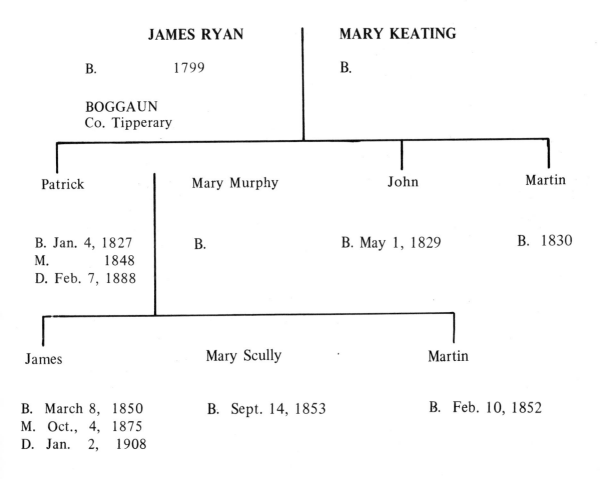

JAMES RYAN　　　　　　**MARY KEATING**

B.　　　1799　　　　B.

BOGGAUN
Co. Tipperary

Patrick　　　Mary Murphy　　　John　　　Martin

B. Jan. 4, 1827　　B.　　　B. May 1, 1829　　B. 1830
M.　　1848
D. Feb. 7, 1888

James　　　Mary Scully　　　Martin

B. March 8, 1850　　B. Sept. 14, 1853　　B. Feb. 10, 1852
M. Oct., 4, 1875
D. Jan. 2, 1908

WILLS

Our next step is to try to locate any wills made by members of the Ryan family of Boggaun. Because of their nature wills are of outstanding value from a genealogical viewpoint in that they provide accurate and detailed information on family relationships. In Ireland up to the year 1858 the administration of wills lay in the hands of the ecclesiastical authorities. In the case of the less well-off wills were normally proved in what was known as the Diocesan Consistorial Court under the jurisdiction of the local bishop. The wills of those who possessed more in the way of material goods had to be sent for probate to the Prerogative Court of the archbishop of Armagh. Since the Ryan family of Boggaun were evidently of small tenant stock any wills made by them would be proved in the Consistorial Court of the diocese of Cashel, within which the townland of Boggaun falls. Indexes to wills probated in many dioceses are now available in handy booklet form; unpublished indexes can be consulted in the Public Record Office. One interesting Ryan testator emerges from the list of Cashel wills, i.e. John Ryan of Gortnaskehy who had his will probated in 1791. Gortnaskehy is sufficiently close to Boggaun to make this particular testator worthy of special note.

If the subject of our search Patrick Ryan — instead of being the son of a tenant farmer as he appears to have been — had been born into the family of a *strong* farmer it is likely that his father's will would be listed among the Prerogative Wills of Ireland. Genealogical abstracts in the form of chart pedigrees were made by Sir William Betham from these wills the originals of which were later destroyed in the Public Record Office fire of 1922. The abstracts covering the period 1536 to about the year 1800 are arranged in alphabetical order and run to well over thirty manuscript volumes. This outstanding collection is housed in the Genealogical Office, Dublin Castle. Before consulting the actual volumes it is advisable to check first a widely available book entitled *Index to the Prerogative Wills of Ireland by Arthur Vicars* to ascertain whether the subject of one's search actually made such a will.

Also at the Genealogical Office is a second and almost equally important collection of will abstracts known as the *Eustace Will Abstracts*. An excellent printed index to the latter collection is available in that office.

If you are still unsuccessful in your search for that elusive last will and testament of your ancestor why not try *A Guide to Copies of Irish Wills by Wallace Clare*. This book is a substantial printed index to wills contained in such sources as learned journals, family histories and rare manuscripts. You will find copies of the book in any reasonably well stocked Irish library.

Still on the subject of wills especially for those made in the 1700's we can recommend the Irish Manuscripts Commission's *Registry of Deeds: Abstracts of Wills edited by P. B. Eustace.* In the early days of the Registry's existence many wills were also apparently registered among the deeds. Genealogical abstracts have been made from these wills to form two large printed volumes covering the period 1708 to 1787. The following is an example of an abstract taken from Vol. 1, page 1:

SULLIVAN, DARBY, Gortnecrehy, parish of Clouncagh, B. of Conelloe, Co. Limerick.

SULLIVAN, DARBY, Gortnecrehy, parish of Clouncagh, B. of Conelloe, Co. Limerick. 22 July 1708. Narrate, 1½p., 4 Nov. 1708. Wife Catherine Sullivan. Sons John and Thomas Sullivan. Third son Daniel, fourth son Dennis Sullivan, Daughter Catherine Sullivan. John Collins, Ballynoe, parish of Clouneilty, B. Conelloe, Co. Limerick, exor.
His real and personal estate in the kingdom of Ireland. Witnesses: Teige Sullivan, Clouny, Co. Cork, Maurice Nash, Ballyhahill, Dnaiel O'Bryan, Curraghnageare, Richard Cantilon, Morenane, Daniel Sullivan, Gortncreghy, John Fitzgerald, Greenhill, Timothy Sullivan, Ahadagh, Derby Sullivan and Matthew Sullivan both of the same, all of the Co. Limerick.
Memorial witnessed by: Daniel Sullivan, John Connell.
1, 247, 151   Thos. Sullivan (seal)
                    a devisee

Name and Place	Nature of Record	Year	Court or Registry
O'Connor, Hugh, Sunningdale, Donnybrook, Co. Dublin, and late of 1 Kenilworth Sq., Co. Dublin.	Probate	1897	P.R.
„ John (Rev.)	Admon.	1812	Prerog:
„ Teresa, Cole's Lane, Dublin ...	Admon. (copy)	1920	P.R.
„ William, Parkgate St., Dublin	„ „	1920	„
O'Conyllan, Teig	Will	d.1672	Tuam Dio.
O'Dell, Constance, Main St., Bandon, Co. Cork.	Probate	1861	Cork D.R.
O'Donnell, Henry Anderson, Limerick City	„	1841	Prerog:
„ William, Ballsbridge, Co. Dublin	Admon. (copy)	1912	P.R.
O'Farrell, George, Carlow	Probate	1846	Prerog:
O'Flinn, Andrew, Ballymoney, Co. Down ...	Admon. W.A.	1868	Belfast D.R.
Ogden, David, Upr. Ballycarney, Co. Wexford.	Probate	1805	Ferns Dio.
Ogle, Henry, Newry, Co. Armagh ...	„	1803	Prerog:
„ Jane, Fathom, Co. Armagh ...	Admon. D.B.N.	1813	Newry exempt
„ John, Newry and Fathom ...	Probate	1799	Prerog:
O'Grady, Eliza, Terenure, Co. Dublin ...	Probate (copy)	1896	P.R.
„ Joseph, Rathdown Road, Dublin ...	Admon.	1898	„
„ Julia, 27 George St., Limerick ...	Probate	1880	Limerick D.R.
„ Maria de la Soledad Isabel Sofia (Hon.)	Will	1889	P.R.
„ William, Dublin	Admon. W.A. D.B.N.	1848 (Orgl. Grant 1825).	Prerog:
O'Hagan, John, Newry, Co. Down ...	Probate	1862	P.R.
O'Hara, Charles, Lisnagarron, Co. Antrim	Grant of Admon.	1891	Belfast D.R.
„ John, Lisnagarron, Co. Antrim ...	Will and Grant	1891	„
„ Mary, Annachmore, Collooney, Co. Sligo.	Probate	1846	Prerog:
„ Patrick, Killadoon, Celbridge, Co. Kildare.	Admon.	1849	„
O'Kearny, Hatton Ronayne, Lr. Glanmire Road, Co. Cork.	„	1904	Cork D.R.
O'Kelly, Patrick, Thomas St., Limerick ...	„	1853	Prerog:
Oliver, Joseph, Tullymore, Co. Armagh ...	Probate	1837	Armagh Dio.
O'Mahony, Thaddeus (Rev.) "Holyrood" Sandymount Ave., Co. Dublin.	„	1903	P.R.
O'Mulrenin, Richard J., South Circular Road, Dublin.	Probate (copy)	1906	„
O'Neill, Anne, Kells, Co. Meath ...	„	1883	„
„ Catherine, Abbottstown, Co. Dublin	Admon.	1862	„
„ Ellen, Carrick-on-Suir, Co. Tipperary	Probate	1865	Waterford D.R.
„ James (Rev.), Dunshaughlin, Co. Meath.	„	1901	P.R.
„ Margaret, Meadstown, Co. Meath	„	1829	Prerog:
„ Nicholas, Ship Street, Dublin ...	Admon.	1817	„
O'Reilley, (or O'Reilly), Daniel Patrick (Rev.), St. Mary's Church, Church St., Dublin.	„	1895	P.R.
O'Reilly, John, 55 Percy Place, Co. Dublin	„	1884	„
Orford, Elizabeth, Rathbride, Co. Kildare	Admon. (unad.)	1841	Prerog:
Ormsby, (alias Elwood), Elizabeth, Strand Hill, Cong, Co. Mayo.	„	1849	„
„ Thomas, Ballinamore, Co. Mayo ...	Admon. W.A.	1836	„
O'Rorke, Owen, 36, 38 and 40 St. Augustine Street, Dublin.	Admon.	1897	P.R.
Orr, Alexander (Rev.), 10 Burlington Place, Eastbourne, Sussex.	Probate	1897	„
„ James, Annarea, Co. Armagh ...	„	1842	Armagh Dio.
„ James Sinclair, Ballyloughan, Co. Armagh (formerly Phibsboro', Dublin).	„	1863	Armagh D.R.

Copy of page 59, 55th Report of Deputy Keeper of Public Records in Ireland, 1928 with list of testators' names.

Particulars of several thousands of more wills made over the past three hundred years can be found in the Reports of the Deputy Keeper of Public Records notably the fifty fifth, fifty sixth and fifty seventh reports. Details such as the name of the testator, his place of residence and date of probate of will are set out in tabular form. You can consult copies of the reports at the National Library and of course at the Public Record Office itself. The actual wills themselves can be inspected at that office which on request will make copies available at a nominal charge.

Wills as we have stated are a wonderful source of information for the pedigree hunter but not always: the following extraordinary will was made in Ireland in 1674:

> I, John Langley, born at Wincanton, in Somersetshire, and settled in Ireland in the year 1651, now in my right mind and wits, do make my will in my own hand-writing. I do leave all my house, goods, and farm of Black Kettle of 253 acres to my son, commonly called stubborn Jack, to him and his heirs for ever, provided he marries a Protestant, but not Alice Kendrick, who called me "Oliver's whelp". My new buckskin breeches and my silver tobacco stopper with J. L. on the top I give to Richard Richards, my comrade, who helped me off at the storming of Clonmell when I was shot through the leg. My said son John shall keep my body above ground six days and six nights after I am dead; and Grace Kendrick shall lay me out, who shall have for so doing Five Shillings. My body shall be put upon the oak table in the brown room, and fifty Irish men shall be invited to my wake, and every one shall have two quarts of the best acqua vitae, and each one skein, dish and knife before him: and when the liquor is out, nail up the coffin and commit me to the earth whence I came. This is my will, witness my hand this 3d of March 1674.
>
> John Langley

The armorial altar tomb of the O'Connor family in Sligo Abbey, 1624, containing the shield and crest of the O'Connors flanked by two figures representing St. Peter and St. Paul. In the centre compartment is a representation of Donough O'Connor and his wife Eleanor Butler kneeling in prayer. In the surrounds are numerous trophies including drum, flag, axe, shield and sword.

MEMORIAL INSCRIPTIONS

It has been said of the Irish that they are in danger of commemorating themselves to death! Be that as it may it is a happy circumstance for the person seeking his or her Irish ancestry that our forebears were generous and diligent in placing memorials over the final resting places of their dear departed. A great variety of such memorials can be seen in our country churchyards from simple iron crosses bearing only a surname to elaborate armorial altar tombs of the great Irish chieftains. Examples of some fine monuments to the families of O'Brien, McMahon, MacNamara, O'Hehir and Considine are to be seen in the Franciscan Abbey Ennis, County Clare. Smith in his *History of Cork* refers to the ancient tombs of the Magners, the O'Callaghans, the Prendergasts, the Donegans, the Meades, the Healeys and the Nagles at Buttevant County Cork. Muckross Abbey near Killarney has been for centuries the traditional resting place of the O'Donoghues, the Falveys and the MacCartheys while the chiefs of the O'Donovan, O'Hea (Hayes) and Collins septs repose in monumental splendour in Timoleague Abbey near Skibbereen, County Cork.

The work of transcribing inscriptions from gravestones in Ireland was begun before the turn of the present century by the Association for the Preservation of the Memorials of the Dead. The published Journal of the Association runs to about a dozen volumes and contains thousands of inscriptions from stones throughout the country. In addition there are numerous illustrations of tablets and monuments as well as many quaint epitaphs, rustic verses and family lore. The library of the Genealogical Office has at least one complete set of this outstanding series the first volume of which appeared in 1888. Here are a few examples taken at random from the Journal:

Kilgefin Churchyard, Co. Roscommon. (Vol. 2 p. 229)

> Erected to the memory of the ancient family of Kilmacor
> by Patrick Hanly. The mothers' names for four generations
> were Anne Dufficy, Kate Cline, Margaret O'Farrell, Anne
> O'Hanley, Mabel McLoughlin, Jane O'Connor.
> Also in fond memory of John Hanly 50 years, and his

children James Hanly 68 years, Bridge Hanly 70, Richard 34, Jane 57, Kate 56, also his affectionate wife Ellen Hanly 64 years, Their dau. Mary 18, his uncles Martin Hanly, Rev. James Hanly P.P. Fairymount.

Parish of Dingle, Co. Kerry. (Vol. 1 p. 87)

To the ultra good life is short and old age rare
Here lies buried
JOHN FITZGERALD, Knight of Kerry,
Sprung from the ancient race of the Knights of Kerry,
Remarkable for the sweetness of his disposition
and the purity of his morals.
He was beautiful in countenance,
Benevolence was in his heart, and truth in his words.
He was upright and agreeable; every
Acquaintance was a friend, not one
An enemy.
Being such a man,
Seized be fever he died prematurely,
in the 35th year of his age,
A. D. 1741
Sacred to the memory of her beloved husband
His grieving wife Margaret erected this monument.

Skibbereen Abbey Churchyard, Co. Cork (Vol. 6 p. 246)

There is a monument in this Churchyard erected by a blacksmith, named Eugene M'Carthy of Skibbereen, to commemorate the burial place of the victims of the famine. . . . . the following inscription appears on a marblet tablet:

Precious in the sight of the Lord is the death of his Saints. Erected to the memory of those departed ones who fell victims to the awful Famine of 1846 and 1847. Eternal Rest grant unto them O Lord and let perpetual Light shine upon them. May they rest in peace. Amen.

Castle Caldwell, Co. Fermanagh (Vol 2 p. 457)

To the
Memory
of
Denis McCabe
Fidler
who fell out of the
St. Patrick's Barge Belong
ing To Sr
James Calldwell Bart

Beware ye Fidlers of ye
Fidlers fate
Nor tempt ye deep least ye
repent too late
You ever have been deem'd to water
Foes
then shun ye lake till it with whisk'y flows
on firm land only Exercise your skill
there you may play and safely drink yr fill
D.D.D.
J.F.

Owing to the absence of early parish registers in Ireland and the non-existence of burial registers gravestone inscriptions are often the only means of tracing earlier generations of many Irish families. On the occasion of a pilgrimage to the burial-place of your ancestors remember to take with you pencil and paper, a small wire brush, a pocket-knife, a piece of cloth and a large sheet of soft brown paper. You may find that you have to contend with an ivy-covered stone or one with a slightly-cut inscription that has all but vanished. If you brush and rub the stone vigorously you will be able to take an impression with the brown paper and so rescue vital details. A further generation added to your family tree should be ample reward for your patience and perseverance. There is no need to be shy in asking the advice and assistance of local people especially in regard to the location of the cemetery which as a rule is located at the site of the ruined old parish church or abbey.

RELIGIOUS CENSUS 1766

Continuing our search for earlier generations of the Ryan family of Boggaun we turn our attention next to the Religious Census of 1766. This census was instituted by the Irish House of Lords and was taken up by the incumbent of each parish who listed heads of households as Catholic or Protestant. Even so the names of small cottiers and labourers rarely appeared on the census lists presumably because they were too poor to be liable for tithe assessment. Fortunately for our purpose many excellent transcripts were made by Tenison Groves, the Belfast genealogist, in the early years of the present century before the destruction of the originals in 1922.

The Tenison Groves notebooks containing many thousands of names from the returns for the dioceses of Armagh, Cashel, Clogher, Cloyne, Connor, Derry, Dromore, Down, Dublin, Ferns, Kildare, Kilmore and Ossory are now in the Public Record Office, Dublin and go a long way towards offsetting the loss of the originals. The returns for Cloyne and Cashel covering the greater portion of Counties Cork and Tipperary are almost complete, and among the heads of families listed for the parish of Killavinogue are James and Thomas Ryan.

HEARTH MONEY ROLLS 1663

Many an ancestry researcher nurtures a quiet ambition to link his forebears with one of the numerous branches of the family tree of a great Irish sept. There is of course an understandable pride in being able to display a lineage of over a thousand years of unbroken descent from an Irish chieftain to whom one owes one's name. Genealogy as we know was a strong point with the ancient Irish and the main lines of the great Irish families are generally speaking well established down to the seventeenth century. But then the old Gaelic order began to crumble with the consequent dispersal of families due to war, confiscation and plantation. For those whose hearts are set on long pedigrees the seventeenth century is indeed crucial to their hopes, the tracing of individuals being particularly tricky at this point in Irish history. Probably the most useful line of enquiry to pursue recordwise for the period is the Hearth Money Rolls.

Hearth Money colloquially known as *Smoke Silver* was a tax of two shillings on every hearth and fireplace established by act of parliament in the reign of Charles II. The purpose of the tax was to help pay for the wars of that penurious Stuart king. Initially the tax was payable on Lady Day and Michaelmas in equal portions, later the entire sum became payable on the tenth of January, yearly. The first collection of tax was made on Lady Day 1663 by the sheriff in each county. The persons liable to pay were entered in lists and these lists became known as the Hearth Money Rolls.

The rolls contain according to counties, baronies, parishes and townlands the names of the inhabitants liable to tax, the number of hearths of which each was possessed together with the amount of tax liability. Although in later days poorer householders were allowed exemption from the tax, at the time the original rolls were compiled no such privilege was in force. Therefore it follows that a list of Hearthmoney payers is practically a list of householders. Accordingly the lists are extremely valuable for the tracing of individuals for genealogical purposes. Moreover the number of hearths with which a person is charged can be taken as an indication of his wealth and standing in the community.

For the statistically minded Sir William Petty in 1660 reckoned that a total of 300,000 hearths in Ireland represented a population of 1,300,000.

In 1788 more than a century after its introduction gross abuses in regard to the administration of the Hearthmoney tax were exposed in Grattan's Parliament by Thomas Connolly, the member from County Kildare. "Was it not a well known fact," said Connolly, "that when a gentleman solicited from the Minister a hearthmoney collection, that instead of its nominal value of £40 he considered it worth from £100 to £200 a year. And how did that arise but by plundering the people by taking indulgence money, and by afterwards taking their pot, their blanket and at last their door, making what return they thought fit to the public treasury".

Bearing in mind our search for earlier generations of the Ryan family we are of course particularly interested in the Hearth Money Rolls for County

PAROCHIA DE KILLEA.

		Hths.	s.
Widd. Juan Boorke, Killonadag	...	1	2
William White	//	... 1	2
Teige Morgin	//	... 1	2
John McLewes	//	... 1	2
Thomas Hackett	//	... 1	2
Daniell Meagher, de Parke	...	1	2
James Meagher	//	... 1	2
William Doghin	//	... 1	2
Ellish Meagher	//	... 1	2
William Costigine	//	... 1	2
Connr Meagher de Garriborlinode	...	1	2
Keadagh Meagher de Skahanagh	...	1	2
Dermott Carroll	//	... 1	2
Dermott Scottye	//	... 1	2
Thomas Meagher	//	... 1	2

BARNAN AND AGHNOMEA PARISHES.

John Ottoway, Killoskehane	...	2	4
Murrogh McReger	//	... 1	2
Donnogh O'Doghon	//	... 1	2
Laghlin Fogerty	//	... 1	2
Roger McMurrogh	//	... 1	2
Roger Shannaghan	//	... 1	2
Laughlin Flanure	//	... 1	2
John McTeige	//	... 1	2
John Meagher Smite	//	... 1	2
Roger McThomas	//	... 1	2
John McGullerneane	//	... 1	2
Edmond Sweeney	//	... 1	2
Phillipp McCormucke	//	... 1	2
Josheph Loyd de Bearnane	...	1	2
James Meagher	//	... 1	2
Darby Meagher	//	... 1	2
Edmond Boorke	//	... 1	2
Edmond Carroll	//	... 1	2
John Carroll	//	... 1	2
Murtagh Kelly	//	... 1	2
John Bryar	//	... 1	2
John Meagher	//	... 1	2
Keadagh Meagher	//	... 1	2
Thomas McKue	//	... 1	2
Teige Shallow	//	... 1	2
Edmond Quirke	//	... 1	2
Theobald Stapleton	//	... 1	2
Phillipp Russhell	//	... 1	2
Nicholas Russhell	//	... 1	2
John Meary, de Aghnemedle	...	1	2
Richd. Douty	//	... 1	2
Thomas Shannaghan	//	... 1	2
Bryan Sweeny	//	... 1	2
Phillipp McThomas	//	... 1	2
Walter Vrino	//	... 1	2
Arthur Kenislye	//	... 1	2
Robt. Bruto	//	... 1	2
Hugh Meagher	//	... 1	2
Roger Shannaghan	//	... 1	2
Richd. Keirwan	//	... 1	2

		Hths.
Derby Banane, de Aghnemedle	...	1
Phillipp McRoger	//	... 1
Derby Shannaghan	//	... 1
John McGillfoile	//	... 1

PAROCHIA DE TEMPLEROE.

Bryan Sweeney, Templeroe	...	1
Patrick Purcell	//	... 1
Edmond Meagher	//	... 1
Wm. McShane	//	... 1
William McGrath	//	... 1
William Gritt		... 1

PAROCHIA DE KILLONINOGE.

Bartholomew Fowkes, Clonmore	...	1
John Ryane	//	... 1
Phillipp Carroll, Ballisorrell		... 1
William Carroll		... 1
Edmond Meagher	//	... 1
Derby McCnoghr	//	... 1
Robert Lunn, Clonbuogh		... 1
William Hude	//	... 1
Daniell Headine	//	... 1
Donnogh Bergine	//	... 1
Therlagh Fitzpatrick, Dromard	...	1
Roger Hamell	//	... 1
Derby Hogane	//	... 1
Wm. McCoreny	//	... 1
William Gormane	//	... 1
John Fighane	//	... 1
Murrogh Reagh	//	... 1
Donnogh Aghjron, Aghanoy	..	1
Donnogh Dulchonty	//	... 1
Edmond McEvoy	//	... 1
Roger Quirke	//	... 1
William Buttler	//	... 1
Walter Buttler	//	... 1
Miles Cleere	//	... 1
William Troe	//	... 1
Teige Agheron	//	... 1

PAROCHIA DE CORBALLY.

David Welsh, Clonkrekin		... 1
Teige Cleary	//	... 1
Teige Hynane	//	... 1
Murrogh Hinane	//	... 1
Phillipp Fihily	//	... 1
Daniell Heanin	//	... 1
Daniell Brimegem	//	... 1
Donogh Milline, Corbally		... 1
William Kissine	//	... 1
Dermott Phichane	//	... 1
William Scully	//	... 1
Daniell McTeige	//	... 1
Dermott McWilliam	//	... 1
David McTeige	//	... 1
Dermott Milline	//	... 1

The Hearth Money Rolls for the parish of Killavinogue, Co. Tipperary, 1665 (above) contain the name of John Ryane.

Tipperary. Happily for our purpose the rolls for that county form the subject of the following book: *Tipperary Families: Hearth Money Rolls, 1665-6-7 by Thomas Laffan, Dublin 1911.* On checking the returns for the parish of Killavinogue, barony of Ikerrin, we observe among the list of taxpayers for that parish the name of John Ryane thus enabling us to roll back the pedigree of the Ryan family to the year 1665.

A TIPPERARY SEPT: THE O'RYANS OF OWNEY

The Ryan family of Boggaun was clearly an offshoot of the O'Mulryans of Owney an important sept whose descendants are today so widely distributed throughout Tipperary and adjoining districts. From time beyond recall the Ryans occupied the tract of land west of a line joining Nenagh and Newport fronting Lough Derg until war and privation forced them far beyond the confines of their ancestral lands. The story of the Ryans of Owney is told in *Records of Four Tipperary Septs by M. Callanan, Galway, 1935* and there is no need to repeat here the wealth of detail contained in that book. As we traverse in spirit the wild country once called Owney we pause for a moment at the ruined Ryan castle of Killoscully before moving southwards over the Keeper Mountains to Foilaclug in the parish of Hollyford where according to local tradition Eamon an Chnoic or Edmond Knock Ryan, the Rapparee, is buried. Further to the west on the Limerick-Tipperary border we enter the now ruined twelfth century cistercian monastery of Abington in a sequestered corner of which a monument to the Ryans bore this inscription —

The most noble William Ryan, chief of the country of Owney, the head and prince of the ancient family of the Ryans caused this monument to be erected to himself, his wife and his children.

The honour of his posterity and praise of his ancestors caused William Ryan to construct this graceful work.

Alas, how much nobility proved in peace and war, how much holy faith, virtue and distinguished fame are enclosed in this sepulchral monument of the Ryans.

If it should be asked why that which is not destined to die should be shut up, the bones alone are covered in the earth but the other parts that know not death will enjoy perpetual day.

The praise, virtue, glory and honour of the Ryan race will live for ever in this honoured name. A.D. 1632.

Records and Record Repositories

What records of a Genealogical nature exist in Ireland and where can they be found?

At the outset it should be realised that Irish records cannot match those of countries say like England or France, certainly not over the last three hundred years. The Irish were not great record keepers, partly due to historical circumstances, partly to the degree of reliance placed on oral tradition. This is best illustrated by the fact that of the hundreds of thousands of people who left Ireland during the period 1845 – 1855 on account of the Famine, scarcely a single record was kept at ports of embarkation such as Queenstown (Cobh), Dublin, Galway, Derry and Belfast. The destruction of the Record Tower in Dublin Castle in 1710 and later on the Public Record Office in 1922 further depleted already lacking primary source materials. Despite these disasters, however, it is surprising how often Irish records can prove adequate when used to the fullest possible extent. The following is a simple guide to Irish libraries, record offices and archives together with a summary of the records they contain.

THE OFFICE OF THE REGISTRAR-GENERAL is located in the Custom House, Dublin. The hours of opening are 9.30 a.m. to 5.00 p.m. Monday to Friday. There is a public counter where one can do one's own research. The Office has records of births, marriages and deaths as from January 1st 1864. In addition Church of Ireland (Protestant) weddings are on record from 1 April 1845. Certified copies of entries in the registers can be procured at a cost of 65p.

THE GENEALOGICAL OFFICE, a state agency under the Ministry of Education, is located in Dublin Castle. This Office incorporates the former

Fenian prisoners in the court-yard of Dublin Castle, 1867 : the centre building now houses the Genealogical Office.

Dublin from the Liffey in the days of sail showing the Custom House. This fine building, the work of the celebrated architect James Gandon, was burned down 25th May 1921.

The Four Courts Building and Public Record Office of Ireland.

Charge on the students of Trinity College, Dublin by the
Metropolitan police 12 March 1858 at the entry of the Earl of
Eglinton into the city.

Ulster Office and Office of Arms. Among the many features of the present office is a unique Heraldic Museum containing many rare and unusual exhibits. The Office and Museum are open to the public 9.30 a.m. to 5.00 p.m. Monday to Friday. There is no admission fee. The Office is the repository of hundreds of manuscripts and printed books which contain the arms and pedigrees of numerous Gaelic, Norman and Anglo-Irish families. There is a specialised research section where genealogical work is carried out by a professional staff at the current rate of £8 per four hours work.

THE PUBLIC RECORD OFFICE is located in the Four Courts Building on Arran Quay and despite its destruction by fire in 1922 is still a happy hunting ground for the family researcher. The Office forms part of the Ministry of Justice and the Minister is ex officio keeper of all public records. Accordingly all correspondence should be addressed to the Deputy-Keeper. The visitor to the Office will be shown to the search room where a magnificent card index gives ready access to the records. Among the chief collections of the Office are Betham's notebooks containing Genealogical abstracts from all Prerogative wills up to the year 1800, the Tithe Composition Applotment Books for all counties of the Republic, Marriage Licence Bonds (Protestant) covering the period 1750 – 1845, Will and Census records not destroyed in 1922, and microfilm copies of many Church of Ireland parish registers. Mechanical copying facilities and clerking services are available at a small charge.

THE REGISTRY OF DEEDS is located in the King's Inn in Henrietta Street off Dublin's Bolton Street. This Office has records extant from 1708, the year of its foundation. It is open to the public daily from 10.00 a.m. to 4.00 p.m. and there is a search room where one can do one's research. A great deal of information of a genealogical nature is contained in its records of Deeds, leases, business transactions, marriage licences and wills. Two indexes, one surnames, the other placenames, provide the key to the source material in the Office.

THE NATIONAL LIBRARY AND ARCHIVES are in Kildare Street by Parliament Buildings. Its recently compiled *Manuscript Sources for the*

History of Irish Civilisation affords an instant index to both domestic and far flung primary source material pertinent to the history of Ireland and her people. The building itself, with its foyer and round reading room, is a good example of old Dublin architecture at its best. Not unnaturally it houses the greatest printed and manuscript collections relating to Ireland in the world. It is open to the public daily from 10.00 a.m. to 10.00 p.m.

THE PUBLIC RECORD OFFICE OF NORTHERN IRELAND has a considerable corpus of Genealogical material of interest to people whose antecedents came from the six north-eastern counties of Ireland. The Office is located in Law Courts Building, May Street, Belfast and the search room is open to the public daily from 9.30 a.m. to 5.00 p.m. There is a magnificent card index to the numerous pedigrees, family notes, wills, land records, deeds, leases, marriage settlements etc. which the Office possesses. Of special interest is the fact that the Office has microfilm copies of Church of Ireland and Presbyterian parish registers for counties Armagh, Antrim, Down, Derry, Tyrone and Fermanagh — the 'Six Counties' as they are called.

THE ULSTER-SCOT HISTORICAL FOUNDATION, also located in Law Courts Building, is the Genealogical arm of the Public Record Office, Northern Ireland. Its purpose is to assist persons of Ulster ancestry to ascertain facts about their ancestors in Northern Ireland. This Foundation will advise visitors on Genealogical matters free of charge. More extensive research is undertaken on a fee-paying basis. Where a written request for a search is made it should be accompanied by a fee of £3. The relevant records will then be examined and a report will be forwarded to the enquirer. Those who have the opportunity and inclination to pursue their own research should note that the Public Record Office, Belfast has prepared an excellent series of short guides on how to use the material available in that Office with separate booklets indicating what records are available for each of the six counties of Northern Ireland.

THE REGISTRAR-GENERAL of Northern Ireland has records of births, marriages and deaths from 1921 onwards as well as the census returns for the years 1931 and 1951. His office is located in Fermanagh House, Ormeau Avenue, Belfast.

TRINITY COLLEGE, DUBLIN, the oldest higher institution of learning in Ireland, houses the Book of Kells, the celebrated illuminated manuscript and crowning glory of Ireland's golden age. The registers of the College from the year of its foundation in 1593 have been published – *Alumni Dublinenses* – containing particulars of some 35,000 students up to about 1860.

THE ROYAL IRISH ACADEMY, 19, Dawson Street has a wide ranging collection of printed and manuscript material of particular interest to the Gaelic scholar. A booklet entitled *The Royal Irish Academy and its Collection* is available free from the Academy.

THE STATE PAPER OFFICE houses the records which formerly belonged to the Chief Secretary's Office. The records include material such as convict papers, convict reference books, criminal index books, registers of convicts sentenced to transportation, registers of convicts sentenced to penal servitude, the 1798 Rebellion papers, proceedings of the Dublin Society of United Irishmen, Fenian and Land League records and papers of the evicted tenants commission. The office is located in the Birmingham Tower, Dublin Castle where the records can be consulted provided they are fifty years old and have been declared public by the Government.

THE LIBRARY OF THE CHURCH REPRESENTATIVE BODY, Braemor Park, Dublin, has a lot of material of special interest to people whose ancestors were in the Church of Ireland tradition. The library possesses extensive lists of clergy of the Church of Ireland many with biographical notes attached which provide a valuable record of the clergy, their careers and their children.

CHURCH RECORDS are of prime importance to the family researcher on account of the late commencement of state records in Ireland. Since as a rule people are baptised and married in their own parishes it goes without saying that parish registers are in the custody of local clergy. Catholic registers date from about 1750 for city parishes but generally speaking books for rural parishes commence much later. Most of the parish books have by now been recorded on film by the National Library of Ireland. A complete list of clergy and parishes will be found in the *Irish Catholic Directory* published annually in January. Protestant registers were dealt a severe blow by the destruction of the Public Record Office in 1922 when more than half the books in the entire country perished in the fire. Most of the existing books have been microfilmed by the two Public Record Offices. The Parish Register Society has printed a number of books mainly relating to Dublin city parishes. The *Irish Church Directory* gives the names and addresses of all Church of Ireland clergy in Ireland.

PRESBYTERIAN RECORDS. The Presbyterian tradition has always been very strong in Ireland ever since the first Minister Edward Brice settled in Ballycarry near Larne in County Antrim in 1613. In 1819 a Presbyterian Synod decreed — "That every minister of this Synod shall keep, or cause to be kept, a regular registry of all marriages celebrated by him, stating the date of each marriage, the names of the parties, the congregations or parishes in which they reside and the names of at least two witnesses present at the ceremony. Each minister is enjoined to register, or cause to be registered, in a book to be kept for that purpose, the names of all the children baptised by him, the dates of their birth and baptism, the names of their parents and the places of residence".

That is not to say that many congregations did not keep records prior to 1819. They did, — and the Presbyterian Historical Society has an impressive list of baptisimal and marriage registers prior to 1820. Also among the Society's records are copies of the Religious Census of 1766 for many parishes in Ulster, lists of Protestant householders for counties, Antrim, Derry and Donegal 1740 as well as a census (or what virtually amounts to one) of Presbyterians taken in the year 1775.

Another source of information are the Certificates of Transference which were given to members leaving a district to show that they were free of church censure. They took the form of brief life histories. The following from the parish of Dundonald, Co. Down will serve as an example:

> Dundonald Aprile 8th 1725 that David Cook and Margaret
> George his wife were orderly persons while with us and
> were admitted to Christian Communion.

You will find courtesy and a feast of information when you visit the Society's headquarters at Church House, Fisherwick Place, Belfast. If you cannot manage a visit to Church House then send a sum of £4 for a report on your family's ancestors. Finally do remember that for historical reasons records of Presbyterian births and marriages will often be found in the registers of the Established Church. So do not overlook that source if your ancestors happened to be of Irish Presbyterian stock.

HUGUENOT RECORDS. Almost three hundred years have passed since the migration to Ireland of a large number of French Protestant refugees known as Huguenots. Exiles for conscience sake they were forced to flee France leaving all their possessions behind. But France's loss — brought about by religious persecution of Louis XIV — was Ireland's gain. Such was the contribution of the 'gentle and profitable strangers' to the culture of their adopted country that the marks of their influence are to this day clearly discernible. D'Olier Street, for example, is named after Jeremiah D'Olier, Governor of the Bank of Ireland, who was High Sheriff of Dublin in 1788. His ancestor, Isaac D'Olier, a Huguenot refugee, settled first in Amsterdam, and afterwards in Dublin.

The refugees who came to Dublin settled for the most part in the 'Liberties' alongside Christ Church Cathedral where they began the manufacture of tabinet since more generally known as Irish poplin. The demand for tabinet was such that in the early 1700's a number of Huguenot artisans left London for Dublin where they extended the manufacture. The Coombe and Weaver's Square became their principal quarters. Up to the beginning of the 19th century this trade was very prosperous but frequent strikes did much to ruin the industry. The manufacture was lost and the 'Liberties', instead of being the richest, became one of the poorest parts of Dublin.

Several well remembered names in Ireland, outstanding in various walks of life, are of Huguenot origin. Richard Chenevix Trench who became Archbishop of Dublin in the last century; Henry Maturin, Senior Fellow of Trinity College; Dion Boucicault, brilliant actor and author of melodramas, (who does not remember *The Wicklow Wedding and The Seachraun!*); and Joseph

Sheridan Le Fanu, the novelist, were all of Huguenot descent. The name of La Touche is inseparably linked with the establishment of banking in Ireland. David Digues La Touche, son of a noble Protestant family that possessed considerable estates near Orleans, accompanied King William to Ireland in 1688. On retiring from military service he founded a silk and poplin manufactory in Dublin. He was entrusted with deposits of money and valuables by his fellow refugees and this suggested the formation of a bank, located near Dublin Castle. The present Munster and Leinster Bank is a lineal descendant of La Touche's concern. He died in 1745

The Huguenot community in Dublin had a number of places of worship notably St. Mary's Chapel in St. Patrick's Cathedral. The formal opening of this Chapel is thus described in the *London Gazette* of the 21st May, 1666:

> "The Archbishop of Dublin, with the Dean and Chapter of St. Patrick's having granted to the French Protestants of this city St. Marie's Chapel, for their Church Assembly, a place depending on this Cathedral, His Grace the Duke of Ormond, Lord Lieutenant of Ireland, who had by his bounty contributed very largely to its reparation, was pleased to countenance their first assembly with his presence, whither he came on Sunday, April 29, his Guard and Gentlemen preceding him, with the Maces and Swords carried before him, accompanied by the Lord Primate of Ireland, the Lord Archbishop of Dublin, Lord High Chancellor of Ireland, the Council of State, and several great Lords and other persons of quality of both persuasions, followed by the Lord Mayor, with the Sheriffs and Officers of the City, who had the Sword and Mace likewise carried before him".

In 1705 a second French congregation met in the new Church of St. Mary's or Mary's Abbey or little St. Patrick's as it was variously styled. This lasted as an independent church until 1716 when it joined itself to St. Patrick's with a common set of church registers. The burial ground of these churches was at the end of Cathedral Lane on the right hand side as you go from

Kevin Street and was a portion of a piece of ground commonly known as the Cabbage Garden — from the plants originally grown in it. It has not been used for burials since the year 1858.

In addition to St. Patrick's and St. Mary's there were two further Huguenot congregations of note in Dublin. One of these congregations met in Wood Street, off Bride Street and was sometimes called the French Congregation of St. Brigide's. The other congregation had its chapel in Lucy Lane, which was afterwards known as Mass Street, and is now Chancery Place. This was also called the French Church by the Inns and the French Church of Golblac Lane. It was sold in the year 1773 to the Presbyterian congregation of Skinner's Row. Its burial ground was in Merrion Row, off St. Stephen's Green, where burials took place up to the early years of the present century.

The Parish registers, containing records of births, marriages and deaths from 1680 to 1830, of all four Huguenot Churches in Dublin have been printed in volumes 7 and 14 of the publications of the Huguenot Society of London. Dublin's Genealogical Office has copies of these volumes.

Outside the Metropolis probably the most celebrated Huguenot settlement was at Portarlington in County Laois formerly Queen's County. The refugees by their industry set a good example to the local people and shortly after their settlement Portarlington became the model town of the County. The refugees as was their practice formed themselves into a congregation and two churches were erected for their accommodation. The old French service was read in these churches down to the year 1817, when service in English took its place, as the French language had ceased to be understood in the neighbourhood. The registers of the French Church at Portarlington are printed in volume 19 of the H.S.L. publications.

A number of smaller colonies of Huguenots were established here and there throughout Ireland where they started various branches of manufacture.. A branch of the linen trade was started at Kilkenny and at Limerick the refugees established the lace and glove trades. The woollen manufacture at Cork was begun by James Fontaine a member of the noble family of de la Fontaine.

Finally we might ask how much do present day prosperous towns such as Waterford, Youghal, Bandon and Lisburn owe to their former Huguenot benefactors.

PALATINE RECORDS

> In the year seventeen hundred and nine
> In came the brass-coloured Palatine
> From the ancient banks of the Swabian Rhine

The traveller in the quiet Irish countryside particularly in Coutny Limerick may occasionally to his surprise chance upon names like Teskey, Switzer, Delmage, Fitzelle, Hartwick, Shire, Sparling, Piper, Embury, Glazier, Miller and Heck. On enquiry he would no doubt be proudly informed by bearers of these names that their forebears were of Palatine stock. Such names of course readily identify a large group of families who settled in Ireland having been forced to flee the Palatinate province of the Rhine because of religious persecution occasioned by the wars of the Spanish Succession.

In September 1709 upwards of eight hundred German speaking Protestant refugees landed at the port of Dublin. As many more sailed directly to North America where they settled principally in Pennsylvania and North Carolina. Those who remained in Ireland were settled mainly on the Southwell (Rathkeale) and Oliver (Kilfinane) estates in County Limerick and to a lesser extent in north County Kerry. They were allowed eight acres of land for every man, woman and child at five shillings rent per acre, the Government undertaking to pay the entire amount of rent for twenty years.

In 1760 John Wesley visited the Palatine community in County Limerick: under the date of July 9 we read in his journal:

> 'I rode over to Killiheen, a German settlement, nearly
> twenty miles south of Limerick. It rained all the way
> but the earnestness of the poor people made us quite
> forget it. In the evening I preached to another colony
> of Germans at Ballygarane. The third is at Court Mattrass,

33

At the Palatine's cottage door.

a mile from Killiheen. I suppose three such towns are scarce to be found again in England or Ireland. There is no cursing or swearing, no Sabbath-breaking, no drunkenness, no ale-house in any of them. How will these poor foreigners rise up in the judgement against those that are round about them.'

Some twenty years later the historian Ferrar following a visit to the same area left us the following account of the Palatine settlement in Co. Limerick:

'The Palatines preserve their language, but it is declining; they sleep between two beds; they appoint a burgomaster to whom they appeal in all disputes. They are industrious men and have leases from the proprietor of the land at reasonable rents; they are consequently better fed and clothed than the generality of Irish peasants. Besides, their mode of husbandry and crops are better than those of their neighbours. They have by degrees left off their sour krout, and feed on potatoes, butter, milk, oaten and wheaten bread, some meat and fowles, of which they rear many . . . The women are very industrious . . . Besides their domestic employments and the care of their children, they reap the corn, plough the land and assist the men in everything. In short the Palatines have benefited the county by increasing tillage and are a laborious and independent people who are mostly employed on their small farms'.

Today their numbers are greatly reduced due to emigration and to the fact that the Government discontinued its original rent-free land scheme. Moreover the brown-eyed dark-haired Palatine girls did not escape the attentions of the local farmers' sons if we are to judge by that well-known Munster ballad entitled *The Palatine's Daughter:*

As I roved out one evening through the woods of Ballyseedy,
Whom should I meet on a cool retreat but a Palatine's
                              daughter ....
You'll find gold and silver, oh! and land without tax or
                              charges,
And a pretty lass to wed if you choose a Palatine's
                              daughter.

If a desire to establish roots is about to send you in quest of your Irish-Palatine forebears you can indulge in a little preliminary armchair research by procuring a copy of *The Palatine Families of Ireland.* This privately printed book is a chronicle of two hundred and six Palatine families who made their homes in places like Rathkeale, Ballingrane, Adare, Killiheen and Kilfinane. The author is Hank Jones, who lives in Studio City, California, U.S.A. Appended to the book is a list of source material dealing with the Palatines in Ireland calculated to keep the most avid researcher busy for a long time.

QUAKER RECORDS. People whose ancestors were in the Quaker tradition in Ireland should have little difficulty in tracing their forebears thanks to the fact that members of the Society of Friends evidently brought to bear on record keeping the same exacting standards that govern the conduct of their everyday lives. After the visit to Ireland of George Fox, founder of the Society in 1669, regular meetings both for worship and business were established and concise and accurate accounts of the proceedings of such meetings made. A few years previously in 1654 William Edmundson, a native of Westmoreland, convened the first settled meeting in Ireland at Lurgan, Co. Armagh attended by Richard and Anthony Jackson, John Thompson, Richard Fayle, John Edmundson and William Moon. Very quickly Meetings were established in all four provinces, the first Leinster Meeting taking place in Dublin about 1655 at the home of Richard Fowkes, a tailor, near Polegate. In Munster there were Meeting Houses in most of the major market towns including Cork, Kinsale, Limerick, Waterford, Youghal and Bandon.

Great value was attached by the Society to the preservation of records of all kinds. Records of births, marriages and deaths in addition to giving the usual details of such events are actually arranged in family groups with a system of page references to individuals born or married later thus making possible the identification of the entire family group.

Records relating to the provinces of Munster, Leinster and Connaught are preserved in the Friends Meeting House in Eustace Street off Dublin's Dame Street. Here one can inspect (on Thursday forenoons, please) huge volumes of births, marriages and deaths from places as far apart as Lisburn in County Antrim to Youghal in County Cork, ranging in date from the mid-1600's to the present day. Among the records housed here are six manuscript volumes of Quaker wills, mainly 17th and 18th century, from the Meetings at Carlow, Edenderry, Mountmellick, Wexford and Dublin. Also in the Historical Library at Eustace Street are some 3,000 letters of and to Friends containing many well known signatures, a few journals and diaries and much correspondence and data relative to relief work, especially that done during the Famine of 1847, together with a large file of manuscript pedigrees compiled by Thomas Webb of Dublin. If for one reason or another you are unable to visit the Society's headquarters in Eustace Street, the library staff will undertake to search the records on your behalf for a fee which by present day standards can only be regarded as nominal.

Records relating to the province of Ulster are held in the Friends Meeting House, Lisburn, Co. Antrim. In the archives here are preserved vital statistics relating to the province of Ulster and beyond, including records of the following Meetings: Antrim, Ballinderry, Ballyhagan, Ballymoney, Coleraine, Cootehill, Hillsborough, Lisburn, Lurgan, Oldcastle and Rathfryland. A most extensive account of the records at Lisburn will be found in the Report of the Deputy Keeper, Public Record Office, Belfast, 1951-53, pp. 29-309. Should you wish to know more about Quaker records we would like to draw your attention to the following book — *Guide to Irish Quaker Records* by *Olive C. Goodbody.* It can be bought at the Government Publications Sales Office, G.P.O. Arcade, Dublin.

ANCESTRY PERIODICALS. Once we find a record of our ancestors instinctively we begin to wonder what manner of men and women were they. What of the faces behind the names? How did the Irish in the past really live? What did they wear? What kind of homes had they? These are the questions which the current (1972) issues of the *Irish Ancestor* helps to answer. This lavishly illustrated twice yearly publication is edited by Miss Rosemary ffolliott, Pirton House, Dundrum, Dublin 14 to whom enquiries regarding subscription rates and so forth should be addressed.

Another useful periodical is *The Irish Genealogist,* journal of the Irish Genealogical Research Society. The object of this society is to promote and encourage the study of Irish genealogy and to make a contribution towards repairing the loss of records sustained in the destruction of the Public Record Office by collecting books and manuscripts relating to genealogy, heraldry and kindred subjects. For those interested in becoming members of the society the address is The Irish Club, 82, Eaton Square, London, S.W.1.

AVAILABILITY OF RECORDS. Those who are giving some thought to tracing relatives and ancestors in Ireland will be encouraged on learning that authorities in Irish libraries, archives and record offices are liberal in regard to making available to members of the public items from their collections for research and study purposes. Short of requesting for private perusal MS. 58 Trinity College Library (this happens to be the Book of Kells!) genuinely interested enquirers can expect to be given facilities to inspect almost any document that is a public record. It is hoped that readers will get a clear idea from the lists that follow of the nature and extent of records available in the various Irish record repositories. These lists can in no sense be regarded as comprehensive but it would be fair to say that they illustrate the amount of record material still available in Ireland despite the ravages of man and time.

LIST BASED ON REPORTS OF DEPUTY
KEEPER, PUBLIC RECORD OFFICE
DUBLIN AND SHORT GUIDE TO
PUBLIC RECORD OFFICE OF IRELAND

MARRIAGE LICENCE BONDS, INDEXES TO:

Armagh, 1727-1845. Cashel and Emily,
1664-1807.
Clogher, 1711-1866. Clonfert, see Killaloe.
Cloyne, 1630-1867. Cork and Ross, 1623-
1845.
Derry (five bonds), 1702, 1705, 1722.
Down, Connor and Dromore, 1721-1845.
Dublin (Marriage Licence Grant Books,
1672-1741.
Dublin (Marriage Licence Bonds), 1718-46.
Elphin, 1733-1845. Kildare, 1790-1865.
Killala and Achonry, 1787-1842.
Killaloe, 1719-1845.
Kilmore and Ardagh, 1697-1844.
Limerick, 1827-1844. Meath, 1665, 1702-
1845.
Ossory, Ferns and Leighlin, 1691-1845.
Raphoe, 1710-1755, 1817-1830. Tuam,
1769-1845.
Waterford and Lismore, 1649-1845.

Valuation and Tax Records

Land Commission: Tithe applotment books,
i.e. books containing particulars of
holdings subject to tithe, giving
occupiers' names, compiled to provide a
basis for tithe commutation, under the
Tithe Composition Acts, 1823 and
subsequently.
Valuation Office: Mainly books compiled c.
1826-51, in the course of work on the
general valuation, giving various
particulars of holdings and tenants,
viz.: field books (4578), house books
(4262), record of tenure books (470).
Quit Rent Office: Records transferred on
the removal of the office to the Land
Commission in 1943, dealing with quit
rents and other land revenues of the
crown, management of crown property and
related matters, from the 17th century
onwards. Includes much material on the
17th century surveys and forfeitures,
especially a set of certified copies of
the Civil Survey of 1654-56 (originals
destroyed, 1922), 83 original Down
Survey and distribution (in which the
changes of ownership brought about by
the 17th century land settlement are
summed up), the crown rental of 1706,
numerous series of letter-books, account-
books, correspondence, memoranda and
files of documents, ranging from 1689
to 1942, with 15 boxes of copies and
extracts from deeds, patents and other
records from the 15th century onwards.
Much of the 17th century material was
formerly in the Headford collection,
belonging to the descendants of Sir
Thomas Taylor, the colleague of Sir

William Petty in the making of the Down
Survey, and was bought in 1837 by the
Commissioners of Woods and Forests, under
whom the Quit Rent Office was at the time
functioning. Much of the earlier material
originated in the Forfeiture Office,
which functioned from 1703 to 1823, in
succession to the Commissioners of
Forfeitures, appointed to administer the
forfeited estates.

Parish Church Records

The position with regard to the custody of
parochial records is that under the
parochial records acts of 1875 and 1876
records of baptisms and burials prior
to 1871 and marriages prior to 31 March,
1845, of the late established church,
were constituted public records, but
where an adequate place of storage was
available locally they were allowed to
remain in the custody of the incumbent
by the authority of a retention order
made by the Master of the Rolls. In 1922
the pre-1871 records of 1006 parishes
were in the Public Record Office, while
the remaining 637 were in local custody
under retention orders (see table in
P.R.I. rep. D.K. 28, appendix) a revised
version of this appendix, indication also
any known copies of destroyed registers,
is available in the search room.

Material now in the Public Record Office is
as follows:

Original registers - 19 parishes (Clogherny,
dioc. Armagh; Aghada, Corkbeg & Inch,
Ballyclogh, Castletownroche, Cloyne,
Fermoy, Macroom, dioc. Cloyne; St. Mary
Shandon, dioc. Cork, vol. 1861-78 only;
Killinick, dioc. Ferns; Inch, dioc.
Glendalough; Clane, Curragh Camp and
Newbridge Garrison, Ballysax marriages
from 1845, dioc. Kildare; Dungarvan,
Templemichael, dioc. Lismore; Clonard,
dioc. Meath; Athenry, dioc. Tuam).
Copies of registers - 27 parishes
(Aghabullog, Carrigtwohill and Mogeesha,
Castletownroche and Bridgetown, Killeagh,
Magourney, Midleton, dioc. Cloyne;
Ahascragh, dioc. Clonfert, formerly
Elphin; Ardcanny and Chapel Russell,
Fedamore, dioc. Limerick; Ashfield, dioc.
Kilmore; Ballymartle, Fanlobbus or
Dunmanway, dioc. Cork; Cloghran, Crumlin,
St. Paul, dioc. Dublin; Clonmore, dioc.
Ferns; Clonmore, dioc. Ossory; Doon, Toem,
Dioc. Cashel and Emly; Dromod and Prior,
dioc. Ardfert; Drumcliff, dioc. Elphin;
Drumcree, Killochonogan, dioc. Meath;
Glengariff, dioc. Ross; Killeigh, dioc.
Kildare; St. Peter (Drogheda), dioc.
Armagh; Templemichael, dioc. Ardagh).
Parochial returns (returns of baptisms,
marriages and burials made by incumbents
on the occasion of a visitation) -
parishes of Innismacsaint, dioc. Clogher,

1660-1866, Inniskeel, dioc. Raphoe,
1699-1700 and 1818-64, and St. Mary's,
Dublin, 1831-70.
Extracts from registers - appreciable
quantity for eight parishes only
(Ballingarry, dioc. Cashel; Carne and
Kilpatrick, dioc. Ferns; Castlerickard,
dioc. Meath; Churchtown, dioc. Cloyne;
Durrow, dioc. Ossory; St. Andrew's and
St. Kevin's, dioc. Dublin).

Census Records

County Antrim, census returns 1851,
parishes Tickmacrevan, Carncastle,
Grange, Kilwaughter, Larne, Craigs,
Ballymoney, Donaghy, Rasharkin, Killead,
Aghagallon, Aghalee, Ballinderry.
County Cavan, census returns 1821,
parishes Annageliffe, Ballymacue,
Castlerahan, Castleterra, Crosserlough,
Denn, Drumlummon, Drung, Larah, Kilbride,
Kilmore, Kinawley, Lavey, Lurgan,
Munterconaght, Mullagh. Census returns
1841, parish Killeshandra.
County Derry, census returns 1831, parishes
Agivey, Macosquin, Ballyaghran, Killowen,
Aghanloo, Tamlaght, Finlagan, Templemore,
Arboe, Termoneeny, Banagher, Glendermot.
County Fermanagh, census returns 1821,
parishes Derryvullen, Aghalurcher.
Census returns 1841, parish Currin.
Census returns 1851, parish Drumheeran.
County Galway, census returns 1821,
baronies Arran and Athenry.
County Meath, census returns 1821,
baronies Upper and Lower Navan.
County Offaly, (King's), census returns
1821, barony of Ballybritt including
town of Birr formerly Parsonstown.
County Waterford, census returns 1841,
parish Lismore.
Complete for all Ireland, census returns
1901.

Wills (Diocesan), Indexes To:

Ardagh, 1695-1858. Ardfert and Aghadoe,
1690-1858.
Armagh, 1677-1858 (M.Y.).
  (and Drogheda District, 1691-1846) (A.Y.)
Cashel and Emly, 1618-1858. Clogher,
1661-1858.
Clonfert, 1663-1857. Cloyne, 1621-1858
(damaged).
Connor, 1622-1858 (and an entry of 1859).
Cork and Ross, 1548-1858 (and two
Probates, 1454, 1470).
Derry, 1612-1858. Down, 1646-1858.
Dromore, 1678-1858 (damaged).
Dublin, 1536-1858 (fragments). (Printed in
appendixes to 26th and 30th Reports of
the Deputy Keeper of the Records).
Elphin, 1650-1858 (fragments).
Ferns, 1601-1858   "
Kildare, 1661-1857   "
Killala and Achonry   "
Killaloe and Kilfenora   "

Kilmore, 1682-1857 (badly damaged).
Leighlin, 1682-1858 (fragments).
Limerick, 1615-1858.
Meath, 1572-1858 (fragments).
Newry and Mourne, 1727-1858 (fragments).
Ossory, 1536-1858 (very badly damaged).
Raphoe, 1684-1858   "   "   "
Tuam, 1648-1858   "   "   "   ,
Waterford and Lismore, 1648-1858 (very
badly damaged).

Collections of Family Papers

Edgeworth papers, late 17th-early 19th
centuries, relating to family property
in Co. Longford and the town of Kinsale,
including a volume of copies of documents
dealing with the management of the
family property compiled by Maria
Edgeworth in continuation of the Black
Book of Edgeworthstown. Sarsfield Vesey
papers, dealing with property of the
Sarsfield and Vesey families in counties
Dublin, Wicklow, Kildare and Carlow,
mainly late 17th and 18th centuries
(deeds 1414-1808). Memo in P.R.I. rep.
D.K. 56, p.342, with list of deeds,
index to correspondence, and some items
printed in full.
Carew papers, relating to Carew family of
Castle Boro, Co. Wexford, 18th and early
19th centuries. Calendared for the
Irish Manuscripts commission by A.K.
Longfield (Shapland Carew papers,
Dublin, 1946).
Monteagle papers, relating to the families
of Spring and Rice and their property in
counties Kerry and Limerick, 1669-1925.
Greville papers, relating to the estates
of the Greville family in Co. Cavan,
early 19th century. Memo in P.R.I.
rep. D.K. 57, p.468.
Hamilton papers, relating the property of
the Hamilton family in counties Armagh
and Down, 17th and 18th centuries.
Bateman papers, relating the property of the
Bateman family in Co. Kerry, 1648-1848.
King-Harman papers, relating the King-Harman
estates in counties Longford, Kildare,
Queen's County and Westmeath, 1656-1893.
Fitzpatrick papers, relating to the property
of the Fitzpatrick family (barons of
Upper Ossory and Gowran), mainly in
counties Leix and Kilkenny, 1574-1842.
Wyche documents, i.e. papers of Sir Cyril
Wyche, Chief Secretary to the Duke of
Ormonde, 1676-82, and Viscount Sidney,
1692-93, and also Lord Justice, 26 June
1693-9 May 1695 and for some time one of
the Trustees for the Sale of Forfeited
Estates. Consists of correspondence,
king's letters, memoranda, accounts and
miscellaneous papers, relating to
forfeitures, military and ecclesiastical
affairs and the administration generally.
Detailed catalogue in search room.
Memorandum with partial catalogue and
some documents printed in full in P.R.I.

rep. D.K. 57, pp. 479-518.

Frazer collection of papers relating to the 1798 period and after. Most of this appears to have originated with the firm of Kemmis, who for some generations acted as solicitors for the crown in criminal causes. It consists of miscellaneous papers relating to the rising of 1798, including a series of reports from an informer, 'J. Smith', and copies of minutes of evidence at courts martial in connection with the rising in Wexford, reports of trials of Ribbon Men in 1840, a series of letters of Sir Jonah Barrington and his family, dealing mainly with his money difficulties, and a brief information in the case of the Queen v. William Smith O'Brien and Thomas Francis Meagher, 1848. Special catalogue in search room. Memorandum in P.R.I. rep. D.K. 55, p.145.

Prim collection of miscellaneous papers relating to the history of Kilkenny in the 17th and 18th centuries. Catalogue in P.R.I. rep. D.K. 58.

A large collection of papers (reports, accounts and correspondence) presented by the Religious Society of Friends, dealing with the work of the society in relieving distress, 1847-65. The Lindsay collection, consisting mainly of material relating to the family of Bermingham of Athenry, Co. Galway, and the claim by Edward Bermingham to the Athenry peerage in 1824, and including a set of copies of parliamentary writs, a visitation book of the diocese of Meath, 1762, a volume of letters and memoranda relating to the Irish Record Commission of 1810-30, and the 8th report of the Maynooth College Commission, 1824. Catalogue in P.R.I. rep. D.K. 56, pp. 58 and 397.

Clifden papers, relating to the property of the Agar family (viscounts Clifden) in and near Gowran, Co. Kilkenny, 1670-1895.

Lenigan papers, relating to the property of the Lenigan family and related families of Evans, Armstrong and Fogarty, in and near Thurles, Co. Tipperary, 18th and 19th centuries.

Osborne papers, relating to the property of the Osborne family, mainly in Co. Waterford, mid. 17th to late 19th century.

Genealogical Collections

Betham genealogical abstracts (214 volumes of abstracts compiled by Sir William Betham for genealogical purposes, mainly from Prerogative wills prior to 1800).

Betham correspondence (eight volumes, dealing with his genealogical researches, including memoranda and extracts from records).

Thrift genealogical abstracts (26 bundles of abstracts made by Miss G. Thrift). Names in testamentary and ecclesiastical

documents abstracted in this collection are included in indexes forming appendix Ib to P.R.I. rep. D.K. 57 and appendices IIc and IId to P.R.I. rep. D.K. 55.

Groves genealogical abstracts (fifteen boxes of abstracts compiled by the late Tenison Groves). List and index of names in search room.

Grove-White parish register extracts (43 volumes of extracts from registers, mainly from Co. Cork).

Crossle genealogical abstracts (19 parcels of abstracts made by the late Philip G. Crossle). Card index in search room.

Miscellaneous Matter

Lists of inhabitants of the baronies of Newcastle and Uppercross, Co. Dublin, c. 1652. M 2467. Copy of a book of survey, Co. Dublin, 1658. M 2475.

Copies of 24 proclamations, miscellaneous subjects, 1652-1691, from originals in the Public Library, Philadelphia. M 3144-3167.

Copy of a list of forfeiting proprietors, from commonwealth council book no. A 35. M 752.

Copies of and extracts from subsidy rolls, hearth money-rolls, and poll-tax assessments and accounts, 1634-99, various places, counties Dublin, Armagh, Fermanagh and Tyrone. M 2468 74.

Volume of notes of receipts of revenue and payments, Dec. 1682 Mar. 1683, by John Price, receiver general. M 2539.

Volume of copies of ecclesiastical instruments and proceedings, principally for the diocese of Dublin, 17th century, with other miscellaneous extracts, including a description of counties Sligo, Donegal and Fermanagh and Lough Erne, by the Rev. William Henry, 1739. M 2533.

Three volumes of copies of petitions, king's letters, bills, acts and correspondence, temp. Chas II-Wm III. M 2458-60.

Volume of correspondence, petitions, etc. (20 items), c. 1678-97, some originals, some copies, including original letter from inhabitants of Belfast declaring readiness to submit to James II, 14 March, 1689. M 2541.

Belturbet corporation minute books, 1708-1798, 4 sheets of corporation minutes, 1660-1664 and a volume of miscellaneous records relating mainly to charitable bequests, mid. 18th century. M 3571-3573, 3606 and 3607.

Copies from parliamentary returns, bundle 73, formerly in P.R.O. relating to the Franciscan order in Ireland, 18th century. M 2928.

Volume containing lists of salaries and pensions payable as on 26 October, 1729. M 2480.

Copy of notebook of Bishop Tenison of

Ossory, describing the state of the diocese, 1731. M 2462.

Census of the diocese of Elphin, prepared for bishop Edward Synge, 1749, arranged by parishes, giving name of head of household, religion, profession, and number of children and others in household. M 2466.

Twenty-three volumes, with a small quantity of papers, relating to the civil administration of the parish of St. Thomas, Dublin, 1750-1864 (mainly applotment books for assessment of taxation, 1823-64, also minute book of the directors of the watch, 1750-1770, grand jury cess book, 1772, register of cholera cases, 1832, deserted children's account book, 1842-64, declarations of finding of deserted children, 1852-63, and applotment warrants and notices to applot, 1764-1832). M 4940-4964.

Volume of copies of material on the history of the liberty of St. Sepulchre, Dublin, 18th century. M 2545.

Extracts from returns, religious census, 1766 (parishes in dioceses of Armagh, Cashel and Emly, Clogher, Cloyne, Connor, Derry, Dromore, Down, Dublin, Ferns, Kildare, Kilmore and Ardagh, Ossory, Raphoe and Cork and Ross). M 2476, 2478, 3582 and 3585.

Test book, 1775-76, containing names of Catholics taking the oath of allegiance under the act 13 and 14 Geo III, c. 35 from a vol. formerly in P.R.O. M 3092. Printed rep. D.K. 59, app. III.

List of freeholders, Co. Meath, 1781, from Headford MS. M 1364.

'Register of popish clergy', diocese of Meath, 1782-3. M 551.

Lists of electors, Co. Longford, 1790. M 2486-88.

Irish civil lists, 1803 and 1818. M 2425 and 2426.

Visitation books, early 19th century (diocese of Armagh, 1819-51, Cashel and Emly 1816, Clogher 1826-61, Dublin and Glendalough 1821-30, Kildare 1823 and n.d., Kilmore 1823, Meath 1823 and 1826, and Ossory 1823 and 1829). M 2491-1529.

Letter books of Lord Francis Leveson-Gower, Chief Secretary, 1829 30. M 736-38.

A number of volumes dealing with army administration in the 18th and 19th centuries, acquired from various sources, including 7 volumes dealing with the Sligo militia, 1855-7 (M 2558-63), an entry book from the Adjutant General's office, Dublin, 1763-65 (M 2554), an entry book of the Lords Justices relating to martial affairs, 1711-13 (M 2553), and 10 vols. relating to the Longford militia, 1791-1860 (M3474-3483).

Accounts of Bryan Bolger, quantity surveyor, Dublin, 1758-1834, of interest for architectural history.

Volume of copies and abstracts of charters and grants, temp. Hen. II - Hen. VIII (Armagh, Cork, Dublin, Drogheda, Kilkenny,

Leitrim, Trim, Waterford, Holy Cross Abbey and Melifont). M 2531.

Volume of transcripts of Dublin charters, Hen. II Eliz., by W. Monck Mason. M 2546.

Volume containing abstracts of entries relating to Ireland in various records now in P.R.O., London, transcript of cartulary of St. Thomas, abstracts of some Irish plea rolls, copy of rental of the lords of Lisnaw, temp. Hen.III, etc. M 2542. Memo in P.R.I., rep. D.K. 57, p.522.

Volume of extracts from statute, justiciary, de banco and memoranda rolls, temp. Edw. I - Edw.IV, in 17th century hand. M 2551.

Volume of abstracts relating to history of Dublin, temp. Hen.III, 17th century, by W. Monck Mason. M 2549. Memo in P.R.I. rep. D.K. 57, p.518.

Letter from an Irish chieftain, Cormacus Thadei, to Thomas, earl of Ormond, n.d., c. 1485-95, asking for funds and various favours. M 2427.

Volume of extracts, in 17th century hand, from patent roll 3 Edw. II, and memoranda rolls and council books, c. 1536-95, dealing with submissions of chiefs, maintenance of troops in Ireland (county cess, hostings, etc.), and copy of instructions from Queen Mary to Lord Deputy Sussex, 20 March, 1557. M 2532.

Small collection of petitions to Lord Deputy Bellingham, 1548-9. M 2439. Replies of the freeholders of the Queen's County to queries regarding remedies for disorders in the county, 1576. M 2440.

Bond of William O'Carroll, chief of his name, to Sir Henry Sidney for a debt of 13 score beeves to the captain of Her Majesty's gallowglasses. M 742.

Desmond survey, 1586 (survey of forfeited lands of the Earl of Desmond, formerly in P.R.O.) - copy of portion relating to Co. Kerry (printed) and Co. Limerick (MS). M 5037, 5038.

Peyton's survey, 1586 (survey of forfeited lands in Co. Limerick, formerly in P.R.O.) - calendar by J. M. McEnery, formerly of the P.R.O. M 5039.

Volume of abstracts of inquisitions, counties Dublin and Wicklow, Hen.VI - Chas. II, by W. Monck Mason. M 2543.

Volume of extracts from records illustrating the history of the Earldom of Ulster (De Lacy and De Burgo), Kildare, Louth, Ormond, Desmond).

LIST BASED ON REPORTS OF DEPUTY KEEPER, P.R.O., N.I., VARIOUS YEARS, PRINCIPALLY 1951-53, WITH APPROXIMATE DATES COVERED BY RECORDS, TOGETHER WITH YEAR AND PAGE OF RELEVANT REPORT.

Acheson family notes, 17c., 1939-45, p.15.
Adair of Co. Antrim, pedigrees and notes, 17c., 18c., 19c., 1935, p.8.
Adams family records, Co. Armagh, 18c., 1951-53, p.30.
Agnew of Cos. Antrim and Armagh 17c., 1951-53, p.31.
Agnew of Co. Down, 17c., 1924, p.10.
Aldworth papers, 17c., 1949-50, p.20.
Alexander of Tyrone, family tree, 18c., 1951-53, p.31.
Alexander of Fermanagh, notes and tree, 1933, p.10.
Allen family of Armagh, 18c., 1951-53, p.32.
Anderson of Cos. Down and Tyrone, 17c., 1951-53, p.33.
Andrews of Antrim and Armagh, 18c., 1951-53, p.33.
Armstrong family notices, 17c., 1951-53, p.17, 35.
Arundell and associated families, 17c., 18c., 1926, p.9.
Ashe of Derry, notes and history, 1948, p.21
Atkinson of Tyrone, 17c., 1951-53, p.37.
Atkinson family pedigree of Co. Down, 18c., 1934, p.28.
Auchmuty genealogy, 17c., 18c., 1951-53,p.38.

Bacon family of Derry, notes and genealogy, 17c., 18c., 1951-53, p.38.
Baillie family history from wills, 17c., 18c., 1951-53, p.39.
Baker of Cos. Tyrone and Armagh, 17c., 18c., 1951-53, p.39.
Barton rentals, 17c., 18c., 19c., 1930, p.10.
Batt historical notes, 17c., 18c., 1951-53, p.19.
Beatty family anecdotes, 1924, p.10.
Beck Pedigree, 1600-1900, 1930, p.10, 26.
Becker notes, 17c., 18c., 1951-53, p.44.
Bell historical notices, 18c., 19c., 1951-53, p.45.
Bellew family tree, 1951-53, p.46.
Bellingham genealogy, 17c., 18c., 1951-53, p.46.
Benson family notes, 17c., 18c., 1951-53, p.47.
Berry of Cavan, Westmeath and King's Co., 1951-53, p.48.
Bigger of Co. Antrim, (1650-1850), 1949-50, pp.35, 351.
Bird family notes, (1740-1900), 1951-53, p.50.
Black family genealogy, 1951-53, p.51.
Blackwood history, (1660-1900), 1938-45, p.19.
Blair family notices, 1929, p.10.
Blennerhasset historical notes, 17c., 1927, p.29.
Bolton of Derry and Antrim, 17c., 18c., 1926, p.8.
Bond of Armagh, 1948, p.29.
Boyd genealogical notes, 1951-53, p.55.

Breden family notes, 17c., 18c., 1951-53, p.58.
Bristow genealogical notes, 17c., 18c., 19c., 1951-53, p.58.
Bullock history and notes, 16c., 17c., 18c., 1928, p.36, 1931, p.32.
Burrows family notes, 17c., 18c., 19c., 1951-53, p.64.
Bury notices, 18c., 1951-53, p.64.

Caldwell family notes, 18c., 1951-53, p.18.
Carson of Co. Monaghan, 1931, p.15.
Cary of Derry, Pedigree, 1951-53, p.71.
Caulfield genealogy, 17c., 1951-53, p.72.
Chambers family history, 17c., 1951-53, p.72.
Chapman of Armagh history, 17c., 1951-53, p.73.
Christy family of Co. Down, 17c., 18c., 1951-53, p.74.
Clarke family of Antrim and Armagh, notes, 1951-53. p.75.
Cowley genealogy, 15c.-18c., 1934, p.9.
Colvin of Armagh, various records, 18c., 1951-53, p.79.
Cooke family records, 16c., 17c., 1951-53, p.82.
Cooper records, lists, Armagh, 17c., 1951-53, p.82.
Cope genealogies, Armagh, 18c., 1951-53, p.82.
Crawford family of Co. Antrim, 17c., 18c., 1949-50, pp.69, 70.
Cunningham of Co. Donegal, (1100-1800), 1951-53, pp.10, 90.

Darley family records, 18c., 1926, p.31.
Davenport family notices, 17c., 18c., 1951-53, p.92.
Davidson of Co. Down, pedigree, 17c., 18c., 1938-45, p.47.
Delafield family history, 1946-47, p.9.
Delap of Cos. Derry and Armagh, 17c., 18c., 1951-53, p.95.
Despard genealogy, 17c., 18c., 1951-53, pp.18, 96.
Dickson, Dixon, notes on family of, Derry, Down and Armagh, 1951-53, pp.96, 97, 98.
Dobbin family notices, 17c., 18c., 19c., 1926, pp.9, 25.
Dobbs family papers, 1951-53, pp.98, 99.
Dobson genealogy, 17c., 1927, p.35.
Douglas history, Tyrone, Armagh, Antrim, 17c., 18c., 19c., 1951-53, p.100.
Downing of Co. Derry, pedigree, 1800, 1951-53, p.101.
Dowse family history, 1927, p.10.
Drennan family deeds, letters, 1928, pp.8, 9, 10.
Drought notes and pedigree, 1938-45, p.15.
Druit of Co. Armagh, 18c., 1951-53, p.102.
Dunbar of Fermanagh, notes, history, genealogy, 1951-53, p.103.

Eames family notices, 17c., 18c., 1951-53, p.105.
Echlin family genealogy 1100-1800, 1951-53, pp.106, 107.
Edwards of Co. Derry, pedigree, 1936, p.9.
Elder of Donegal, family notices, 19c.,

Public Record Office, Belfast

1951-53, pp.10, 108.
Ellis records, 1951-53, p.107.
Emison family records, lists, 1946-47, p.9.
Ewarts genealogy, (1700-1900), 1930, p.10.

Faris family records, (1600-1800), 1951-53,
  p.110.
Fawcott of Antrim and Armagh, 1951-53, p.111.
Ferrard family papers, 16c., 17c., 18c.,
  1926, p.8.
Finnis notices, (1600-1800), 1951-53, p.113.
Fisher of Co. Armagh, 17c., 1951-53, p.114.
Fletcher family notes, 1951-53, pp.114, 115,
  116.
Forsythe of Derry County, 18c., 1951-53,
  pp.117, 118.
Fox family records, Co. Armagh, 18c.,
  1951-53, p.118.
Frith lists, notes, (1600-1800), 1951-53,
  p.120.

Getty family of Belfast, bible and notes,
  19c., 1951-53, p.123.
Gibson records, Cos. Armagh and Down,
  1951-53, p.123.
Gilbert family records, Co. Armagh, 1951-53,
  p.123.
Gordon Clan of Co. Antrim, 1935, p.12.
Graham family notices, 1934, pp.56, 57.
Greer genealogy, various counties, 17c.,
  18c., 1951-53, pp.17, 130, 131.
Gregg of Derry and Antrim, various dates,
  1951-53, p.132.
Grierson of Scotland and Ireland, (1500-
  1800), 1951-53, p.132.

Hall of Cos. Antrim and Monaghan, 18c.,
  1951-53, p.135.
Hamilton family history, in extenso,
  1951-53, pp.136, 137.
Hanna family tree, 1946-47, p.6.
Hare genealogical records, 17c., 1951-53,
  p.139.
Harman notices, 1951-53, p.140.
Harrison family of Co. Armagh, 18c.,
  1951-53, p.141.
Haughton records, Antrim and Armagh, 1951-53,
  p.142.
Heather family notices, 18c., 1951-53, p.144.
Henderson family tree, various counties,
  18c., 1927, p.7.
Hewitt of Antrim and Armagh, 17c., 18c.,
  19c., 1951-53, p.146.
Hill of Cos. Antrim and Down, 17c., 18c.,
  1951-53, p.148.
Hillary etc., of Armagh and Down, 1951-53,
  p.148.
Hobson family records, Tyrone, Antrim,
  Armagh, 1951-53, p.150.
Hogg of Cos. Armagh and Antrim, 18c., 1951-53,
  pp.150, 151.
Holmes genealogy, 17c., 18c., 1951-53, p.19.
Houston family records, 1927, pp.7, 41.
Hughes genealogical chart, 17c., 18c., 1932,
  p.9.
Hull family of Co. Down, 1932, p.12.
Hume records, 1951-53, p.155.
Hunter of Cos. Antrim, Down and Armagh,
  1951-53, p.155.

Irwin, Irvine, etc., genealogy, various dates,
  1951-53, pp.20, 158.

Jackson family documents, early dates, 1951-53,
  pp.20, 159.
Johnston of Co. Down, genealogical notes,
  (1000-1800), 1946-47, p.68.
Johnstone family records, 16c., 17c., 18c., 1928
  p.65.
Jones genealogy, 17c., 18c., 1951-53, p.163.

Kellett family history, 18c., 1951-53, p.165.
Kenah, notes and history, 1951-53, p.166.
Kennedy of Clogher and Derry, family trees,
  1938-45, p.16.
Kerr genealogy, (1100-1900), 1951-53, p.167.
Kilpatrick family of Donegal, 18c., 19c.,
  1951-53, p.10.
King family notices, various dates, 1951-53,
  pp.16, 18, 168, 169.
Kirk of Cos. Antrim and Armagh, 18c., 1951-53,
  pp.170, 171.
Kirkpatrick pedigree etc., (1300-1800), 1951-53,
  p.170.
Knight family records, 18c., 1951-53, p.170.
Knox genealogy, various dates, 1948, p.6.

Langtree family notes, 18c., 1951-53, p.172.
Lecky genealogical notes, Donegal, 18c., 1951-53
  p.10.
Lewis family records, 18c., 1938-45, p.15.
Lombard history, 17c., 1951-53, p.180.
Lowry family genealogy, (1600-1900), 1931, p.13.
Luther genealogy, 17c., 1951-53, p.182.
Lynas etc., of Armagh, various dates, 1951-53,
  pp.178, 182.

McDonald of Fermanagh, pedigree, 18c., 19c.,
  1938-45, p.60.
McNeill, notes and pedigree, (1400-1900), 1951-5
  p.21.
Magennis etc., 1951-53, p.199.
Magrath family notes, 17c.-19c., 1951-53, p.199.
Maitland of Co. Down, pedigree, 18c., 1938-45,
  p.6.
Marsh family chronicle, 17c., 18c., 1951-53,
  p.202.
Marshall of Armagh and Antrim, various dates,
  1951-53, p.203.
Matthews family notices, various dates, 1951-53,
  pp.204, 205.
McAskie family, notes etc., 18c., 1951-53, p.184
McBride records, Armagh, 16c., 17c., 1951-53,
  p.184.
McCance and allied families, early dates, 1925,
  pp.7, 8, 9.
McGready of Co. Down, family tree, (1700-1900),
  1930, p.10.
McCullogh genealogy and notices, 18c., 19c.,
  1951-53, pp.18, 188.
McGusty family records, (1600-1850), 1951-53,
  p.192.
McNeil etc., family chronicle and notes, (1400-
  1900), 1951-53, p.196.
McQuiston Family, births, and deaths, 1690-1883,
McTier of Belfast, notes etc., 17c., 18c., 1929,
  pp.10, 28.
Mercer family of Down and Armagh, various dates,
  1951-53, p.207.

Meredith of Cos. Antrim and Down, assorted records, 1951-53, p.207.

Miller family records, some early, 1951-53, p.209.

Milliken chronicle, Down and Armagh, 1951-53, p.210.

Montgomerty family notices and pedigrees, most extensive, 1951-53, pp.212, 213; 1946-47, p.95; 1938-45, pp.16, 17.

Moore pedigree, 17c., 18c., 1951-53, p.215.

Morrison of Cos. Tyrone and Armagh, various dates, 1951-53, p.217.

Mulholland family notices, extensive, 1951-53, pp.21, 219.

Nesbitt genealogy, (1600-1850), 1951-53, p.223.

Nicholson of various northern counties, early date, 1951-53, pp.225, 226.

Nixon family documents, middle dates, 1924, p.10.

Parkinson family papers, Co. Louth, 1951-53, p.233.

Patterson Records, some early, mainly Armagh, Antrim and Tyrone, 1951-53, pp.234, 235.

Person family of Armagh, early dates, 1951-53, p.237.

Phillips of Derry, notes, early date, 1927, p.4.

Pillar of Armagh, Tyrone and Down, middle date, 1951-53, p.238.

Pim family tree, (1600-1900), 1951-53, p.17.

Porter of Armagh, various records, early date, 1951-53, p.240.

Purdy of Co. Tyrone, notes, early date, 1951-53, p.243.

Ray or Rea or Ray of Cos. Down and Armagh, early date, 1951-53, pp.244, 245, 246, 247.

Reade family chronicle, (1600-1900), 1951-53, pp. 246, 247.

Richardson of Cos. Armagh, Down and Tyrone, various dates, 1951-53, pp.248, 249.

Robinson records, assorted, middle date, 1951-53, p.250.

Rogers family records, Antrim, Tyrone, Down, and Armagh, various dates, 1951-53, p.252.

Rowan of Co. Antrim, family tree, (1500-1900), 1938-45, p.19.

Savage family records, very extensive, 1951-53, pp.79, 125, 257.

Shaw family documents, various dates, 1951-53, p.260.

Smyth records, notes, pedigrees, various dates, 1951-53, pp.264, 265.

Stephens of Armagh, pedigree, 18c., 1951-53. p.269.

Stephenson family records, middle dates, 1925, pp.7, 8; 1937, p.8.

Stewart genealogical notices, very extensive, 1946-47, p.118; 1938-45, pp.13, 16.

Stone family pedigree, (1300-1800), 1951-53, pp.19, 271.

Stouppe documents, middle dates, 1925, pp. 7, 8.

Swanzy deeds and notes, middle dates, 1951-53, pp.19, 274.

Tandy family notices, (1600-1800), 1951-53, p.275.

Taylor documents, notes, etc., early dates, 1951-53, pp.19, 276.

Thompson family documents, extensive, 1951-53, pp.16, 21, 278.

Travers family charts, 17c., 18c., 1951-53, p.283.

Turner of Armagh and Down, middle dates, 1951-53, p.285.

Van Homrigh genealogy, 17c., 18c., 1951-53, p.287.

Walker family records, Cos. Down, Tyrone and Monaghan, 1951-53, p.289.

Wardell genealogy, 18c., 1951-53, p.293.

Watson documents, early dates, 1925, pp.7, 8.

Webb family records, 17c., 18c., 1951-53, p.294.

West family tree, 1951-53, p.296.

Wilkinson family notices, Cos. Antrim and Armagh, 1951-53, p.301.

Wilson papers, pedigrees, etc., very extensive, 1925, pp.8, 9; 1951-53, pp.303, 304.

Wray documents and history, early dates, 1946-47, p.9.

Young historical notices, 1924, p.10; 1951-53, p.308.

MAJOR COLLECTIONS

Antrim Deeds - papers of the Earl of Antrim covering period 1610-1784; contains 360 documents relating to his estates in Cos. Antrim and Derry. Index to deeds in D.K's Report, 1928, Appendix B.

Armagh Manor Rolls - (microfilm), original collection in Armagh Library; contains accounts of court cases held on manors or estates.

John Mitchel Letters - copies of letters written by Mitchel while in exile first in Van Diemen's Land (Tasmania) and later in America.

Downshire Letters, 18th century - Marquis of Downshire collection; records relating to the rise of the United Irishmen.

Paterson Collection 1737-1888 - papers relating to the affairs of the Irwin family of Carnagh, Co. Armagh.

Massereene Tithe Book, 17th century - mainly a register of deeds affecting the estate of Viscount Massereene and Ferrard.

Findlay and Williams Collection - military records 1727 2863, consisting of militia and army lists.

Genealogical Office, Dublin

Kings, Princes, Chieftains.......a book of pedigrees and notes on Gaelic families including O'Brien, O'Connor, O'Melaghlin, MacMurrough, O'Neill, O'Donnell, MacDonlevy, MacLoughlin, O'Carroll, MacCarthy, MacDermott, O'Phelan, O'Farrell, Magennis, Maguire, O'Kelly, O'More, O'Reilly, O'Rourke, O'Sullivan, Brennan, Callaghan, O'Donoghue, O'Donovan, O'Gorman, Murphy, O'Shea, O'Toole, Fox and Fitzgibbon M.610.

Prerogative marriage licences, 1600-1800 M.605-607.

Limerick freeholders with exact addresses and occupations, 1829. MS. 623

Genealogical collections - a book of pedigrees, families include Cusack, Dillon, Lee, Sarsfield, Redmond, Arthur, MacCarthey, Taaffe, Mitchell, French, Hamilton, Gravett, Butler, Armstrong, Birchenshaw, Griffith, Bathe, St. John, Beckford, Campbell, Tuite. M.647.

The Palatines.......a book of notes on the German colony in Co. Limerick. M.540.

Obituaries from newspapers, mainly 17th, 18th centuries. M.546-551.

Co. Down wills, 1646-1858. M.472.

Kilkenny, Tipperary, Limerick families, pedigrees and notes - Andrews, Baker, Brereton, Briscoe, Cave, Cochrane, Comerford, Dodwell, Drew, Eaton, Elliott, George, Greene, Haughton, Hoare, Holmes, Langley, Lewis, Lloyd, Nelligan, Nixon, Osborne, Pigott, Rothe, St. Leger, Southwell, Sweetman, Walker, Walsh, Wheeler, Whitelaw, Wilson. M.708.

Wills, abstracts from prerogative wills of Ireland by Sir William Betham, very extensive, 17th, 18th, 19th centuries. M.223-256.

Freeholders, Co. Clare, 1829; Queen's County, 1758; Kilkenny, 1775; Donegal, 1761; Fermanagh, 1788; Meath, 1775; Roscommon, 1780; Tipperary, 1775; Longford, 1836; Armagh (Poll Book), 1753; Westmeath (Poll Book), 1761. M.442-444.

Book of genealogies and pedigrees of the following families - Armit, Brabazon, Benn, Bowen, Bray, Bloomfield, Beatty, Carney, Cuthbert, Cox, Cain, Dorman, D'Olier, Davys, Erck, Eager, Edgeworth, Fleming, Ford, Gregg, Gahan, Gamble, Greene, Gilbert, Goslin, Hearn, Humfrey, Henchy, Hatch, Hendrick, Jones, Lloyd, Little, Latham, Loughnan, Lambert, McGusty, Meadows, Mason, Manley, Noy, Parsons, Purcell, Preston, Pim, Redmond, Ridgeway, Rowan, Smith, Sloan, Talbot, Wilson, Wallis, Walker, Wall. M.384.

Funeral books, arms and genealogies of thousands of families, mainly 16th, 17th centuries. M.64-79.

Directories for year 1809 following towns - Belfast, Cork, Waterford, Limerick. M.542.

Freemen, roll for city of Dublin, 1468-1774.

Louth, county, poll tax, 17th century,

transplantation lists, 1656; book of postings and sales, 1703; book of survey and distribution, 1659; Grand Jury members, 1861, 1879. M.541.

Religious census 1766, returns for over sixty parishes in various counties. M.536-537.

Ossory (mainly Co. Kilkenny) marriage licence bonds, mainly 17th and 18th centuries. M.612-617.

Pedigrees of O'Dwyer, Grace, Heard, Cummins, Power, Slack. M.412.

Grants of arms etc. from 1552; card index in office.

Walker pedigree with tabulated pedigrees of associated families - Cooper, Sisson, Turner, Crampton, Marsh, Wall, Roper, Thompson, Garston, Digby, French, Verner, Jervis, Meredyth, Ribton, Sale. M.505.

Linea Antiqua (Roger O'Ferrall), original plus copy in three volumes by Sir William Betham, most extensive work containing genealogies and arms of Irish families.

Book of wills, pedigrees, notes etc. on the following - Farmer, Gamble, Nicholls, St. Leger, Weekes, Purdon, Leader, Donovan, Chinnery, Jephson, Aldworth, North, Hansard, Lloyd. M.523-524.

Dublin marriage licences, with dates and places of marriage, mainly 17th and 18th cent. M.473-5.

Anglo-Irish families, short pedigrees based on wills (originals destroyed), about 3,000 families, 16th, 17th, 18th centuries M.215-219.

Crown Jewels, report of the commission into disappearance of Irish crown jewels from Dublin Castle, 1908. M.507.

Book of genealogies, several families including - Rogers, Esmonde, Codde, Phaire, Hill, Jacob, Symes, Newton, King, Naper, Redmond, Moore. M.279.

Gordon family, extensive history, biography, notes. M.702 A.

Militia lists, 1761, following counties - Limerick, Cork, Tipperary, Kerry, Derry, Louth, Wicklow, Monaghan, Roscommon, Down, Donegal, Dublin, Tyrone. M.608.

Butler of Ormond, memoirs and commentary. M.711.

Army lists, 1746-1772, reviews at Tullamore, 1770; Dublin, 1771; Bandon, 1769; Cork, 1722; Drogheda, 1770; Birr, 1769; Thurles, 1772; Galway, 1771; Gort, 1769; Athlone, 1770; M.579.

Notices and wills of - Blain, Nixon, Gaven, Bowyer, Rolleston, Spunner, Bingham, Becher, Martin, Brett, Orr. M.520.

Blennerhasset pedigree, 15th cent. onwards, with allied families - Bayley, Conway, Herbert, Peppard, Lacy, Babington, Brown, Spring. M.562.

Davys, Co. Longford, notes and history. M.653.

Donnellan family, family tree, 1500-1900. M.467.

Library of Trinity College, Dublin

LIST BASED ON CATALOGUE OF MSS. IN
LIBRARY OF TRINITY COLLEGE, DUBLIN
COMPILED BY T. K. ABBOTT.

M.58   Book of Kells, 9th cent. illuminated manuscript, made and long preserved in Columcille's monastery at Kells, Co. Meath, where it remained till 1541 when the last abbot, Richard Plunket was forced to give up the abbey and its property. In 1568 the MS. was in the hands of Gerald Plunket, a harbour-master at Dublin. Later it was acquired by Richard Ussher, the primate, and from his library it entered Trinity College. MS. consists of 339 leaves of thick glazed vellum written in red, black, purple and yellow inks. There were at least two artists. It contains the four gospels, short account of Hebrew names and charters bestowing grants of land on the Abbey of Kells. Has been described as the most beautiful book in the world.

M.52:   Book of Armagh, made in 807 by the scribe Ferdomnach. MS. contains the New Testament in Latin, the Confession of St. Patrick and an account of the life of St. Martin of Tours.

M.57   Book of Durrow, so called from Durrow in Co. Offaly, like Kells, a Columban institution. MS. dates from 6th-7th cent. and is the oldest known Irish book. It contains a copy of the Gospels in Latin, an explanation of Hebrew names, epistle of St. James and summaries of the Gospels with symbols of the Evangelists. Book of Durrow used to possess a cover now lost, made by Flann, son of Malachy, King of Ireland.

M.804:   Collection of Genealogical and Historical Tracts - descent of Fitzpatrick, genealogy of Kavanagh, notice of Birminghams who changed their name to MacFeorais, genealogy of Reynolds from Milesius to a chief called Megranall, a catalogue of the Kings of the race of Ir who ruled over all Ireland.

M.1440:   Historia et Genealogia Familiae de Burgo (Burke), with an account of the high connections of the Burkes in England, France and Ireland, and description of the property and rights of MacWilliam Burke. Contains nine pictures full-length portraits of Burkes in complete armour, the first being Richard Mor, also a roll of arms of various branches of the de Burgos.

M.1280:   Collection of Romances, Historical Poems and Genealogies - pedigrees of O'Duffy, O'Murrigan, O'Donnellan, O'Hamill.

M.1294:   Caithreim Turlogh:- pedigrees of various branches of the O'Brien family, also O'Gorman, O'Loughlin and MacBrody.

M.1326:   Medical Treatise - with the names of physicians O'Fergus, O'Callanan and O'Cannavan, noted physician of West Connaught.

M.1336:   Brehon (Old Irish) Law Tracts - relative duties of the chieftain and his subjects; laws relating to property, theft, evidence; article on the rights of poets; scripture genealogies; list of women celebrated in Irish history; pedigrees of O'Dooley, O'Linchy, O'Coffey, O'Driscoll, O'More and other families of Leix.

M.1419:   History of O'Rody family - poems, songs and notes.

M.1429:   Collection of Irish Deeds - with details of wills, mortgages, covenants, indentures, early 16th centuary.

M.1296:   History of the Irish race - account of the Milesians; pedigrees of M'Carthys, O'Sullivan Mor, Beare and Moyle; O'Keeffe, MacGillicuddy and O'Cahillfamily trees; pedigree of the O'Donoghues for twenty seven generations showing stem of the two main branches, O'Donoghue of the Glens and O'Donoghue of the Lakes; a short account of English families in Ireland; article on the early inhabitants of Ireland; genealogies of the following - O'Moriarty, O'Donovan, O'Cullen, O'Brien, MacMahon, O'Kennedy, MacNamara, O'Dea, MacGrath, MacCoghlan, MacConry, O'Quin, MacClancy, O'Carroll, O'Meagher, O'Hara, O'Gara, Magennis, lord of Iveagh, O'Conor Kerry, O'Conor Corcamroe, O'Loughlin of Burren, O'Neill, MacSweeney of Fanad, of Doe and of Bannagh; O'Donnell, O'Shaughnessy, MacDonnell, Earl of Antrim, Maguire, MacMorough, MacGiollapatrick, O'Mulrian, O'Melaghlin, O'Mulloy, O'Mulvey, MacAllin, now Campbell.

M.1079:   Scottish Records - pedigrees of various Scottish families including MacLeoid; description of the Shrine of Adamnan, 9th abbot of Iona.

M.1071:   Journal of events in Ireland in 1641 by O'Mellan, chiefly those in which the O'Neills were concerned but list of names include many other families.

M.1318:   Yellow Book of Lecan - historical poems about many Irish families including MacMahon of Oriel and O'Kelly of Hy-Maine; sketch of the history of the Jews from Abraham to David; account of the celebrated trees of Ireland knocked by a storm in 665; description of Cruachan, ancient palace and cemetery

Registry of Deeds, Dublin

Land Index Volumes arranged by Counties and Cities with dates.

Vol.	1	Cos. Antrim, Armagh, 1708-1738.
"	2	Cos. Armagh, Cavan, 1739-1810.
"	3	Co. Clare, 1708-1738.
"	4	Cos. Clare, Kerry, 1739-1810
"	5	Co. Cork, 1810-1819.
"	6	Cos. Clare, Kerry, Limerick, 1811-1820.
"	7	Cos. Antrim, Down, 1811-1820.
"	8	Co. Cork, 1780-1809.
"	9	Co. Cork Towns, 1780-1809.
"	10	Co. Antrim, 1739-1810.
"	11	Co. Down, 1739-1810.
"	12	Co. Cork, 1820-1828.
"	13	Cos. Tipperary, Waterford, 1708-1738.
"	14	Cos. Kerry, Limerick, 1708-1738.
"	15	Cos. Carlow, Dublin, 1708-1738.
"	16	Cos. Carlow, Laois, 1739-1810.
"	17	Cos. Clare, Kerry, Limerick, 1821-1825.
"	18	Cos. Meath, Laois, 1811-1820.
"	19	Cos. Donegal, Sligo, 1739-1810.
"	20	Cos. Cavan, Down, 1821-1825.
"	21	Co. Galway, 1826-1828.
"	22	Cos. Clare, Kerry, Limerick, 1826-28.
"	23	Cos. Down, Cavan, 1826-28.
"	24	Co. Galway, 1811-20.
"	25	Co. Leitrim, 1811-20.
"	26	Co. Cork, 1739-1779.
"	27	Cos. Kildare, Kilkenny, Offaly, 1708-1738.
"	28	Co. Offaly, 1739-1810.
"	29	Co. Kildare, 1739-1810.
"	30	Co. Kilkenny, 1739-1810.
"	31	Cos. Kilkenny, Kildare, Offaly, 1811-1820.
"	32	Cos. Kilkenny, Kildare, Offaly, 1821-1825.
"	33	Cos. Kilkenny, Kildare, Offaly, 1826-1828.
"	34	Co. Dublin, 1739-1806.
"	35	Liberties of Dublin, 1739-1810.
"	36	Co. Dublin, 1807-1819.
"	37	Co. Dublin, 1820-1828.
"	38	Cos. Mayo, Roscommon, Sligo, 1708-1738.
"	39	Cos. Mayo, Roscommon, Sligo, 1739-1810.
"	40	Cos. Mayo, Roscommon, Sligo, 1811-1820.
"	41	Cos. Donegal, Roscommon, Sligo, 1821-1825.
"	42	Cos. Donegal, Sligo, Mayo, 1826-1828.
"	43	Cos. Fermanagh, Derry, Monaghan, Tyrone, 1708-38.
"	44	Cos. Fermanagh, Derry, City, 1739-1810.
"	45	Cos. Monaghan, Tyrone, 1739-1810.
"	46	Cos. Monaghan, Tyrone, 1811-1820.
"	47	Cos. Fermanagh, Derry, 1811-1820.
"	48	Cos. Fermanagh, Derry, Monaghan, 1821-1825.
"	49	Cos. Derry, Tyrone, Fermanagh, 1826-1828.
Vol.	50	City of Cork, 1810-1819.
"	51	City of Cork, 1820-1828.
"	52	Cities of Kilkenny, Derry, Drogheda, 1780-1810.
"	53	Cities of Limerick, Waterford, 1780-1810.
"	54	Cos. Leitrim, Longford, 1739-1810.
"	55	Co. Galway, 1708-1738.
"	56	Co. Galway, 1739-1810.
"	57	Cos. Leitrim, Longford, Galway, 1821-25.
"	58	Co. Tipperary, 1739-1810.
"	59	Co. Tipperary, 1739-1810.
"	60	Cos. Waterford, Tipperary, 1811-1820.
"	61	Cos. Waterford, Tipperary, 1821-1825.
"	62	Cos. Waterford, Tipperary, 1826-1828.
"	63	Cos. Westmeath, Wexford, Wicklow, 1708-1738.
"	64	Cos. Wicklow, Waterford, 1739-1810.
"	65	Co. Wexford, 1739-1810.
"	66	Co. Westmeath, 1739-1810.
"	67	Cos. Wexford, Wicklow, 1811-1820.
"	68	Co. Westmeath, 1811-1820.
"	69	Athlone, Mullingar, 1821-1825.
"	70	Cos. Westmeath, Wexford, Wicklow, 1825.
"	71	Cos. Louth, Meath, Leix, 1708-1738.
"	72	Co. Meath, 1739-1810.
"	73	Co. Louth, 1738-1810.
"	74	Cos. Carlow, Louth, Meath, Leix, 1821-25.
"	75	Cos. Meath, Louth, Leix, 1826-1878.
"	76	Co. Limerick, 1739-1810.
"	77	Cos. Armagh, Cavan, 1811-1820.
"	78	Cos. Antrim, Armagh, 1821-25.
"	79	Cos. Armagh, Antrim, 1826-28.
"	80	City of Cork, 1739-1779.
"	81	Co. Carlow, 1811-1820.
"	82	Cos. Cavan, Donegal, Down, 1708-1738.
"	83	City of Cork, 1779-1810.
"	84	Cities Limerick, Waterford, Derry, 1811-1820.
"	85	Cities Waterford, Drogheda, Limerick, 1821-25.
"	86	Cities Kilkenny, Waterford, Derry, 1826-28.
"	87	City of Dublin, 1708-1738.
"	88	City of Dublin; A-J, 1739-1779.
"	89	City of Dublin; K-Z, 1739-1779.
"	90	City of Dublin; A-J, 1780-1792.
"	91	City of Dublin; K-Z, 1780-1792.
"	92	City of Dublin, 1793-1806.
"	93	City of Dublin, 1807-1819.
"	94	City of Dublin, 1820-1828.
"	95	Co. Antrim, 1828-1832.
"	96	Co. Armagh, 1828.
"	97	Co. Carlow, 1828-1832.
"	98	Co. Cavan, 1828-1832.
"	99	Co. Clare, 1828-1832.
"	100	Co. Cork, 1828-1832.

EXTRACTS FROM THE CATALOGUE OF MANUSCRIPTS
in the possession of the Representative
Church Body prepared by Rev. Chancellor
J. B. Leslie D. Litt.

(O.) stands for original; the rest are
copies.
(C.) Copyright reserved.
(Tr.) Transcript.

Aghalow and Carnteel Parishes, Religious
Census, 1766, with names of Householders,
(Groves Tr.).

Ahoghill Religious Census, 1766, with names
of Dissenters, Papists & Churchpeople,
(do.).

Ardagh Diocese, Summary of Religious Census,
1766, some names given, (do.).

Ardbraccan Parish, Religious Census, 1766,
giving names of Protestants, (do.).

Ardee Parish, Religious Census, 1766,
names, (do.).

Ardtrea Parish, Religious Census, 1766,
names by townlands, (do.).

Armagh County, Hearth Money Return, 1640,
of Lurgan, Derrynoose & Tynan, (do.).

Armagh Diocese, Drogheda Rural Deanery
Return, 1802.

Armagh Diocese, Parliamentary Return re
Churches, 1768, (Groves Tr.).

Armagh Diocese, Religious Census of 1766
under Parishes, (do.).

Armagh Diocese, See Rent Rolls, 16th &
17th Cent., (Groves Tr.).

Aughnamullen Parish, Religious Census,
1766, by townlands, (Groves Tr.).

Bagot Family, see Drury Papers.

Ballinlanders Marriage Register, 1852-77.

Ballyburr (Ossory), Tithe Composition
Book, 1828, (O.).

Ballymakenny (Armagh), Religious Census,
1766, giving names (Groves Tr.).

Ballymodan (Cork), copy Baptismal Registers,
1695-1793, by Rev. W. W. Stewart.

Ballynascreen (Derry) Religious Census,
1766, giving names of Protestants,
(Groves Tr.).

Ballynaslaney, Co. Wexford, Religious
Census, 1766, some names given,
(Groves Tr.).

Beaulieu (Armagh), Religious Census 1766,
with names, (Groves Tr.).

Boho (Clogher), Religious Census, 1766,
with names, (Groves Tr.).

Bovevagh (Derry), Religious Census, 1766,
names by townlands, (Groves Tr.).

Butler, Isaac, Journal 1744, in Armagh
Library, extracts re Clergy, Monumental
Inscriptions, &c., (Groves Tr.).

Carlingford (Armagh), Religious Census,
1766, names by townlands, (Groves Tr.).

Carte Papers, extracts showing the names
of Clergy in Ireland 1647.

Cassidy, William, "Inscriptions on
Tombstones in Lambeg Church-yard,"
(printed copy).

Castledawson (Derry), Religious Census,
1766, (in Ardtrea Lists, Groves Tr.).

Charlestown (Co. Louth), Religious Census,
1766, names, (Groves Tr.).

Clergy of Church of Ireland, Biographical
index by Canon J. B. Leslie. 4 volumes.
(O.).

Clerical Obituaries, 18th Century, (Lodge
MS. in Armagh Library).

Clonkeehan Parish, Co. Louth, Religious
Census, 1766, names. (Groves Tr.).

Clonmore (Ossory), Religious Census, 1766,
two names & numbers, (Groves Tr.).

Cong (Tuam), combined Register, 1745-1759,
(O.).

Connor Diocese, Parliamentary Return re
Churches, 1768, (Groves Tr.).

Cork Diocese, Religious Census, 1766,
(Groves Tr.).

Creggan (Armagh), MS. History of Parish by
Rev. Samuel Nelson, Presbyterian
Minister (ob. 1847).

Crumlin (Dublin), Religious Census, 1766,
names of families (Groves Tr.).

Darver, Co. Louth, Religious Census, 1766,
names, (Groves Tr.).

Derry Diocese, Parliamentary Returns 1768.
"   "   Religious Census, 1766 by
parishes, giving names of Church Clergy
& other Ministers, (Groves Tr.).

Derryloran (Armagh), list of Protestant
Householders, 1740, from Hearth Money
Return, (Groves Tr.).

Derryloran (Armagh), Religious Census,
1766, names by townlands, (Groves Tr.).

Derrynoose (Armagh), list of Protestant
Householders, 1740, (do.).

Derryvullen (Clogher), Religious Census,
1766, names by townlands, (do.).

Desertcreat (Armagh), list of Protestant
Householders, 1740, (do.).

Desertmartin (Derry), Religious Census,
1766, names of "Protestants," Dissenters
& Papists given.

Donaghcloney (Dromore), extracts from
Parish Register, (Swanzy Collection).

Donaghmore (Armagh), copy of Parish
Register with Index, 1741-1825, made
by Capt. Ynyr A. Burges, D.L.

Donnybrook Parish (Dublin), Religious
Census, 1766, summary by townlands,
(Groves Tr.).

Drogheda Rural Deanery Return, 1802.

Dromiskin, Co. Louth, Religious Census,
1766, names, (Groves Tr.).

Dromore Diocese, Religious Census of
Seapatrick, 1766, (names) & summary of
other parishes (do.).

Drumachose (Derry), Religious Census,
1766, names of Church, Dissenting and
Popish families, by townlands (Groves
Tr.).

Drumglass·(Armagh), Religious Census,
1766, names by townlands, (do.).

Drumglass (Armagh), extracts from Parish
Register, 1685-1779.

Drury Family Papers, including entries

from Parish Registers of Ballysonnan, Durrow, Fountstown, Nurney, re Baggot, Gatchell, Harte, Hoysted, Kelly, Phillips, Stack & Toomey families, and biographical notices of 24 clergy.

Dublin Diocese, Grant Book, 1660-97, Calendar of, (C.), (Leslie Collection from Records lost in P.R.O.).

Dublin Diocese, twenty one Marriage Licences early 18th Cent., St. Mary's Parish, and Arklow. Memoranda & Plea Rolls, 1464-1546, extracts.

Dublin Diocese, Religious Census, 1766, summaries by Parishes.

Dunganstown Churchyard, plan of same made by Prof. Stanley Lane Poole, with names of families buried, 1643-1908.

Dunleer Parish Register (now lost), extracts from, (Swanzy Collection).

Durrow (Ossory), Parish Registers (lost), extracts copied by late Canon P. B. Wills.

Edermine (Ferns), Religious Census, 1766, names of Protestant families, (Groves Tr.).

Eglish (Armagh), Parish Registers, 1803-1935.

Ematris (Clogher), Religious Census, 1766, by townlands, (Groves Tr.).

Great Connell (Kildare), Tithe Composition Book, 1833, (O.).

Groves Transcripts of Hearth Money Returns, 1740, 1766, & Subsidy Roll, 1634, made by Tenison Groves, B.E., fully indexed, bound in 1 vol., 4to.

Hearth Money Returns, 1664-5, 1740 & 1764, indexed under Dioceses & Parishes.

Kilbroney (Dromore), Religious Census, 1766, names, (Groves Tr.).

Kildemock (Co. Louth), Religious Census, 1766, with names, (Groves Tr.).

Kildress (Armagh), Religious Census, 1766, names by Townlands, (do.).

Killaloe, Bp. Worth's Account Book of the Diocese 1661, (has much information about Clare families) (O.).

Killeagh Parish Register, extracts from, (Swanzy Collection).

Kilmore Diocese, Parish Register of Kilmore, Co. Cavan, extracts from, 1705-1875.

Kilmore Diocese, Religious Census, 1766, summary of Parishes, (Groves Tr.).

Kilrush (Killaloe), Parish Registers, 1741-1841. (O.).

Kilshanning Church and Churchyard, Co. Cork, copy of Inscriptions in, (Swanzy Collection).

Kinawley (Kilmore), Religious Census, 1766, names of Protestants, (Groves Tr.).

La Touche Family, genealogy (MS copy of printed work).

Leck (Derry), Religious Census, 1766, names by townlands, (Groves Tr.).

Long MSS., Deeds & old newspapers deposited by late Mrs. Long of St. Michan's, Dublin.

Lurgan (Kilmore), Religious Census, 1766, names of Protestant families, (Groves Tr.).

Magharafelt (Armagh), Religious Census, 1766, with names, (Groves Tr.).

Midleton (Cork), Parish Register (lost), extracts from, (Swanzy Collection).

Militia Chaplains in 1761, (Groves Tr.).

Modreeny Tithe Payers, 1839. (O.).

Monaghan, Religious Census, 1766, by townlands, (Groves Tr.).

Mullabrack Marriage Register, 1767-1811.

Newtownhamilton Baptismal Register, 1823-26 (typed copy).

Offerlane Tithe Composition Book, 1828. (Ö. in Ossory Collection).

Omeath, Co. Louth, copy of Parish Register, 1845-1936, by Rev. E. G. Ward, M.A.

Ossory, Grant Book, Marriage Licences, 1738-1804.

Philipstown, Co. Louth, Religious Census, 1766, names, (Groves Tr.).

Preban (Ferns), Tithe Composition book, 1824.

Raphoe Diocese, Religious Census, 1766, with names of Clergy & Summary, (Groves Tr.).

St. Peter's, Dublin, Marriage Licences, 1787-1824.

Seapatrick (Connor), Religious Census, 1766, names, (Groves Tr.).

Seaver Pedigree, in Swanzy Collection.

Shankill (Lurgan), Dromore Diocese:-
(1) Protestant Householders, 1740, (Groves Tr.).
(2) Subsidy Roll 1634, names by townlands.

Shanlis, Co. Louth, Religious Census, 1766, names, (Groves Tr.).

Shrule, Co. Longford, list of Protestant Parishioners, 1731.

Shrule (Ardagh), Religious Census, 1766, (Groves Tr.).

Smarmore, Co. Louth, Religious Census, 1766, names, (Groves Tr.).

Stickillen, Co. Louth, Religious Census, 1766, names, (Groves Tr.).

Swanzy Collection, transcripts &c., made by late Very Rev. H. B. Swanzy, M.A., M.R.I.A., Dean of Dromore, including:-
(I) Chancery Bills, 1667-1839, names of Parties, 1 vol.
(II) Chancery & Exchequer Bills, surnames of 3 vols.
(III) Down & Connor, First Fruit Returns, 1675-9.
(IV) Exchequer Bills, 1676-1834, names of Parties, 1 vol.
(V) Prerogative Marriage Licences A to D, list of, 2 notebooks.
(VI) Registry of Deeds, extracts with Indes of names 1 vol.
(VII) Wills, 800 summaries, typed in dictionary order.

Adair Narrative: Progress of Pres. Ch.
in Ireland (1623-1670).

Aghadowey, Co. Derry: Commonplace Book,
Rev. J. McGregor.

Antrim Book by Rev. R. Magill: Bapt. and
Marr. Regs. for parish Millrow, Co.
Antrim, 1820-39.

Antrim County: Hearth Money Rolls, 1669,
transcript copy.

Antrim Town: Bapt. and Marr. Regs.
1674-1736.

Antrim County: Protestant householders,
1740, transcripy copy.

Army lists, 1642.

Armagh Town: Bapt. and Marr. Regs.
1707-1728, 1796-1808.

Aughnacloy, Co. Tyrone: Committee Book,
1743-82.

Ballina, Co. Mayo: Subscription list for
erection of church at Ballina, 1849.

Ballymoney, Co. Antrim: Bapt. Reg. from
1817.

Bambridge, Co. Down: Marr. Reg. 1753-1794.

Bangor, Co. Down: Marr. Reg. from 1808
and outline history of congregation.

Belfast: Rosemary St. Ch. Bapt. Reg.
from 1722.

Campbell Mss.: Campbell genealogical
table by Dr. Campbell.

Carnmoney, Co. Antrim: Bapt. Reg. from
1708, Marr. Reg. from 1708, also
memoranda and session books containing
Bapt. and Marr. Registers from 1776.

Carrigart, Co. Donegal: Bapt. Reg.
1844-84 with history of congregation by
Rev. Francis McClure.

Castledawson and Magerafelt, Co. Derry:
Registers and session books, some very
early.

Castlereagh, Co. Down: Bapt. Reg. from
1809, Marr. from 1816.

Coleraine, Co. Derry: Meeting house
account book, 1802-35, Marr. Regs.
1809-1840.

Cullybackey, Co. Antrim: Bapt. Reg.
from 1812.

Down County: Subsidy Roll, 1663.

Drumaul, Randalstown, Co. Antrim: List
of seat-holders 1842.

Drumbo, Co. Down: Bapt. Regs. from 1764,
Marr. from 1787.

Dublin (Abbey Church): Bapt. Regs. from
1779, Marr. from 1805.

Derry County: List of Protestant householders 1740.

Dissenters lists 1704-1782, 1775 list
very comprehensive.

Donegal County: Hearth Money Rolls, 1669,

Derryvalley, Co. Monaghan: Bapts. from
1816.

Donegore, Co. Antrim: Bapts. and Marr.
from 1806.

Dromara, Co. Down: Marr. from 1817.

Donacloney, Co. Down: Bapts. from
1798.

Derry County: Hearth Money Rolls, 1663.

Dundalk, Co. Louth: Bapt. and Marr. Regs.
from 1819.

Dungannon, Co. Tyrone: Bapt. and Marr.
Regs. from 1790.

Enniskillen, Co. Fermanagh: Marr. Reg.
from 1819.

Fourtowns, Co. Down: Notices of Marriages
1845-61.

Frankford or Castleblaney, Co. Monaghan:
Marr. Reg. 1820-34.

Gervagh, Co. Derry: Bapt. and Marr. Regs.
from 1795.

Hamilton Estate: Rent Rolls, 1670, with
lists of tenant holders in parishes of
Bangor, Holywood, Dundonald, Ballywalter
and Killyleagh, Co. Down.

Killeshandra, Co. Cavan: Bapt. and Marr.
Regs. from about 1740.

Killyleigh, Co. Down: Transcript copy Regs.
very early c. 1692.

Larne, Co. Antrim, poll list 1833.

Lisburn: Bapt. Regs. from 1692, Marr. from
1688.

Lurgan, Co. Armagh: Bapt. Regs. from 1746.

Maghera: Sketch of its history by Rev.
R. L. Marshall.

Muster Rolls 1631.

Mountmellick, Co. Laois: Regs., history,
statistics, bapt. 1849-96.

Rathfriland, Co. Down: Marr. Regs. from
1763, bapt. from 1804.

Reid Mss.: Misc. papers relating to Irish
affairs and history of Pres. Ch. in
Ireland.

Rowan: Genealogical tree from 1660.

Scarva, Co. Down: Bapt. Reg. 1807-34,
Marr. Reg. 1825-45.

Templepatrick: Session book 1688-97 with
names of donors.

Tyrone County: Hearth Money Rolls, 1666.

Ulster Plantation: List of Scottish
freeholders, notes on the plantation of
Ulster.

Waterford: Bapt. Reg. 1770, Marr. Reg.
from 1761.

Workman: History of the Workman family of
Belfast by Rev. A. Rose, 1920.

Wills: Copies of certain wills from
originals in P.R.O. Dublin by Rev. J. E.
Boggis.
          Copy of Mulligan Wills, Diocese of
Connor, 18th century.
          Copy of will of Thomas Fulton of
Co. Derry, 1688.

COUNTIES OF IRELAND AND THEIR DIOCESAN JURISDICTIONS

County	Dioceses
Antrim	Connor, Derry, Down, Dromore
Armagh	Armagh, Dromore
Carlow	Leighlin
Cavan	Ardagh, Meath, Kilmore
Clare	Killaloe, Kilfenora, Limerick
Cork	Cork, Ross, Cloyne, Ardfert
Derry	Armagh, Connor, Derry
Donegal	Clogher, Derry, Raphoe
Down	Connor, Down, Dromore
Dublin	Dublin
Fermanagh	Clogher, Kilmore
Galway	Clonfert, Elphin. Killaloe, Tuam
Kerry	Ardfert
Kildare	Dublin, Kildare
Kilkenny	Leighlin, Ossory
Laois (Queens)	Dublin, Kildare, Leighlin, Ossory
Leitrim	Ardagh, Kilmore
Limerick	Cashel, Emly, Killaloe, Limerick
Longford	Armagh, Meath
Louth	Armagh, Clogher
Mayo	Killala, Achonry, Tuam
Meath	Armagh, Kildare, Kilmore, Meath
Monaghan	Clogher
Offaly (Kings)	Clonfert, Kildare, Killaloe, Meath, Ossory
Roscommon	Ardagh, Clonfert, Elphin, Tuam
Sligo	Ardagh, Elphin, Killala
Tipperary	Cashel, Killaloe, Waterford and Lismore
Tyrone	Armagh, Clogher, Derry
Waterford	Waterford and Lismore
Westmeath	Ardagh, Meath
Wexford	Dublin, Ferns
Wicklow	Dublin, Ferns, Leighlin

PUBLISHED DUBLIN PARISH REGISTERS (CHURCH OF IRELAND) IN PUBLICATIONS OF IRISH MEMORIALS ASSOCIATION/DUBLIN PARISH REGISTER SOCIETY

St. John, marr., bapt., bur., 1619-1699, vol. 1.

St. Patrick, marr., bapt., bur., 1677-1800, vol. 2.

St. Peter and St. Kevin, bapt., marr., bur., 1699-1761, vol. 9.

St. Michan, bapt., marr., bur., 1636-1685; 1686-1700, vols. 7, 3.

St. Catherine, bapt., marr., bur., 1636-1715, vol. 5.

Parish of Monkstown, bapt., marr., bur., 1699-1786, vol. 6.

St. Nicholas without, bapt., marr., bur., 1694-1739, vol. 10.

St. Bride, bapt., marr., bur., 1632-1800, vol. 11.

St. Mary, Donnybrook, marr., 1712-1800,
vol. 11.

St. Nicholas within, marr., 1671-1800, vol. 11.

Parish of Finglas, burials, 1664-1729, vol. 11.

St. Michael. marr., 1656-1800, vol. 11.

St. Michan, marr., 1700-1800, vol. 11.

St. John, marr., 1700-1798, vol. 11.

St. Nicholas within burials, 1671-1823, vol. 11.

St. Audeon, burials, 1672-1692, vol. 12.

St. Mary, Crumlin, marr. and bapt. 1740-1830, vol. 12.

St. Andrew, marr., 1801-1819, vol. 12.

St. Catherine, marr., 1715-1800.

St. Ann, Dawson St., marr., 1719-1800.

St. Luke, marr., 1716-1800.

St. Werburg, marr., 1704-1800.

St. Mary., marr., 1697-1800.

HEARTH MONEY ROLLS

Counties Antrim, 1669, Derry, 1663, Down (Subsidy Roll 1663), Tyrone, 1666 – transcripts in Presbyterian Historical Society, microfilms of same in Public Record Office, Belfast.

Counties Donegal and Armagh, transcripts in Genealogical Office.

County Dublin, 1664, printed in Journal of Kildare Archaeological Society, vols. 10, 11 (1927-30).

County Monaghan, printed in The History of County Monaghan etc., by D. C. Rushe, Dundalk, 1921.

County Tipperary, printed in Tipperary Families etc., edited by Thomas Laffan, Dublin, 1911.

County Wicklow, printed in Journal of Royal Society of Antiquaries of Ireland, vols. 5, 6.

County Louth, printed (in part) in History of Kilsaran etc. by James B. Leslie, Dundalk, 1908.

County Fermanagh, printed in Enniskillen, Parish and Town, by W. H. Dundas, 1913.

IRISH PROVINCIAL NEWSPAPERS

County	Name of Newspaper	Where Published
Antrim	Belfast News-letter	Belfast
Armagh	Guardian	Armagh
Carlow	The Nationalist and Leinster Times	Carlow
Cavan	Anglo-Celt	Cavan
Clare	The Clare Champion	Ennis
Cork	Weekly Examiner	Cork
Derry	Derry Journal	Derry
Donegal	Donegal Democrat	Ballyshannon
Down	Leader	Dromore
Fermanagh	Impartial Reporter	Enniskillen
Galway	Connaught Tribune	Galway
Kerry	Kerryman	Tralee
Kildare	Leinster Leader	Naas
Kilkenny	Kilkenny Journal	Kilkenny

Leitrim	Leitrim Observer	Carrick-on-Shannon
Laois	Leinster Express	Portlaoise
Limerick	Limerick Leader	Limerick
Longford	Longford Leader	Longford
Louth	Dundalk Democrat	Dundalk
Mayo	Western People	Ballina
Meath	Meath Chronicle	Navan
Monaghan	Monaghan Argus	Monaghan
Offaly	Midland Tribune	Birr
Roscommon	Roscommon Herald	Boyle
Sligo	Sligo Champion	Sligo
Tipperary	Tipperary Star	Thurles
Tyrone	Dungannon Observer	Dungannon
Waterford	Munster Express	Waterford
Westmeath	Westmeath Examiner	Mullingar
Wexford	Free Press	Wexford
Wicklow	Wicklow People	Wicklow

ROYAL IRISH ACADEMY

Book of Lecan, illuminated 15th cent book on Gaelic Law, traditions and genealogy by Giolla Iosa MacFirbis. M.535

Book of Genealogies by MacFirbis, O'Curry transcript, M.583.

Genealogy of the O'Donnells with poems. M.545

Book of Munster, genealogies of principal southern families. M.484

Deeds, Roscommon County, 1812. M.24 Q.35

Tree of Life of the Fitzgeralds with notes on allied families Roche, Barry, Butler. M.673

Book of O'Conor Don, poems, topography on allied Connaught families. M.625

A survey of Co. Westmeath, 1741. M.H.I.2

Purcell family papers, Co. Tipperary. M.4 A.42

Notebook of John Philpot Curran. M.12 B1 10

Dublin City Memoranda Rolls, 1447-1745. M.12 C 18

Clonmel Freeholders, 1776. M.12 D 36

Burke family notes, Cos. Mayo, Galway, Sligo. M.1001

Papers relating to Sarsfield family of Co. Cork. M.12 K 20

Survey of County Cavan, C. 1835. M.14B7

Genealogies of O'Reilly and Maguire families.

Book of the O'Lees of Hy-Brasil. M.454

Genealogical papers of O'Connor and MacDermot families. M.1219

O'Clery: Book of Genealogies - story of the Irish race. M.790

O'Reilly Papers: Genealogy and spreading branches of the House of O'Reilly. M.1038

Genealogy of Anglo-Irish families. M.247

Papers of the MacNamaras of Tulla, Co. Clare, their castles etc. M.1040

Pedigrees of O'Neill, MacSweeney, O'Cathain, O'Hagen, MacLochlainn, O'Ferguson, etc. M.621

Clare genealogies - MacNamara, Clancy, O'Grady, O'Quin, O'Dea, MacCoghlan. M.1212

Genealogical poem on the O'Rourkes, O'Reillys, McGaurans, etc. M.471

Munster Families: Dal gCais and derived families. M.622

King of Ireland, lists, notices, history. M.667

NATIONAL LIBRARY OF IRELAND

Pedigrees of Irish Families, Madden and Betham. M.110

Nugent and Dillon family notes. M.122

Magee genealogies (extensive). M.127

Book of Irish Felonies. M.1597

Dodwell-Brown Diary, 1788. M.1598

Convict Register, 19th century. M.3016

Mayo county, Staffords' Survey (copy). M.5160

Clonmel assizes, 17th and 18th centuries 2 vols. M.4908-9

Bulmer family chronicle. M.5220

Limerick county, estate maps, 1747. M.1790

Dublin guilds, history, (Evans). M.738

Society of Friends Minutes 1673 1708. M.94

Derry, Book of Plantation, 1609. M.27

Tipperary County, 'Down' Survey, 1655-56. M.95

Nugent Pedigrees. M.126

Wills and Administrations, 1632-1894, 2 vols. M.142-3

Leitrim estate rental, 1844. M.179

Longford County, Cromwellian Settlement, M.768

Dublin voters lists, 1832. M.783

Meath county, Freeholders list, C.1775 M.788

De Angelo (Nangle) Family pedigree, also Nagle Peppard, Jordan, Costello. M.475

Ballymodan (Bandon, Co. Cork) history (Knox) 1834. M.675

Lenihan family history book. M.763

Down county, estate rolls, 18th century. M.784

Donegal, Poll of Electors, 1761. M.787

Loughrea, Co. Galway, Town Rate book, 1854, 1887. M.92

Cork and Tipperary counties, statistical survey 18th, 19th centuries. M.96

Limerick, city assembly book, 18th century. M.89

Cusack family history, (extensive). M.2116

Wexford, Quit Rents, early date. M.1782

DIRECTORIES

Directories of Ireland, 1846, 1879: I. Slater.

Irish Directory (market towns, seats, houses) 1814: Ambrose Leet.

Landowners of Ireland, 1878: Hussey de Burgh

Irish telephone Directory (annual).

Irish Catholic Directory (annual)

Irish Church Directory (annual).

Dublin City Directory (Wilson's) from 1751, (Thom's) from 1844.

Belfast Almanacs from 1770.

Cork and southern town's directory, 1787.

Pedigrees in Printed Books

Reynell	Co. Westmeath Ir.B.			1890
Rice	Mount Rice. Kildare L.P. III. 203			
Robinson	Dublin Ir.B.			1888
Robinson	Rosmead. Westmeath B.C.G.			757
Rochfort	Carrick L.P.			15
Rowan	Antrim B.C.G.			594
Rowe	Hackney and Shacklewell L.P. II. 331			
Ryan	Kilgera, Kilkenny B.C.G.			192
Ryves	Rathsallagh, Co. Wicklow Ir.B. 1888			

St. George. Bt. Carrick on Shannon L.P.
 I. 114
St. George. Knt. Dunmore. Galway L.P.
 III. 284

Sarsfield	Lucan Kild.J. IV.			116
Saunders	Saunders' Court, Co. Wexford Ir.B. 1890			
Saunders	Saunders' Grove Kild.J. IX. 125, 133			

Shawe
Shane. Bt. Kilmore and Bishopstown L.P.
 I. 104

Shaw	Dublin B.C.G.			456
Southwell. Knt. Mereworth, Kent. L.P. VI. 4				
Southwell	Woodrising, Norfolk L.P. VI. 6			
Southwell	Barnham L.P. VI.			14
Span	Longford B.C.G.			745
Staunton	Galway Ir.B.			1888

Stewart, Bt. Newtown Stewart, Tyrone L.P.
 VI. 243

Stopford (Bishop)	L.P. III.			121
Sutton	Castletown Kild.J. II.			366
Talbot	Belgard Kild.J. IV.			131
Talbot	Carton Kild.J. IV.			5
Taylor	Swords, Co. Dublin Ir.B.			1888
Temple	Mount Temple. Westmeath L.P. V. 234			
Tennison	Donoughmore, Wicklow B.C.G.			508
Tuite. Bt.	Sonna L.P. III.			25
Tynte	Ballycrenane Kild.J. VIII.			223
Usher	Dublin L.P. IV.			311
Ussher	Mt. Ussher, Co. Wicklow Ir.B. 1888			
Vernon	Clontarf, Dublin B.C.G.			198
Vincent	Dublin Kild.J. V.			79
Wall	Johnstown, Co. Wicklow Kild.J. VI. 382			
Warburton	Garryhinch, King's Co. B.C.G.			804
Waring	Pottlerath, Kilkenny B.C.G.			757
Waterhouse	Castlewaterhouse L.P. II.			391

Wemys, Knt. Danesfort, Co. Kilkenny L.P.
 VI. 74

Wemys	Danesfort, Co. Kilkenny Ir.B. 1888			
Wentworth	Fyanstown, Meath B.C.G.			95
Wesley	Dangan, Meath L.P. III.			67
Wheeler	Grenan, Kilkenny L.P. II.			247
Whaley	Whaley Abbey L.P. VI.			71
White	Pitchfordstown. Kildare L.P.			

	I. 248			
Whyte	Leixlip Kild.J. II.			397
Whyte	Redhills, Cavan L.P. II.			296
Williams	(Lord) Thame L.P. IV.			281
Wogan	Blackhall Kild.J. III.			87
Wogan	Rathcoffey Kild.J. III.			79
	V.			110
Wolfe	Kildare B.C.G.			723
Worth	Rathfarnham L.P. VI.			245
Worth	Dublin Kild.J. VI.			233
Wilson	Ballycloughan, Antrim B.C.G.			61
Wilson	Scarr. Wexford B.C.G.			662
Winter	Agher. Meath B.C.G.			792
Wray	Castle Wray B.C.G.			642
Wrixon	Ballygiblin. Cork B.C.G.			143
Wybrants	Danesfort, Co. Kilkenny Ir.B. 1888			

LIST OF PEDIGREES CONTAINED IN
VISITATION OF IRELAND, EDITED
BY F. A. CRISP, PRIVATELY
PRINTED, 1911.

Vol. 1 Belmore, Earl of
Bowen-Colthurst of Oakgrove and
 Dripsey Castle, Co. Cork.
Burke of Elm Hall, Co. Tipperary.
Burtchaell of Brandondale, Co.
 Kerry.

Cooke-Trench of Millicent, Co.
 Kildare.
Cooper of Cooper Hill, Co. Limerick.

Drever

Gillman of Clonteadmore, Co. Cork.
Greene, formerly of Greenville, Co.
 Kilkenny.
Greer of Sea Park, Carrickfergus,
 Co. Antrim.
Greeves of Strandtown, Co. Down.

Hore of Pole Hore, Co. Wexford.

Jackson of Tighnabruaich, Belfast,
 Co. Antrim.

Lowry of Pomeroy House, Co. Tyrone.

Macpherson, formerly of Londonderry.
Massy-Westropp of Attyflin,

O'Callaghan-Westropp of Maryfort,
Owden, formerly of Brooklands,
 Co. Antrim.

Paterson, formerly of Plaister and
 Swillymount, Co. Donegal.
Powerscourt, Viscount.

Roberts of Glassenbury, Co. Kent,
 Britfields Town, Co. Cork, and of
 the City of Cork.

Somerville of Clermont, Co. Wicklow.
Stackpoole of Eden Vale, Co. Clare.
Stubbs of Danby, Co. Donegal.

Tuthill, formerly of Kilmore, Co.
Limerick.

Vigors of Burgage, Co. Carlow.

Whitla of Ben Eadan, Co. Antrim.

Vol. 2 Ardilaun, Baron

Blood of Ballykilty, Co. Clare.
Butcher of Danesfort, Killarney,
Co. Kerry.

Carroll of Hyde Park, and of
Carrollina, Co. Cork.
Chenevix-Trench, Archbishop of Dublin
Crawford of Stonewold, Ballyshannon,
Co. Donegal.
Crozier of Gortra House, Co.
Fermanagh.
Cullen of Corry, Co. Leitrim.

Grierson of Baldonell, Co. Dublin.
Guinness of Dublin.

Hudson-Kinahan of Glenville, Co.
Cork.

Iveagh, Baron
Longworth-Dames of Greenhill, King's
County.

Macartney, formerly of Rosebrook,
Co. Armagh.
Monck, Viscount
Montgomery of Grey Abbey, Co. Down.
Montgomery of New Park, Moville,
Co. Donegal.

O'Connell of Lakeview and Ballybeggan,
Co. Kerry.

Peacocke, Archbishop of Dublin.
Pigott of Tincurry, Co. Tipperary,
and of the Manor House, Dundrum,
Co. Down.

Sharman-Crawford of Crawfordsburn
and Rademon, Co. Down.
Stoney of The Downs, Co. Wicklow.

Westropp of Ballyvolane, Co. Cork.
White of Lough Eske Castle, Co.
Donegal.

Vol. 3 Alexander of Ahilly, Co. Donegal.
Ashtown, Baron

Ball
Barry of Sandville, Co. Limerick.
Bayly of Ballyarthur, Co. Wicklow.
Berry, formerly of Eglish Castle,
King's County.

Clements of Ashfield Lodge, Co. Cavan.
Coote of Ballyfin, Queen's County.

Deane-Drake of Stokestown, Co.
Wexford.

Filgate of Lissrenny, Co. Louth.

Galt of Ballysally, Co. Derry.
Grogan of Moyvore, Co. Westmeath and
Ballyntyre Hall, Co. Dublin.

Harman of Palace and Carrigbyrne,
Co. Wexford.

Hatton of Clonard, Co. Wexford.
Homan-Mulock of Bellair, King's
County.
Hussey-Walsh of Cranagh and
Mulhussey, Co. Roscommon.

Lefroy of Carrig-glas Manor, Co.
Longford.
Leitrim, Earl of
L'Estrange of Moystown, King's
County.

Mansergh of Grenane, Co. Tipperary.

Orpen-Palmer of Killowen, Co. Kerry.

Smyth of Ardmore, Co. Derry.

Vincent of Summerhill, Co. Clare.

Westropp of Fortanne, Co. Clare.
Wright, formerly of Golagh, Co.
Monaghan.

Vol. 4 Annesley, Earl
Athlumney, Baron

Bewley
Blake of Corbally, Co. Galway.
Bowen of Bowen's Court, Co. Cork.

Cavan, Earl of
Casey of The Donaghies, Raheny, Co.
Dublin.

Dillon, Viscount
Dillon, formerly of Rathmoyle, Co.
Roscommon.

Fuller of Glashnacree, Co. Kerry.

Gosford, Earl of
Greene of Millbrook and of
Hallahoise, Co. Kildare.

Heaton-Armstrong of Roscrea, King's
County.

Kelly of Mucklon, Co. Galway, and of
Kilcash, Co. Roscommon.
Kirkpatrick of Mohill, Co. Leitrim.

Lyons of Old Park, Belfast, Co.
Antrim.

Molony of Cragg, Co. Clare.
Moore, formerly of Kilcurry,
Taghshinny, Co. Longford.

O'Donovan of Clan Cathal, Co. Cork.
O'Reilly, formerly of Baltrasna,
Co. Meath.

Reeves of Besborough, Co. Clare.

Sandes of Greenville, Co. Kerry.
Shackleton of Ballitore, Co. Kildare.
Swanzy of Newry, Co. Armagh.

Wade of Clonebraney, Co. Meath.
West
Wicklow, Earl of
Wilson of Currygrane, Co. Longford.

Vol. 5 Battersby of Loughbawn, Co.
Westmeath.
Bingham of Bingham Castle, Co. Mayo.
Borrowes of Gilltown, Co. Kildare,
Baronet.

Bourke
Burke of Ballydugan, Co. Galway.

Crookshank of Drumhalry and
Birrenagh, Co. Longford.

De Burgh of Oldtown, Co. Kildare.
Delany of Bagnalstown, Co. Carlow.

Edgeworth of Kilshrewly, Co.
Longford.

Finny of Leixlip, Co. Kildare.

Guillamore, Viscount

Henn of Paradise Hill, Co. Clare.
Honan

Lucan, Earl of

Maturin and Maturin-Baird of
Newtown Stewart, Co. Tyrone.
Morony of Odell Ville, Co. Limerick.

O'Connor of Rockfield, Co. Dublin.
O'Grady of Kilballyowen, Co.
Limerick.

Persse

Sligo, Marquess of
Smythe of Barbavilla, Co. Westmeath.
Spedding of Ballynamudagh, Co.
Wicklow.
Swanzy of Avelreagh, Co. Monaghan.

Taaffe of Smarmore, Co. Louth.
Talbot of Castle Talbot, Co. Wexford.

Uniacke

Vol. 6   Ashbourne, Baron

Barry of Castle Cor, Co. Cork.
Bellew, Baron
Boyle of Limavady, Co. Londonderry.
Brown (now Gardner-Brown), formerly
of Peter's Hill, Belfast, and of
Solitude, Co. Antrim.

Chambers of Fosterstown, Co. Meath.
Coplen-Langford of Kilcosgriff,
Co. Limerick.

Edgeworth of Edgeworthstown, Co.
Longford.

Farran
Fox of Kilcoursey, King's County,
and of Galtrim, Co. Meath.

Higginson of Lisburn, Co. Antrim.
Hurly, formerly of Bridge House,
Co. Kerry.

Inchiquin, Baron

Lecky of Beardiville, Co. Antrim.
Leslie of Glasslough, Co. Monaghan,
Baronet.
Lisle, Baron
M'Cance of Knocknagoney, Holywood,
M'Cance of Suffolk, Dunmurry, Co.
Antrim.
Macaulay
MacDermot of Coolavin, Co. Sligo.
Magee

Meadows of Thornville, Co. Wexford.
Morgan of Old Abbey, Co. Limerick.

Ogilby of Ardnargle, Limavady, and
of Pellipar, Dungiven, both Co.
Londonderry.

Plummer

Scott of Castle House, Lisburn, Co.
Antrim, Baronet.
Shawe-Taylor of Castle Taylor, Co.
Galway.

Westropp of Mellon, Co. Limerick.
Wilson of Daramona House, Co.
Westmeath.
Wolseley of Mount Wolseley, Co.
Carlow, Baronet.

THE IRISH GENEALOGIST

Birch family of Birchgrove, parish of
Tullylish, Vol.3, No.5, 1960.
Mulloy of Kells, Co. Meath, do.
Dillon family of Roscommon, Vol.2, No.12,
1955.
Elrington family of Ireland, Vol.1, No.9,
1941.
Boyle-Roche family pedigree, Vol.2, No.8,
1950.
Irwin of Roxborough, Co. Roscommon, Vol.1,
No.2, 1937.
Lennon of Cloncullen, Co. Westmeath, Vol.2,
No.2, 1944.
Grierson of Co. Meath, Vol.3, No.4, 1959.
Nicholson of Brickeen, Co. Sligo, Vol.2,
No.2, 1944.
Charleton of Clonmacnoise, Vol.4, No.2, 1969.
Herrick family of Co. Cork, Vol.3, No.8,
1963.
Wood of Co. Sligo, Vol.3, No.8, 1963.
Aylward of Ireland, Vol.4, No.3, 1970.
Goodall of Co. Wexford, Vol.3, No.12, 1967.
Conron family of Co. Cork, Vol.3, No.9,
1964.
Lambert of Brookhill, Co. Mayo, Vol.3, No.10,
1965.
Peyton of Co. Roscommon, Vol.2, No.2, 1944.
Phibbs of Cos. Sligo and Leitrim, Vol.2,
No.2, 1944.

THE IRISH ANCESTOR

Crone family of Co. Cork, Vol.1, No.2, 1969.
Odell of Co. Limerick, do.
Brewster of Co. Kerry, Vol.3, No.2, 1971.
Brereton of Cos. Kildare and Carlow, Vol.3,
No.2, 1971.
Blaney of Co. Armagh, Vol.3, No.1, 1971.
O'Higgins of Ireland and Chile, Vol.2,
No.2, 1970.
Dexter of Dublin and Kildare, Vol.2, No.1,
1970.
Hillas of Co. Sligo, Vol.4, No.1, 1972.
Moncton of Co. Limerick, Vol.4, No.1, 1972.

Family History in Printed Books

Irish Families: Dr. E. MacLysaght, Dublin, 1972. Articles on the 300 best known Irish names - Ahearne, Athy.......MacWard, Woulfe.

Suppliment to Irish Families: Dr. E. MacLysaght, Dublin, 1964, history of 500 Irish families - Abraham. Aiken........ ..... Uriel, Wiley.

Memoirs of the Archdales: Henry Archdale, Enniskillen, 1925, pedigrees of the following - Archdale, Audley, Barrington, Blackwood, Damer, Dawson, Dunbar, Edwards, Gore, Humphreys, Mervyn, Montgomery, Porter, Price, Sexton, Stewart.

Families of French and Nixon: Henry B. Swanzy. 1908. Historical notes on the following families - French, Nixon, Erskine, Meade, Enery, Swanzy.

An Account of the families of Lennard and Barrett: Thomas Barrett-Lennard, 1908, contains history of Lennard, Barrett, Fynese.

Roots in Ulster Soil: T. H. Mullen, Belfast, 1967. Commentary on the following - Mullen, Barbour, Black, Forsythe, Wallace, Brown, Henderson, Anderson, Holdom.

The Leslies and their forebears: Pierce Leslie Pielou, Dublin, 1935. Contains history of Leslie, Pielou and allied families.

History of Maunsell or Mansel: Robert G. Maunsell, Cork, 1903, genealogy of following - Crayford, Gabbelt, Knoyle, Persse, Toler, Waller, Warren, White, Winthrop.

History of the County Dublin: F. E. Ball, Dublin, 1902.

Vol 1. Families dealt with - Allen, Archibold, Bee, Byrne, Cheevers, Crehall, Bathe, Dungan, Espinasse, Fitzsimons, Goodman, Hacket, Jessop, Kennedy, Mapas, Plunkett, Proud, Powell, Pocklington, Talbot, Walsh, Watson.

Vol 2. Borr, Bret, Brigg, Bruns, Cusack, Deane, Dobson, Downes, Harold, Loftus, Moenes, Ussher, Walsh, North.

Vol 3. Allen, Bulkelley, Clinch, Curran, Dawe, Domville, Howell, Preston, Purdon, Roberts, Russell, Taylor.

Vol 4. Annesley, Brereton, Browne, Carberry, Deane, Fagan, Finlay, Forster, Gallane, Harte, Luttrell, Miles, Molyneux, Says, Scurlock, Sedgrave, Slingsby, White, Wilkinson.

History of Armstrong: William R. Armstrong, Pittsburg, Pennsylvania, 1969, with accounts of the following - Stevenson, Bell, Johnston, Dunlap, Duncan, Brown.

History of Clonmel: William P. Burke, Waterford, 1907, with historical notes on - Alcocke, Bagwell, Baron, Brenock, Burke, Butler, Foley, Hamerton, Hely-Hutchinson, Leynagh, Moore, Osborne, Perry, Riall, Vaughan, Wall, White.

The Book of McKee: Raymond W. McKee, Dublin, 1959, with history of Mackey, O'Neill and McKee families.

History and Genealogy of the Pomeroy family: W. Pomeroy, U.S.A., 1958, contains genealogy of - Pomeroy, Holmes, Smyth, Gilbourne, Deane, Towgood.

The Seagrave Family 1066-1935: Charles W. Seagrave, London, 1936, with extensive history of Seagrave and allied families.

Memorials of Adare Manor: Earl of Dunraven, Oxford, 1865, contains pedigrees of - Edwin, O'Donovan, Quin, Scrope, Wyndham.

History of the Town and County of Wexford: Philip H. Hore, London, 1911, among the families treated - Kavanagh, Peppard, Devereux, Masterson, Codd, Wadding, Roche, O'Byrne, Kinselagh, Colclough, Cox, Meadows, Chambers, White, McCarte, MacMurrough, Anglesey, Harvey, Stafford, Harper.

Pedigrees from Ulster: R. M. Sibbett, Belfast, 1931. Families treated - Baird, Wauchop, Cochran, Gibson, Wasson.

The Wrays of Donegal: C. V. Trench, Oxford, 1945, with history of - Wray, Donnelley, Johnston, Waller, MacDaniel, Atkinson, Jackson.

The History of the County of Monaghan: E. P. Shirley, London, 1879, with notices and family trees of - MacKenna, Leslie, Ancketill, Dawson, Corry, Madden, Burnet, Cairns, Westerna, Lucas, Fleming, Foster, Owen, Montgomery, Blaney, Devereux, Shirley, Ferrer, Seymour, MacMahon.

History of County Mayo: Hubert T. Knox, Dublin, 1908, with genealogical tables of the following families - O'Conor, Donnell, McWilliams, Bourke, Gibbons, Walter, Barrett, Jordan, Costello, MacEvilly, Staunton.

History and Topography of County Clare: J. Frost, Dublin, 1883. Contains history of three hundred Clare families including, O'Davoren, O'Loughlin, O'Hynes, MacNamara, MacClancy, O'Grady, O'Dea, O'Griffin, O'Quin, MacBrody, MacGorman, MacCurtin, O'Brien, O'Connor.

Three Hundred Years in Innishowen: A. Young, Belfast, 1879, with pedigrees, trees, engravings, portraits, arms of Young, Hart, Harvey, Doherty, Knox, Montgomery, Cary, Davenport, Benson, Vaughan, Latham, MacLaughlin, Hamilton, Skipton, Richardson, Stuart, Gage, Boyd, Crofton, Day, Staveley, Laurence, Homan, ffolliott, Cuff, Synge, Nesbitt, Ball, Chichester, Smith, Ussher, Torrens.

The Fermanagh Story: Peter Livingstone, Enniskillen, 1969, with history of over three hundred County Fermanagh families - Aiken, Bannon, Breen .... Winslow.

History and Antiquities of the Diocese of Kilmacduagh: J. Fahy, Dublin, 1893, with history and legends of the following families - O'Connor, O'Loughlin, O'Daly, O'Shaughnessy, Burke.

Annals of Westmeath: James Woods, Dublin, 1907, with accounts of the following - Petit, Nugent, Delamer, Ledwith, Naper, O'Melaghlin, MacGeoghegan, Tyrrell, O'Conor, Malone, Piers, Tuite, de Lacy, Fenelon, Fallon.

Blake Family Records: Martin Blake, London, 1905, with genealogies and arms of the tribes of Galway - Athy, Blake, Bodkin, Browne, D'arcy, Deane, Font, French, Joyce, Kirwan, Lynch, Martin, Morris, Skerritt.

History of the Corry Family: Earl of Belmore, London and Dublin, 1891. Contains historical notes on - Corry, Crawford, Johnston, Anketill, Mervyn, Leslie, Armor, Lowry, Eccles, Shepherd, Dawson.

The Pooles of County Cork: R. ffolliott, pr. pr., 1956, with history and anecdotes of - Poole, Bernard, Hungerford, Hewitt, Baldwin, Morris, Lackey, Barry, Townsend, Jellett, Morgan, Wynn, Waring, Lucas, Hayman, Holmes, Meade, Casey, Daunt, Nesbitt, Becher, Moore, Boyle, Somerville.

The History of Sligo, Town and County: T. O'Rorke, Dublin, n.d., with historical notes on - O'Hara, Filan, Jones, Fibbs, MacDonagh, O'Connor, Meredith, O'Gara, MacDermott, O'Dowd, MacDonnell, MacSweeney, Crofton, O'Rorke.

History of Enniskillen: W. C. Trimble, Enniskillen, 1921, with much genealogical information on the following - Frith, Gamble, Quinton, Kerr, Dundas, Edmonson, Crook, Walmsley, Whitten.

The Ulster Clans: T. H. Mullin, Belfast, 1966, contains extensive history of - O'Neill, MacLoughlin, O'Kane, McCloskey, O'Mullan, Magilligan, O'Mellan, O'Hagan, O'Quin.

A Genealogical History of the Tyrrells: Joseph H. Tyrrell, pr. pr., with chart pedigrees of the following - Ashe, Aylmer, Blood, Carlisle, de Clare, Edgeworth, Giffard, Hassard, Haughton, Head, Loftus, Longcake, Lucas, de Nogent, O'Reilly, Pilkington, Rochford, Sarsfield, Senlis, Tuite, Thompson, Warren.

Old Kerry Records: Mary A. Hickson, London, 1872, with notes on - Aylmer, Blennerhasset, Brown, Daly, Fagan, Gould, Hussey, Nagle, Sigerson, Skiddy, Tuohy, Wall.

O'Kief Coshe Mang, Slieve Lougher and Upper Blackwater, Ireland: Albert Casey, Alabama, U.S.A. A most extensive work running to 14 vols. on Cork and Kerry families, based on baptismal records, deeds, wills, gravestone inscriptions etc.

History of Queens County: Daniel O'Byrne, Dublin, 1856. Contains a history of the ancient septs of that county - Brennan, Byrne, Delaney, Dempsey, Duff, Dunne, MacEvoy, Gorman, Fitzpatrick, Kelly, Lawlor, More.

History and Antiquities of Kilkenny: William Healy, Dublin, 1893, with histories of the following families - Archdeacon, Archer, Bryan, Butler, Blanchfield, Blake, Comerford, Dalton, Fitzgerald, Forstall, Grace, Lincoln, Leslie, O'Neil, St. Leger, Lawless, Purcell, Ryan, Rochford, Shortal, Strange, Sweetman, Walsh.

Ball Family Records: William Ball Wright, York, 1908, with genealogical memoirs of - Ball, Blackall, Delahoyd, Feltus, Paumier, Wright.

The Roll of the House of Lacy: de Lacy - Bellingari, Baltimore, 1928, with pedigrees, military memoirs and notices of the following families - Browne, Croke, Hartnett, O'Dell, de Lacy, Naughton/Norton.

The History of the Moore Family: Countess of Drogheda, Dublin, 1906, contains chart pedigrees of - Moore, Clifford, Loftus.

History of Ely O'Carroll etc.: John Gleeson, Dublin, 1915. Contains much information on north Munster families including O'Carroll, O'Meagher, Ryan, Kennedy, Butler, Hogan, MacEgan, O'Meara, Jordan, Foyle and Fitzpatrick.

The Barringtons: Amy Barrington, Dublin, 1917. Contains pedigrees of the following families - Barrington, Bewley, Malone, Shackleton, Mark, Strangman, Pim, Wakefield, Grubb, Abraham, Leadbeater and Carleton.

Memoirs of the Binghams: Rose McCalmont, London, 1915, with notices of - Bingham, Ramsey, Carden, Mills, Yelverton, Wake, Trenchard.

The Tiernan and other Families: Charles B. Tiernan, Baltimore, 1901, with genealogy of the following - Tiernan, Somerville, Bolling and Bernard.

Vicissitudes of Families: Bernard Burke, London, 1896, with commentary on several families including - Percy, Neville, Cromwell, Stuart, O'Neill, de Vere, Doddington, Lindsay, Mitton, Baird and Maguire.

Families of Ballyrashane (Ulster): T. H. Mullin, Belfast, 1969, with family trees of the following - Simpson, Rankin, Greer, Stuart, McCollum, Atchison, Reid, Huston, McConaghy, MacAfee, McCurdy, Norris, Lynn, Barr, Curry, Parkhill, Eaton, Chestnutt, Anderson, Stirling, McIntyre, Ross, Boyce, Jamison, Quin, Carson, Workman, Morrow, Campbell, Moore, Williamson, McClelland, Pollock, Eccles, Irvine, Witherow, Patton, McKinley, Blair, Ferguson, Godfrey, Calvin, Dunlop, Logan, Nevins, Walker, Sloan, Lees, Hemphell, Sinclair, Lyle, Getty, Boyd, Auld, Watton.

History of Irish Brigades in the Service of France: John C. O'Callaghan, London, 1885, most extensive; among families treated - Barrett, Bellew, Cantillon, Drumgold, Grattan, Lally, Luttrell, MacSheehy, O'Farrell, Shortall, Williams, Wogan.

Common Elements in Irish Placenames

Ath, Agh, (ath): a ford, shallow part of a river.

Agha, (achadh): a field, level meadow.

Alt, (alt): an eminence, high place, side of a glen.

Anna, Annagh, (eanach): a moor, marsh, soft terrain.

Ard, (ard): a height, top, summit, lofty, higher ground.

Bally, (baile): town, village, homestead.

Ballagh, (bealach): a roadway, passage, gap, pass.

Barn, Barna, (bearna): pass or gap in hill or mountain.

Barr, (barr): top, head, summit.

Bawn, Baun, (ban): small field, enclosure, white coloured.

Beagh, (beithe): abounding with birch trees.

Bell, (beal): mouth, entrance, estuary.

Ben, (beann): peak, pointed hill.

Boher, (bothar): road, way, passage, lane.

Boley, (buaile): place for milking cows, booley or dairy place.

Brack, (breac): speckled, spotted, spotted (with stones, furze) hill.

Bun, (bun): end, bottom, of hills or mountains.

Caher, Cahir, (cathair): stone fort, abode, city.

Cam, (cam): crooked.

Cappa, Cappagh, (ceapach): plot of ground laid out for tillage.

Carn, (carn): heap of stones, rocky summit.

Carrick, Carrig, (carraig): a rock, crag or stone.

Carrow, Carhoo, (ceathramhadh): quarter, measure of land.

Cashel, (caiseal): wall, bulwark, castle.

Cavan, (cabhan): a hollow plain.

Clar, (clar): plain, flat piece of land.

Clash, (clais): furrow, deep ditch.

Clogh, (cloch): stone, rock, cliff.

Clon, Cloon, (cluain): plain, lawn, meadow.

Cool, (cul): back, corner, angle.

Cor, Corr, (cor): a round hill.

Cosh, Cush, (cos): leg, foot, at the foot of, beside.

Creeve, (craobh): branch, bough, tree, bush.

Croagh, Crogh, (cruach): rick, stack, piled-up hill.

Cross, (cros): a cross.

Cuil, Cuill, (coill): a wood.

Curra, Curragh, (currach): bog, marsh, soft plain.

Derry, (doire): an oak, oak wood.

Doo, (dubh): black.

Doon, Dun, (dun): a fortress.

Dreen, Drin, (draighean): blackthorn.

Drom, Drum, (druim): the ridge of a hill.

Eden, (eadan): the forehead, brow of a hill.

Esker, (eiscir): ridge of sand hills, ridge of mountains.

Farn, (fearn): alder tree, place abounding in alders.

Farran, (fearann): land, ground, country.

Freagh, (fraoch): heather, heath, a heathy place.

Gal, Gall, (gall): stranger, foreigner.

Garran, Garraun, Garrane, (garran): grove, wood, copse.

Garry, (garrdha): garden.

Glas, (glas): green; of mountain, stream or meadow.

Glan, Glen, (gleann): valley, glen.

Gol, Goul, Gowl, (gabhal): fork, the fork of a hill.

Gort, Gurt, (gort): a field or garden.

Graigue, (graig): village, manor.

Greenan, (grianan): sunny place, bower, summer house.

Illan, Illaun, (oilean): island.

Inis, Inish, Inch, (inis): an island, a field near a river or lake.

Kell, (caol): narrow, slender, straight.

Kil, Kill, (cill): a church or small monastery.

Knock, (cnoc): hill, hillock.

Lack, Leck, Lick, (leac): stone, flagstone, slate.

Laght, (leacht): a grave, pile of stones in memory of the dead.

Lis, Liss, (lios): earthen fort, fortified place, ancient palace.

Lough, (loch): a lake.

Lag, Leg, Lug, Lugg, (lag): a hollow, glen.

Lear, Lyre, (ladhar): a fork, forking of glens or rivers.

Maghera, (machaire): a plain, level ground.

Maul, Meel, (meall): a hillock, eminence.

Meen, (min): a smooth spot on a hill presenting a green surface.

Mon, (moin): turf, peat, bog.

Money, (muine): brake, shrubbery, a hillock.

Moy, (magh): a plain, plain of hills.

Muck, (muc): a pig or boar.

Mullagh, (mullach): top, summit, height, top of a hill.

Park, (pairc): field, meadow.

Poll, Pol, Poul, (poll): hole, pit, a measure of land.

Port, (port): a harbour, bank or landing place.

Rath, (rath): earthen fort with trees, a fortress.

Ring, Rin, Rinn, (rinn): a headland, promontory.

Roe, Roo, (ruadh): red, gorse clad hill.

Ros, Ross, (ros): a promontory, isthmus, a grove or wood.

Scart, (scairt): a thick tuft of shrubs or bushes.

Shan, (sean): old, e.g. Shanbally, "old town".

Sra, Sragh, Srah, (srath): a field on the bank of a river.

Tawnagh, Tawny, (tamhnach): a small field.

Temple, (teampall): a church or temple.

Ti, (tigh): a house.

Tir, (tir): land, country, region.

Tober, (tobar): well, fountain, spring, source.

Tom, (tuaim): a grave or tumulus.

Ton, (toin): backside.

Toor, (tuar): a place for bleaching clothes.

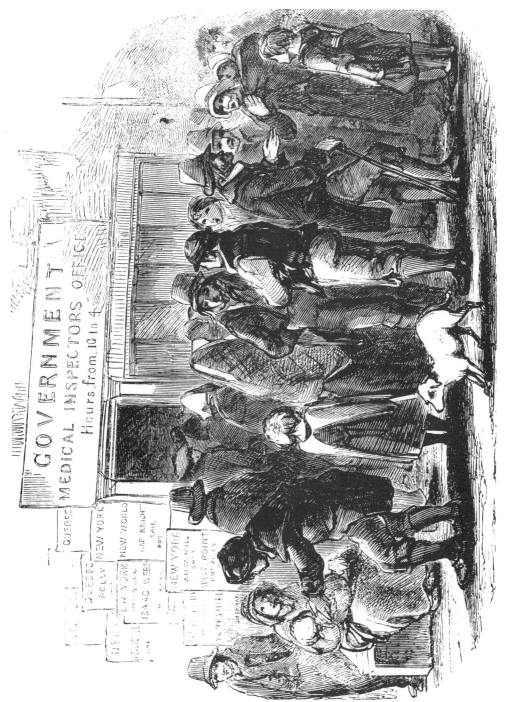

The Government inspector's office.

Preliminary Research in One's

Home Country

It frequently happens that people of Irish descent seeking ancestors and relatives in Ireland lack the essential information necessary for commencing a search in Ireland. There is little use, for example, in attempting to trace 'John Gallagher who left Ireland about 1850 for America' since a hundred persons could be found to fit such a set of circumstances.

Much time and expense can be saved during an Irish tour and the chances of success greatly enhanced if an effort is made beforehand to ascertain as much as possible about family connections in one's own country, with special reference to the original ancestor. Failure to check such personal records as early nostalgic letters from the homeland, old diaries and the family bible may mean overlooking precious original information not elsewhere available. Sometimes the gravestone of the original settler gives specific though not always accurate information. Since a vast number of Irish emigrants settled in the United States, Australia, Canada and England, a word on the official genealogical records of these countries may prove helpful.

AMERICAN RECORDS

For the average American enquirer the most critical factor in bridging the gap between the United States and Ireland is the date and place of arrival in America and the exact part of Ireland from which the original ancestor came. Due to a breakdown in family tradition it often becomes necessary to consult American immigration entry forms, census returns, passenger lists, etc. These records are housed in the U.S. National Archives in Washington D.C.

PASSENGER LISTS

The Archives has incomplete series of customs passenger lists and immigration passenger lists of ships arriving from abroad at Atlantic and Gulf of Mexico ports. The following table shows the dates of passenger lists and related indexes in the Archives:

Port	Customs passenger lists	Immigration passenger lists	Indexes
Baltimore	1820–91	1891–1909	1820–1952
Boston	1820–74 and		1848–91 and
	1883–91	1891–1943	1902–20
New Orleans	1820–1902	1903–45	1853–1952
New York	1820–97	1897–1942	1820–46 and
			1897–1943
Philadelphia	1800–82	1883–1945	1800–1948
Certain minor ports	1820–73	1893–1945	1890–1924

Supplementing the indexes listed above is a general index to quarterly reports of arrivals at most ports except New York, 1820-74.

A customs passenger list normally contains the following information for each passenger: his name, age, sex, and occupation, the country from which he came, and the country to which he was going, and, if he died in passage, the date and circumstances of his death. The immigration passenger lists that are more than 50 years old (those less than 50 years old are not available for reference purposes) vary in information content but usually show the place of birth and last place of residence in addition to the information found in the customs passenger lists. Some of the immigration passenger lists include the name and address of a relative in the country from which the passenger came.

The Archives will search the customs passenger lists if in addition to the name of the passenger and the name of the port of entry an inquirer can supply the following information: the name of the vessel and the approximate date of its arrival or the name of the port of embarkation and the exact date of arrival. It will also search the immigration passenger lists over 50 years old if an inquirer can give the full name and age of the passenger and names and ages of accompanying passengers, the name of the port of entry, the name of the vessel, and the exact date of arrival. The Archives will also consult such indexes as it has to the names on the customs and immigration passenger lists provided an inquirer can supply the name of the port of entry and the supposed year of arrival.

Positive microfilm copies of passenger lists more than 50 years old are available for use in the Archives microfilm reading room by researchers or their agents.

CENSUS RETURNS

A census of the population has been taken every 10 years since 1790. The Archives has the 1790-1870 returns, a microfilm copy of the 1880 returns, and the surviving fragment of the 1890 returns. The 1790-1840 returns show the names of the heads of households only; other family members are tallied unnamed in age and sex groups. The 1850-90 returns include the name age and State, Territory or Country of birth of each free person in a household. Additional information is included with each succeeding census.

The available returns for the 1790 census were published by the Federal Government in the early 1900's. The published census returns for 1790 are for Connecticut, Maine, Maryland, Massachusetts, New Hampshire, New York, North Carolina, Pennsylvania, Rhode Island, South Carolina, and Vermont. Returns for each State are listed in a separate, indexed volume. The returns for the remaining States — Delaware, Georgia, Kentucky, New Jersey, Tenessee, and Virginia — were burned during the War of 1812.

The Archives staff will, free of charge, search for a specific name, in any index it has. For returns not indexed, the staff can make a very limited search for a particular name in a given year's returns if provided with the

State and County in which the person lived. If the county had a large population, particularly after 1850, the specific town or township is needed. If the residence was in one of the larger cities, the street address or ward is also needed. This information can be found in city directories and ward maps that are normally available in city and State libraries, historical societies, and archives. When a requested entry is found, the fee for a photocopy of the census page on which it appears will be given. If the search is too extensive for the Archives staff to undertake, the fee for a microfilm copy of the related census returns will be given.

MILITARY SERVICE RECORDS

Registers of enlistments in the U.S. Army, 1798-1914, and compiled military service records of volunteers, 1775-1903, including records of service in the Army of the Confederate States of America, are in the Archives. The registers relate to service performed in both peacetime and wartime. They usually show for each recruit his name, age, place of enlistment, regiment or company, and date and cause of discharge, or, where applicable, date of death or date of desertion and of apprehension after desertion. The compiled military service records normally show the soldier's rank, military organization and term of service. Occasionally they also show his age, the place of his enlistment, and the place of his birth.

NATURALIZATION RECORDS

The Archives has naturalization proceedings of the District of Columbia courts, 1802-1926. These records show, for each person who petitioned for naturalization, his age or date of birth, his nationality, and whether citizenship was granted. The Archives has also photo-copies and indexes of naturalization documents, 1787-1906, filed by courts in Maine, Massachussetts New Hampshire and Rhode Island. These records were copied and indexed by the Work Projects Administration in the late 1930's. The Archives will search these records for information about naturalizations that occurred before September 17, 1906, if given the full name of the petitioner and the approximate date of naturalization.

LAND RECORDS

The land records in the Archives (dated chiefly 1800-1950) include donation land entry files, homestead application files, and private land claim files relating to the entry of individual settlers on land in the public land States. There are no land records of the Thirteen Original States and Maine, Vermont, West Virginia, Kentucky, Tenessee, Texas, and Hawaii. Records for these States are maintained by State officials, usually in the State capital. The donation land entry files and homestead application files show, in addition to the name of the applicant, the location of the land and the date he acquired it, his residence or post office address, his age or date and place of birth, his marital status, and if applicable, the given name of his wife or the size of his family. If an applicant for homestead land was of foreign birth, his application file contains evidence of his naturalization or of his intention to become a citizen. Supporting documents show the immigrant's country of birth and sometimes the date and port of arrival. Genealogical information in records relating to private land claims varies from the mention of the claimant's name and location of the land to such additional information as the claimant's place of residence when he made the claim and the name of his relatives, both living and dead.

AUSTRALIAN RECORDS

Australians of Irish descent recall with pride names such as Charles McMahon, speaker of the Assembly, Victoria, Robert Burke-O'Hara celebrated explorer, Paddy Hannan, first man to ride into Kalgoorlie and after whom Hannan Lake in that district is today named, Charles O'Connor, Coolgardie water-works engineer and countless more whose names loom large across the pages of Australian history. They are fortunate in that their country's libraries and archives are storehouses of genealogical source material in the form of shipping lists, census returns etc. which the serious enquirer would do well to consult before commencing searches in Ireland. Many of them are the descendants of thousands of unfortunate men women and children who for trivial and sometimes obscure offences were forced to wear the convict chain in Van Dieman's Land. The following is one of thousands of records to be found in the State Library of Tasmania —

> "A convict named . . . . . was transported per "Duke of Richmond" arriving Hobart Town on 2nd January 1844. He was tried in Tipperary on the 2nd August, 1843, and was sentenced to fourteen years transportation for "assaulting a habitation". He was well conducted in prison and never convicted before. His occupation was a quarryman aged twenty five years . . . . . . was single when transported, his native place was . . . . . . "

It is scarcely necessary to point out the genealogical value of such a record which for obvious reasons is not quoted in full.

Until December 1825, Van Dieman's Land was a dependency of New South Wales which meant that up to that time Sydney was the administrative centre for the Island. Nevertheless under various immigration regulations Hobart retained files of arrivals, containing information on their places of origin, ports of embarkation, sailing and arrival dates and so on.

An index of shipping covering the period 1803-57 is available at the State Archives in Hobart, a copy of which may be inspected at the National Library in Canberra.

The Registrar-General of Tasmania has records of births, marriages and deaths from 1838 onward, also records for Churches in existence in the island for the period 1804-1838.

By the time the last convict ship sailed into Sydney Cove in June 1849 more than ninety thousand persons had been transported from these islands to New South Wales.

The 1828 Census of New South Wales is a list over 35,000 persons living in the colony at that time. The census gives information relating to age, trade, residence, religion, if living in the colony or elsewhere, together with land and stock held and the name of the ship in which the settler arrived. Members of the same family are bracketed together, e.g.

> "McDermott, of Sydney, lodgers, Castlereagh Street, Edward 45, 'Minerva' 1719, Ann 44, 'Speke' 1809. Margaret 16".

The Census returns may be consulted at the Mitchell Library in Sydney. Once the name of the ship is known or indeed the approximate date of arrival, the passenger list of the relevant vessel should then be inspected. Again the Mitchell Library has the records.

One final source of considerable genealogical (and physical!) weight. It is the New South Wales Government gazette 1832-1886, a multi-volume work much of which has been indexed. The gazette has thousands of entries relating to land grants, will probates, titles and many other official and semi-official matters. Copies are available in the major Australian Libraries.

CANADIAN RECORDS

Many an Irish famine emigrant caught his first glimpse of the New World as his ship approached St. John's or Halifax or Quebec whence many moved on to eventually settle in various parts of the North American continent. A recent statistic has shown that some twenty per cent of the present population of Canada is composed of Irish stock. Strong trading links between St. John's, New Foundland and sea coast towns in south west Cork were a feature of Irish commercial life in the early years of the nineteenth century.

The Irish-Canadian who because of a breakdown in family tradition has to seek a lead on his Irish antecendents in Canadian records might well begin by consulting the Census of 1851. The returns are in the Dominion Public archives in Ottawa.

Registration of births, marriages and deaths in Canada is governed by the Vital Statistics Act of the particular Province. Alberta, for example, has registers which date from 1885 — in the custody of the Deputy-Registrar General, Edmonton. The civil registers of Ontario go back to 1869 and there are Church records as far back as 1812. Quebec has probably the oldest of all Canadian records where Catholic and Protestant Church registers extend back to 1617, when the French colony was established.

ENGLISH RECORDS

A short account of genealogical research facilities in England is included here for two reasons: first a large number of people of Irish descent are now resident there due to the proximity of the two islands, and secondly because many records of Irish interest, e.g. Crown books, police, army and navy enlistments etc. were transferred to London on the establishment of the Irish Free State in 1922.

London as the seat of government has the outstanding record repositories such as the Public Record Office, the National Central Library, the British Museum and the General Register Office.

The General Register Office is located in Somerset House and the Registrar has the following records —

1. Records of Births, Marriages and Deaths, registered in England and Wales from 1st July 1837.
2. Marine Register Book — records of Births and Deaths at sea since 1st July 1837.
3. Non-Parochial Registers, mainly prior to 1837. These are mostly registers kept by nonconformist bodies and in some cases go back as far as 1642.
4. Army Returns — Births, Marriages and Deaths in the Army Registers extending as far back as 1761.
5. Consular Returns — vital statistics of British subjects in foreign countries since July 1849.

Parish registers, as in Ireland, are kept in parish churches throughout the country, the custodian being the incumbent, who is legally entitled to charge a small fee for searching the records. Books begin at various dates, many reach back to 1750, a few are considerably older.

The Public Record Office, Chancery Lane, has millions of documents relating to the actions of the central government and the courts of law of England and Wales from the eleventh century, of Great Britain from 1707, and of the United Kingdom from 1801 to the present day. It will be recalled that Ireland was part of the United Kingdom until 1921.

Of particular interest from an Irish point of view are the census returns for the years 1841 and 1851 which give among other details an indication of the birthplace of persons in the household.

Two London based societies provide expert advice and assistance on matters genealogical, viz.

The Society of Genealogists,
37, Harrington Gardens,
London S.W. 7.

The Irish Genealogical Research Society
The Irish Club
82 Eaton Square
London S.W. 1.

ANTRIM

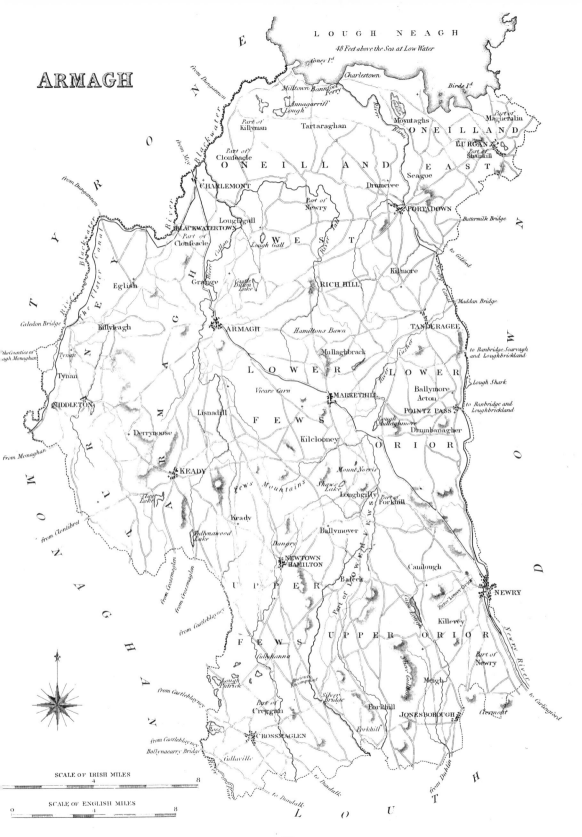

ARMAGH

LOUGH NEAGH

48 Feet above the Sea at Low Water

CARLOW

CAVAN

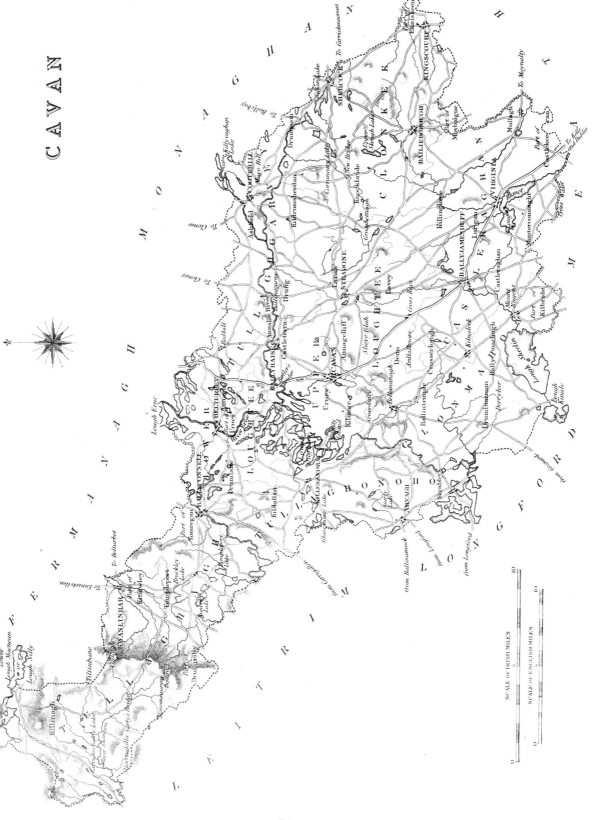

SCALE OF IRISH MILES

SCALE OF ENGLISH MILES

73

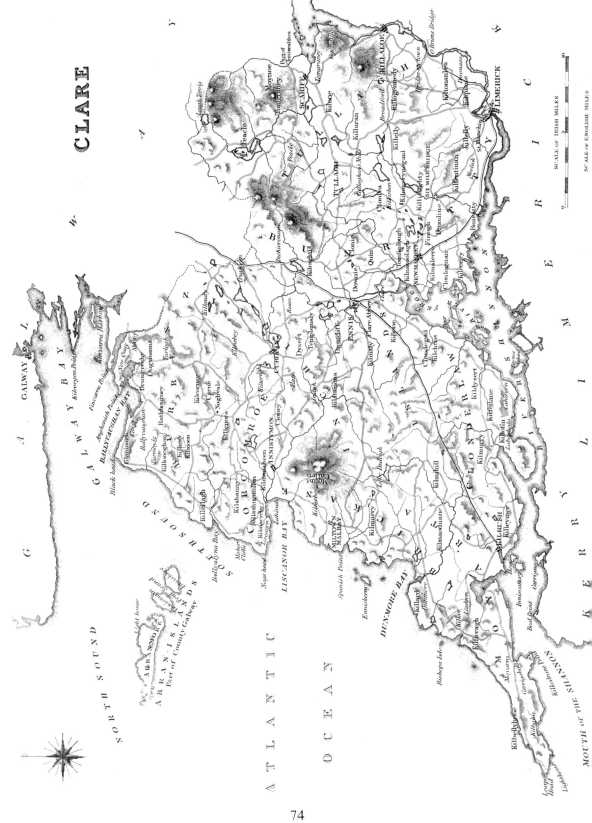

CLARE

CORK

Reference to the Baronies.

1 Duhallow
2 Orrery and Kilmore
3 Fermoy
4 Condons and Clangibbons
5 West Muskerry
6 East Muskerry
7 Barretts
8 Barrymore
9 Kinnatalloon
10 Bear
11 Bantry
12 East Carbery
13 Kinalmeaky
14 Kinalea
15 Imokilly
16 West Carbery
17 Ibane and Barryroe
18 Courcey's
19 Kinsale
20 Kerricurrihy

SCALE OF IRISH MILES

SCALE OF ENGLISH MILES

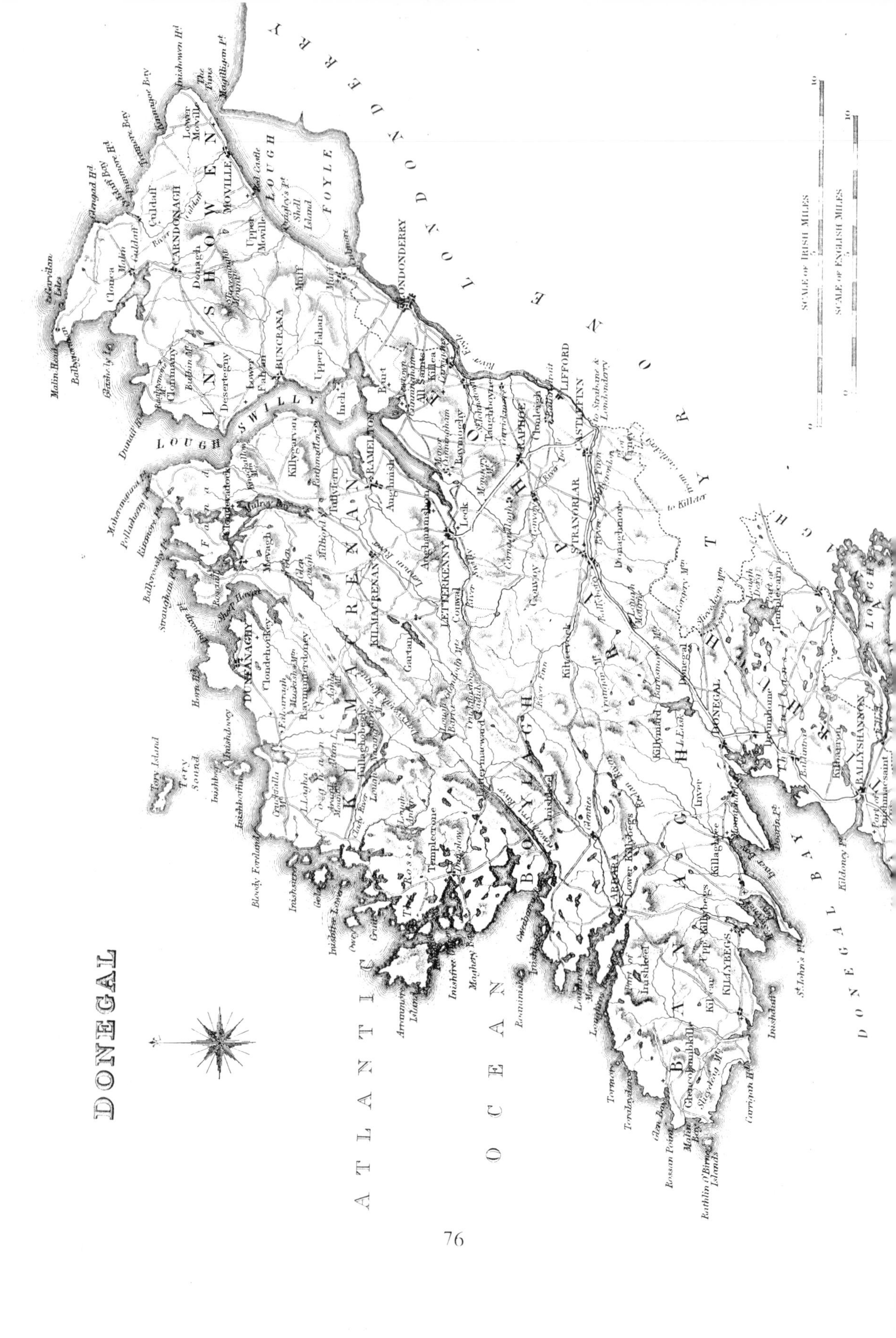

DONEGAL

SCALE OF IRISH MILES

SCALE OF ENGLISH MILES

ATLANTIC

OCEAN

LONDONDERRY

LOUGH FOYLE

LOUGH SWILLY

INNISHOWEN

CARNDONAGH

MOVILLE

Lower Moville

Upper Moville

BUNCRANA

INNISKEEL

KILMACRENAN

LETTERKENNY

RAPHOE

LIFFORD

CASTLEFINN

STRANORLAR

BANAGH

TIRHUGH

KILLYBEGS

BALLYSHANNON

DONEGAL

DONEGAL BAY

DUNFANAGHY

Tory Island

Inishbofin

Aranmore Island

Bloody Foreland

DOWN

ANTRIM

BELFAST LOUGH

Grey Point

Bangor Bay

Groomsport Point

New Island

Lighthouse Island

Copeland Island

New Harbour

BANGOR

Crawfordsburn

Hollywood

DONAGHADEE

Knockbreda

Newtownbreda

BELFAST

BALLYMACARRET

Dundonald

NEWTOWN ARDS

LOWER

ARDS

COMBER

Part of
Ballywalter

GREY ABBEY

Part of
Lambeg

Part of
Drumbeg

CASTLEREAGH

Tullynakill

Inishargy

KIRKCUBBIN

St Andrews

LISBURN

Drumbo

Kilmood

Ardmillan

Ballyhalbert

to Antrim

to Glenavy & Antrim

to Lisburn & Belfast

to Lisburn & Belfast

Navigation

Blaris

MOIRA

Part of
Shankill

Drumore

SAINTFIELD

Killaney

Killinchy

Ardkeen

Part of
Castleboy

Cleghy
Bay

Part of
Witter

LURGAN

Magheralin

HILLSBOROUGH

Annahilt

Ardquin

Ballyphilip

KILLYLEAGH

PORTAFERRY

DROMORE

Waringstown

Donaghcloney

LOWER IVEAGH

Magheradrool

Ballynahinch

Crossgar

Kilmore

Strangford

Part of
Ballyquintan

Tullylish

Magherally

Dromore

KINELARTY

Inch

Part of
Witter

GILFORD

Garvaghy

Dromara

Part of
Saul

Ballyculter

BANBRIDGE

Seapatrick

Loughinisland

STRANGFORD LOUGH

Ballyquintin Pt.

Scarvagh

DOWNPATRICK

Part of
Kilclief

Mill Quarter
Bay

Killard Point

LOUGHBRICKLAND

Lough
Brickland

LECALE

Down

Part of
Kilclief

Aghaderg

Annaclone

Part of
Newry

Ballee

Dunsfort

Guns Island

UPPER

IVEAGH

Drumgooland

Clough

Part of
Rathmullan

Bright

Boat Harbour

Donaghmore

Drumballyroney

CASTLEWELLAN

Kilmegan

Ballykinlar

ARDGLASS

Dundrum

Tyrella

Killough

RATHFRILAND

Drumgath

Maghera

Boat Harbour

Killough Bay

Ringford Point

Bryansford
River Shimna

Black Rock

DUNDRUM BAY

Saint Johns Point

Hilltown

Kilcoo

NEWRY

Clonduff

Dunmore Head

MOURNE

River Apueking

Clonduff

Clonallan

Kilbroney

Kilkeel

Annalong

WARRENSPOINT

ROSSTREVOR

Killowen Point

CARLINGFORD

KILKEEL

LOUTH

CARLINGFORD

Green Castle
Point

LOUGH

Coast Guard Station

Old Lighthouse

Cranfield Point

IRISH CHANNEL

SCALE OF IRISH MILES

0   5   10

SCALE OF ENGLISH MILES

0   5   10

77

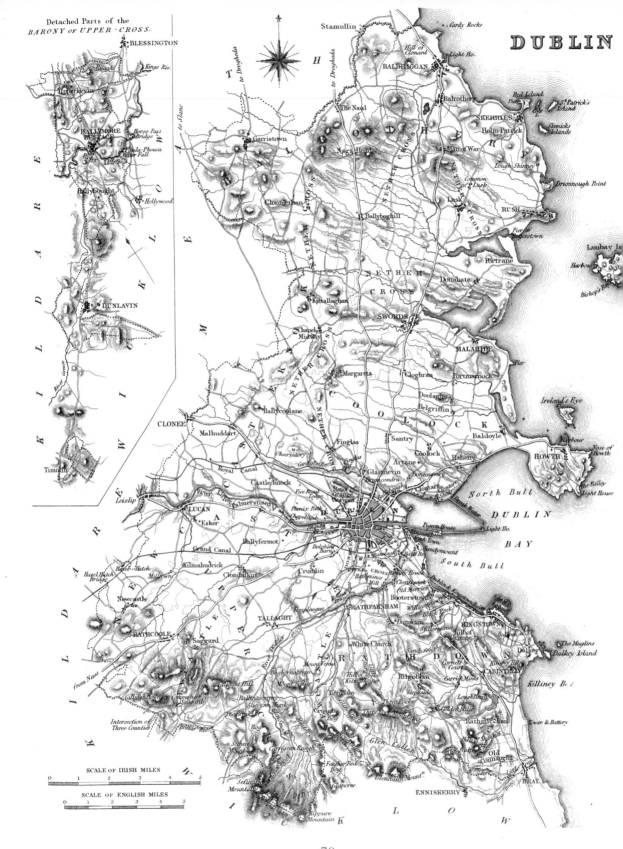

DUBLIN

SCALE OF IRISH MILES

0 1 2 3 4 5

SCALE OF ENGLISH MILES

0 1 2 3 4 5

78

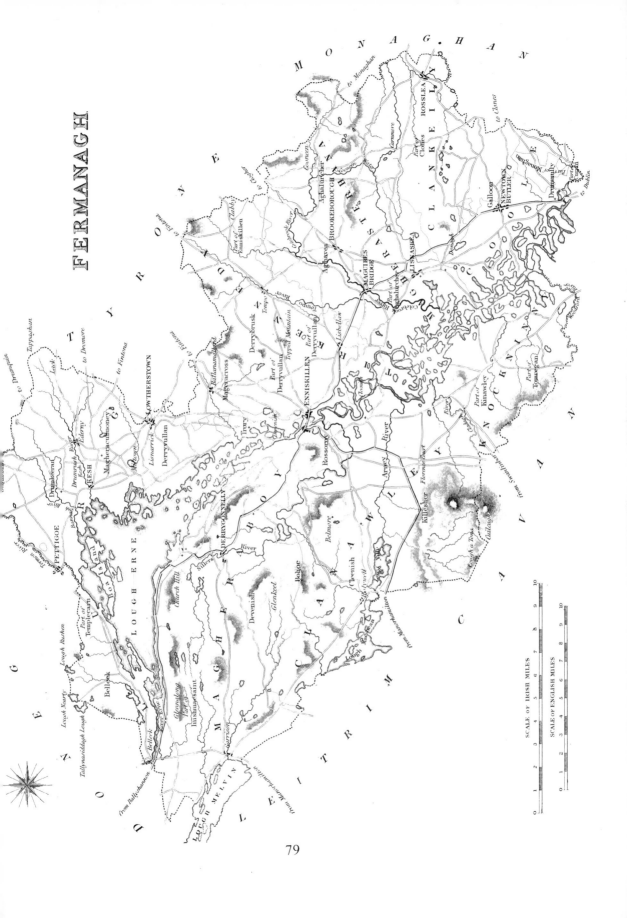

FERMANAGH

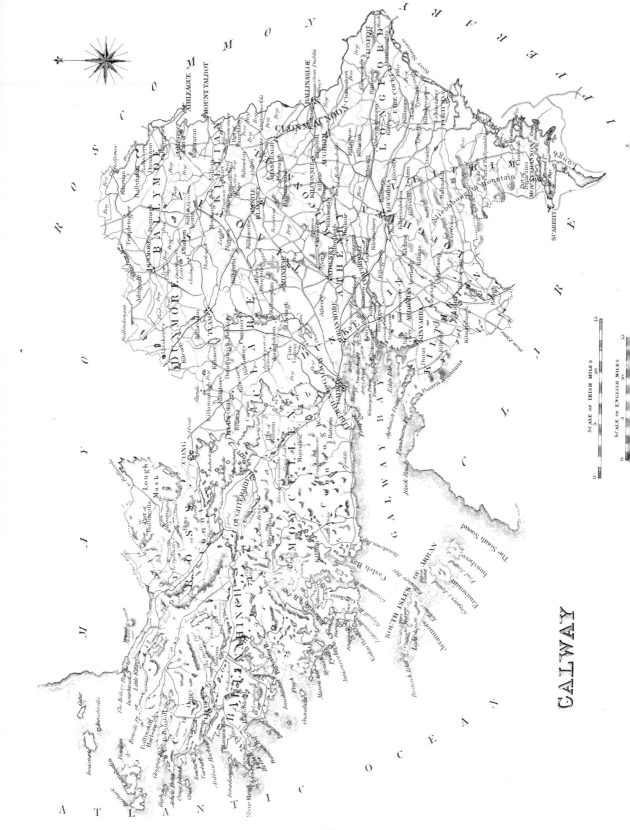

GALWAY

KERRY

81

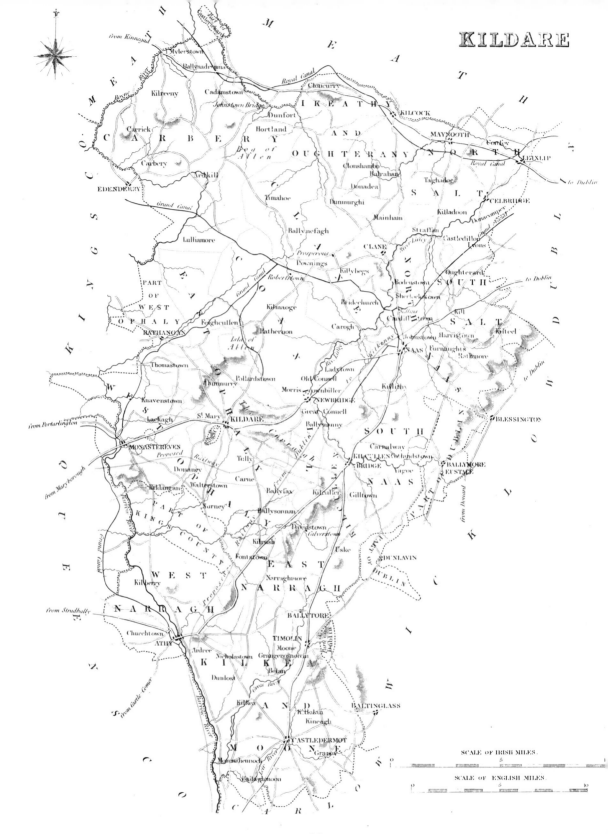

KILDARE

SCALE OF IRISH MILES.

SCALE OF ENGLISH MILES.

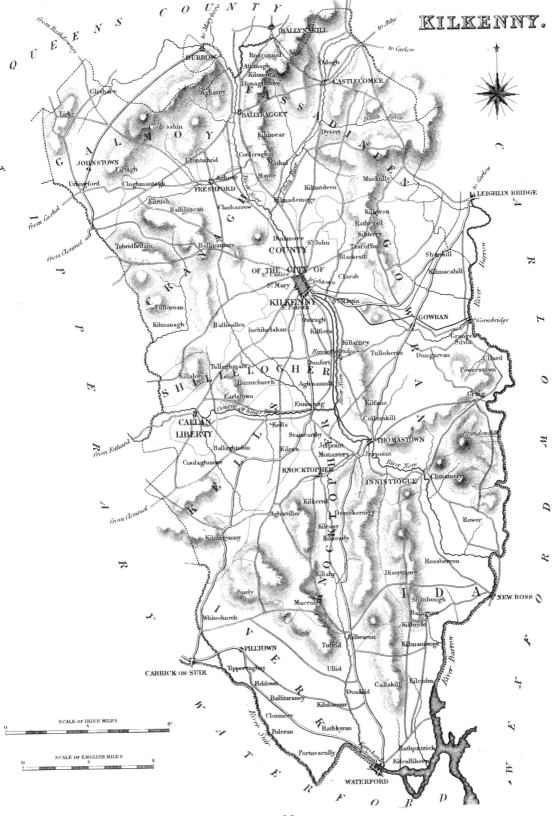

KILKENNY.

QUEENS COUNTY

from Rathdowney

to Maryboro

to Athy

to Carlow

BALLYNAKILL

Rosconner
Attanagh
DURROW
Kilmeenan
Donaghmore

Clough

CASTLECOMER

Glashare

Agharny

Firke

Cooleashin

BALLYRAGGET

Dinin River

to Carlow

JOHNSTOWN

Fartagh

Kilnocar

Dysert

Urlingford

Cloghmantagh

Clontubrid

Cooleraghin

Mothel

Muckally

LEIGHLIN BRIDGE

FRESHFORD

Mayne

Kilmodeen

Kilrush

Aghour

Aghour

Kilmademoge

Killyran

Balliloscan

Clashacrow

Tubridbritain

Ballinamore

Rathcool

Kilderry

Shankill

River Barrow

Tulloroan

Dunmore

St. John

COUNTY

Tascoffin

Blackrath

Kilmacahill

OF THE CITY OF

St. Canice

St. Mary

CITY OF

Irishtown

Clarah

Kilmanagh

KILKENNY

St. Patrick

St. Martin

GOWRAN

Goresbridge

Ballikallen

Inchihelahan

Outragh
Kilfiera

Killarney

Grange
Silvia

Ullard

Tullaghman

Bennetsbridge

Tulloherin

Dungarvan

Powerstown

Killalos

Burntchurch

Dunfert
Aghmamull

Craig

Earlstown

Ennisnag

Kilfane

Ballhtobin

Onrue or Kings River

Kells

Coltonkill

Brandon Hill

CALLAN
LIBERTY

Stancarthy

Kilree

Jerpoint
Monastery

THOMASTOWN

Jerpoint

River Nore

Clonamery

Coolaghmore

KNOCKTOPHER

Kilkerril

INNISTIOGUE

Kilnagranny

Aghaviller

Demekernery

Rower

Kileasy
Kilready

Rossbercon

Buely

Killahy

Diserunore

Shanbough

NEW ROSS

Muccully

Ballyguan

Whitechurch

Kilbride

Kilbeacon

Kilmanwoge

PILTOWN

Tubrid

Kileolm

CARRICK-ON-SUIR

Tippercaghny

Ullid

Gallskill

Fiddown

Dunkild

Ballitarsney

Kilmacour

Clonmore

Rathkyran

Poleran

Portnescully

Rathpatrick

Kilculliheen

WATERFORD

WATERFORD

SCALE OF IRISH MILES
0   4   8

SCALE OF ENGLISH MILES
0   4   8

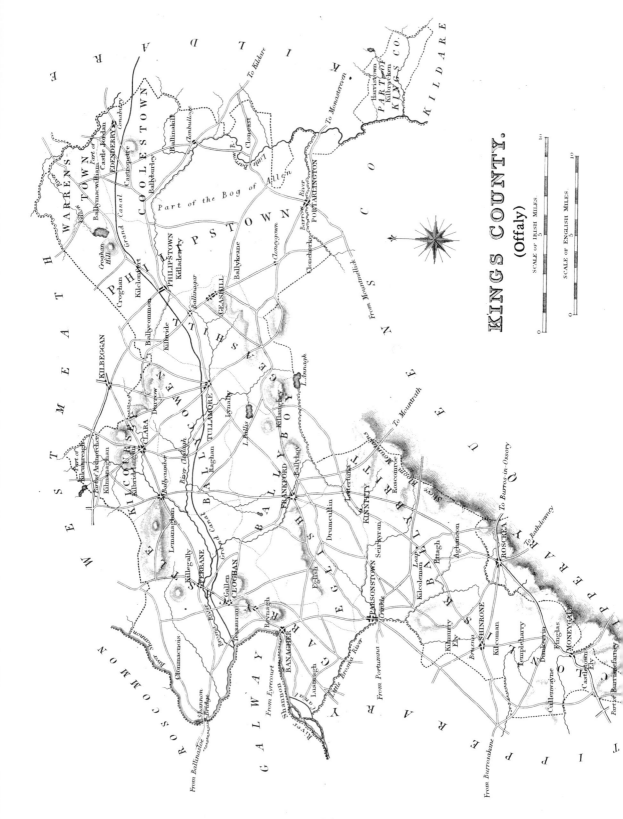

KINGS COUNTY.
(Offaly)

SCALE OF IRISH MILES.

SCALE OF ENGLISH MILES.

84

LEITRIM

Donegal Bay
to Ballyshannon
to DONEGAL
to Ballyshannon
Bundiff
from Sligo
Kinlough
FERMANAGH
MELVIN
Glenaniff
Rossinver
Lough Iron
Castlegal
Truskmore
Keelasnet
Glenkeel
Doory
Lurganboy
Mullind
Lough Gilly
from Sligo
from Sligo
Drumlease
MANOR HAMILTON
Cloncare
Benbo
R. Bonet
DROMAHAIRE
Killargy
Kiltenumory
DROMAHAIRE
L. Clean
Innismagrath
CAVAN
Kilvloy
Slieveaneiran
Drumreilley
LOUGH ALLEN
Bencroy
Barlunny Mountain
Oughteragh
Ballinamore
Newtowngore
Black Glen
Ballintra
Drumshambo
Dallnbridge
Crohabrigan
Fenagh
Drumreilly
Carrigallen
Carrigallen
LEITRIM
Leitrim
Kiltoghart
River Shannon
CARRICK ON SHANNON
MOHILL
Cloone
Mohil
Kilcone
from Boyle
Jamestown
DRUMSNA
Mohil
MOHILL
Ballynebir Bridge
Annaduff
Lough Sallagh
Ballinamuck
ROOSKY
Drumod
Drumlish
to Longford
LONGFORD

SCALE OF IRISH MILES.
0   5   10

SCALE OF ENGLISH MILES.
0   5   10

85

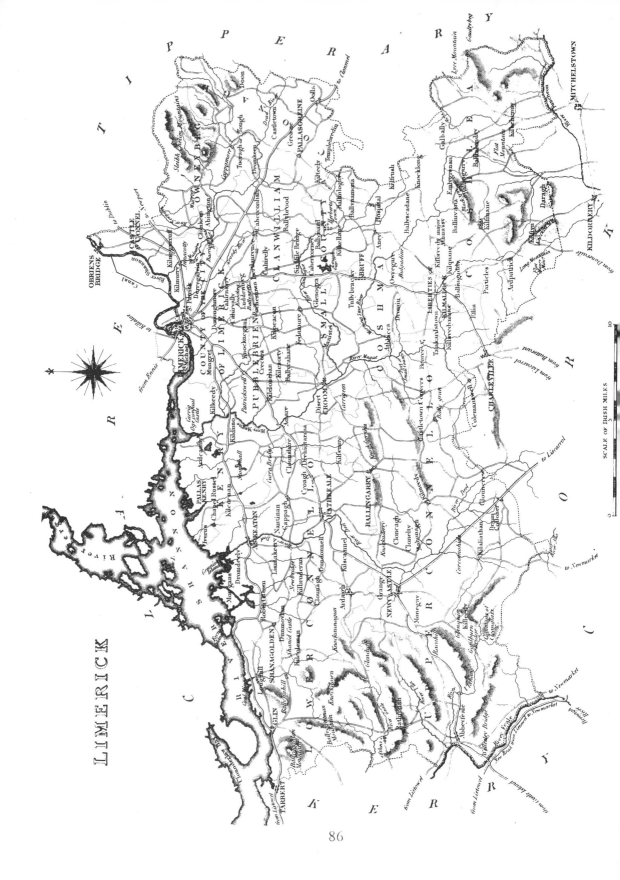

LIMERICK

LONDONDERRY

SCALE OF IRISH MILES

SCALE OF ENGLISH MILES

87

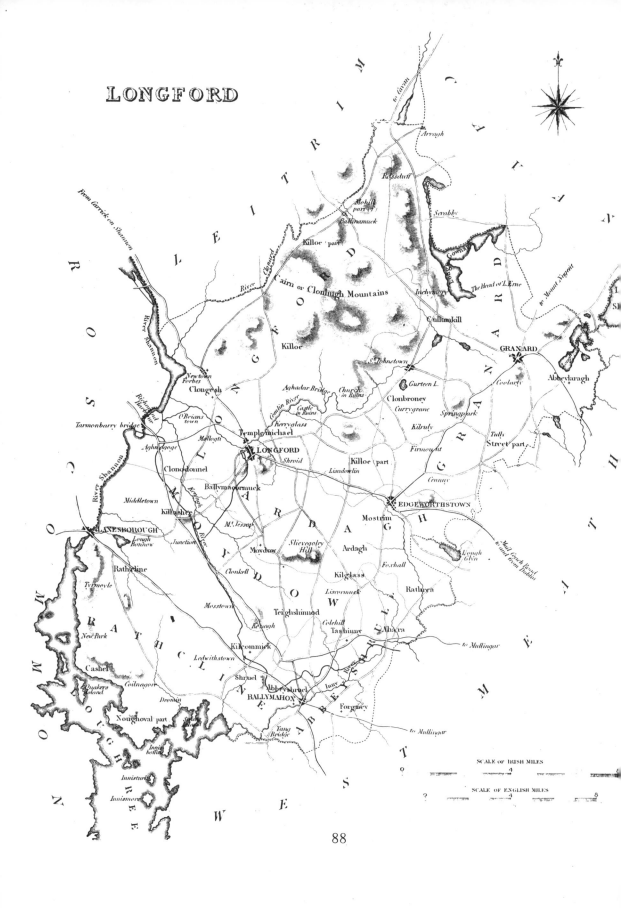

LONGFORD

88

LOUTH

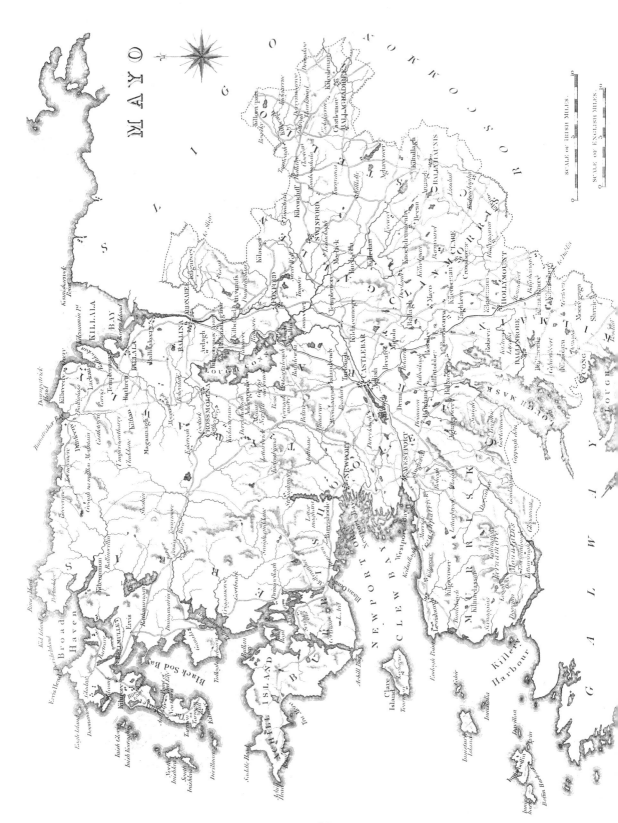

MAYO

SLIGO

ROSCOMMON

GALWAY

90

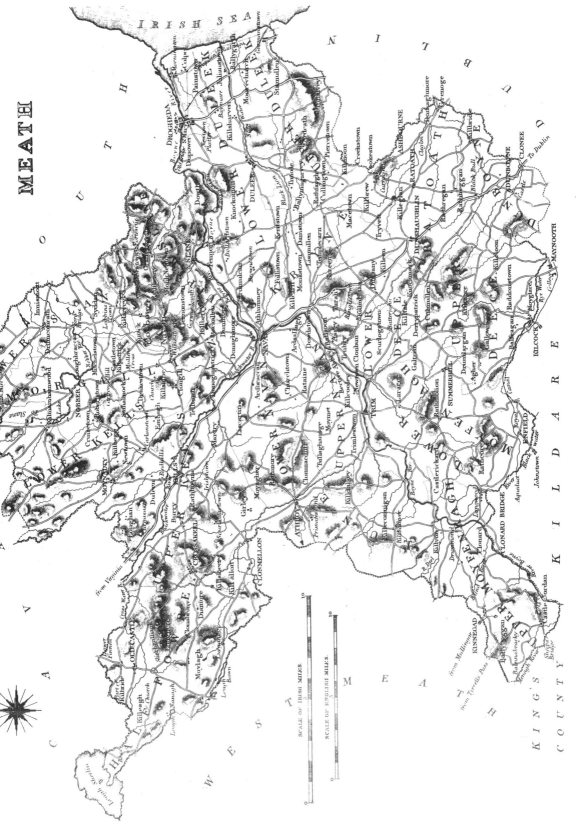

MEATH

IRISH SEA

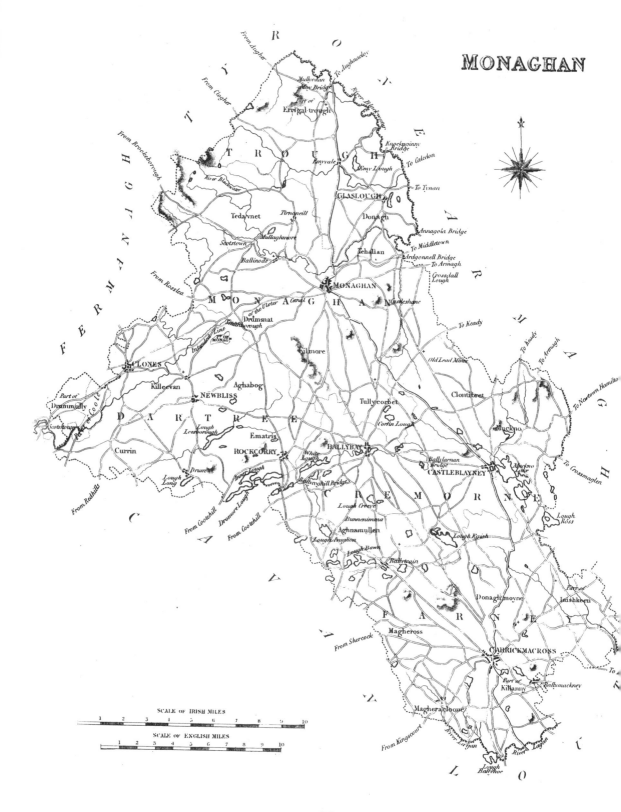

MONAGHAN

From Clogher
From Aughnacloy
To Aughnacloy
River Blackwater
Mulkedan
New Bridge
Part of
Errigal trough
From Brookeborough
T Y R O N E
Knockninny
Bridge
Emyvale
Emy Lough
To Caledon
GLASLOUGH
To Tynan
Tedavnet
Tirnoneill
Donagh
Annagola Bridge
Scotstown
Mullaghmore
To Middletown
Ardgonnell Bridge
Ballinode
Tehallan
To Armagh
From Rosslea
M O N A
G H A
MONAGHAN
Grosedall
Lough
of the Ulster Canal
Drimsnat
To Keady
Smithborough
Racksheane
MOYE
Internal Line
Silmore
Old Lead Mines
To Keady
To Armagh
CLONES
Killeevan
Aghabog
Tully-corbet
Clontibret
To Newtown Hamilton
NEWBLISS
Part of
Drummully
Lough
Leerstonough
Cortin Lough
Muckno
Scotshouse
D A R T R E E
Ematris
White
Lough
BALLYBAY
Ballylarnan
Bridge
Muckno
Lough
Currin
ROCKCORRY
CASTLEBLAYNEY
To Crossmaglen
Drum
Long
Lough
Dromore Lough
Ballreaghill Bridge
Lough Ross
From Redhills
Lough Green
C A V A N
From Cootehill
From Cootehill
Lough Bawn
C R E M O R
N E
Burneninima
Aghnamullen
Lough Aughon
Lough Fea
Donaghmoyne
Part of
Inishkeen
Ballytrain
F A R N E Y
Magheross
From Shercock
CARRICKMACROSS
Part of
Killanny
Ballymackney
Maghera-cloone
From Kingscourt
River Lagan
River Lagan
Lough
Ballyhoe
L O U T H

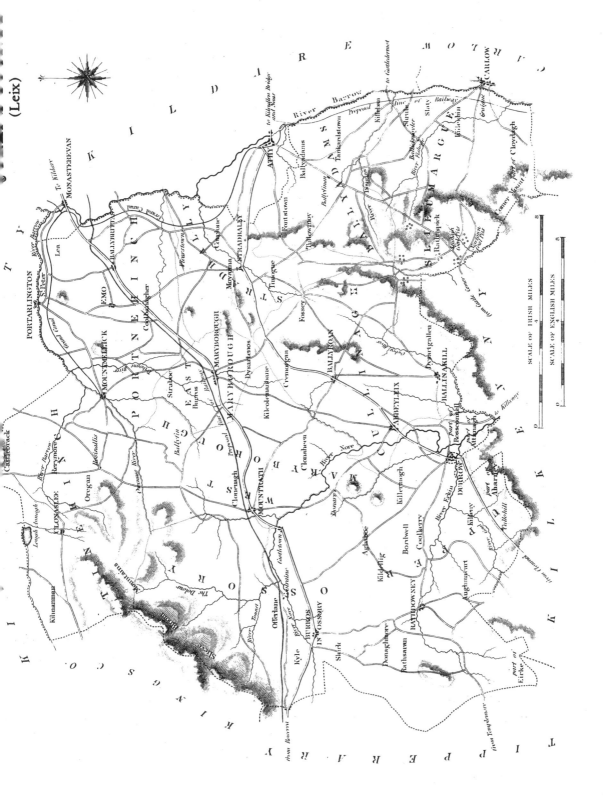

(Leix)

ROSCOMMON

SLIGO

LEITRIM

Slieve Curlagh

Lough Allen

Ballyfarnon

Lough Skean
Kilronan
Drumshambo

Lough Meelagh
KEADU

Shannon

to Sligo

River

Lough
Oakport

Lough
Gara

Battle Bridge

Kilbrine

Lough

BOYLE

Ardcarney
LEITRIM

Part of
Sligo

Eastersnow
Tumna
CARRICK
on Shannon

Kilnuch

JAMES
TOWN
DRUMSNA

BALLAGHADERREEN

Ballinavohor
Kilnamanagh

Kilcola

Goghan
Killummod

Kilmore

Lough Boderig

Lough
Bofinn

from Swineford

Tibohine

FRENCHPARK

Kilnacumse
ELPHIN

Aughrim

Cloonaft

Carnadoe
Bridge

Killglass

PART OF

ROOSKEY

Lough Errit

Ballygloss

Lough Glin

Belanagare

Lough
Bally
Shankhill
Creeve

Kilmustian

Tully

from Swineford

B
Loughglin

Kilcorkery

Donane Lough
Lough
Innes

from Ballyhaunis

Lough Acdurn

Baslick
TULSK
Ogulla

STROKESTOWN
Bumlin

OBBER

Castlerea
Kilkeevan

Castle Plunket
Kilcoosty
Monfinlough

Lisonuffy

TARMONBARRY

Kilullagh

Ballytough
Slieveadeyn

Killukin

Kilbride

Tuam

River Feurish
Erra

River Shannon

Ballintobber

Ardclare
Clontuskert

BALLYMOE

Oran

HALF BALLYMOE

Kilgeffin

PART OF
BALLINTOBBER
LANESBOROUGH

ROSCOMMON
Kilteevan

Donamon

Fuerty

Hine

Gregg

River
Porterin

Kilmaine

ATHLEAGUE
Killenvoy

Tessaragh

St Johns

Inchboffin

from Ballinamona
MOUNT TALBOT
Rahara

Lough
Funcheon

Taghboy

Kilto

Gilleenerwan
Lough

Ballyforan
Bridge

Dysart
Cam
Bridgeswell

Millitown
Pass

St Peters

ATHLONE
St Marys

Ballyneeny

Carrured
Taughmaconnell

Drum

Long
Island

Ballygill
Bridge

from Ahascragh

Creagh
Moore

River

Commaliagle
River

BALLINASLOE
MOYCARNON

Seven Churches
Ruins

KINGS Co

River Shannon

SHANNON BRIDGE

SCALE OF IRISH MILES

SCALE OF ENGLISH MILES

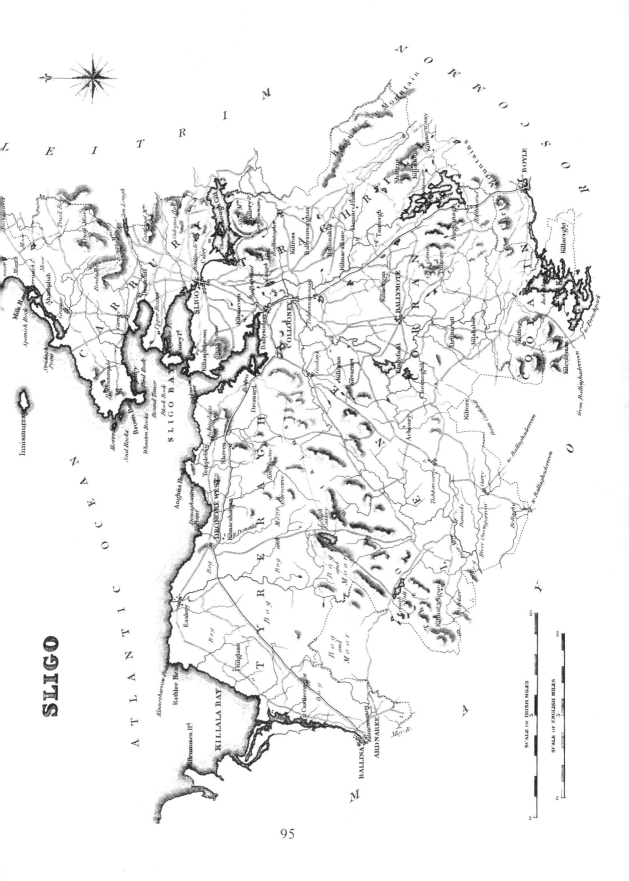

SLIGO

95

TIPPERARY

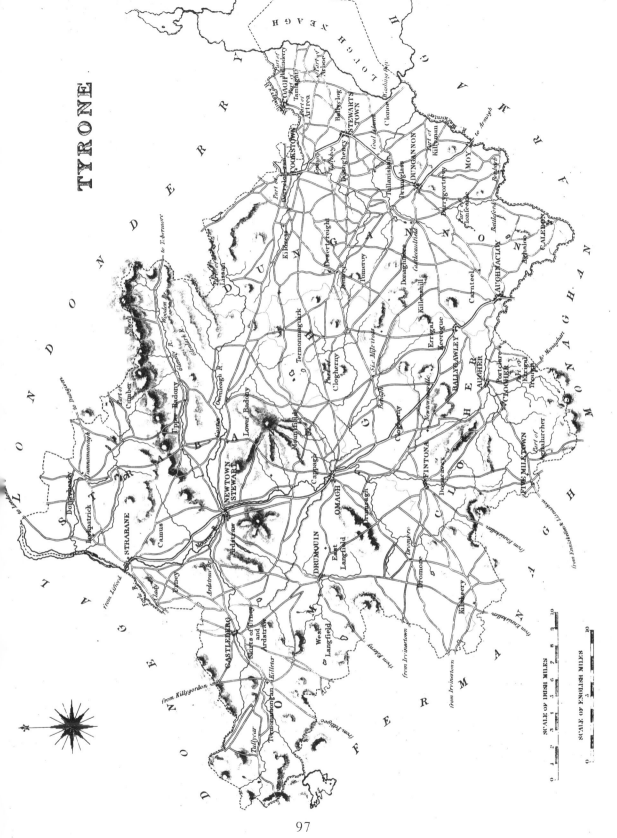

TYRONE

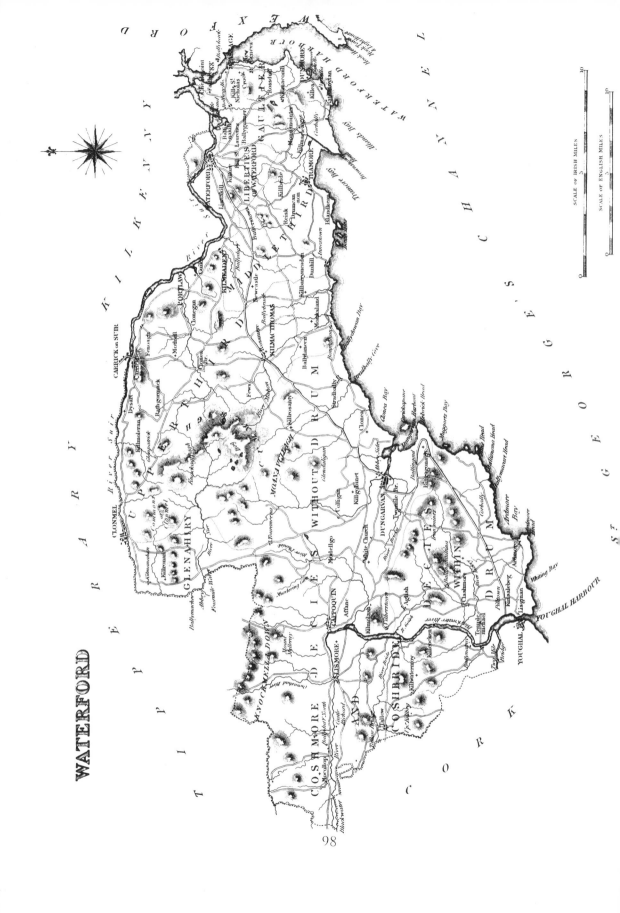

WATERFORD

SCALE OF IRISH MILES

SCALE OF ENGLISH MILES

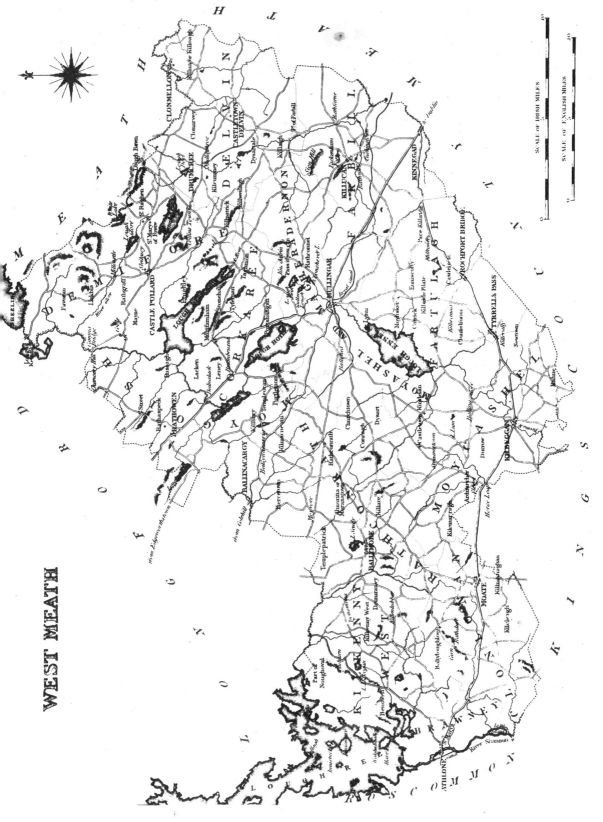

WEST MEATH

99

WEXFORD

SCALE OF IRISH MILES

SCALE OF ENGLISH MILES

WICKLOW

SCALE OF IRISH MILES

SCALE OF ENGLISH MILES

101

Departure of the Nimrod and Athlone steamers with emigrants on board from Queenstown, Co. Cork.

Emigrant Passenger Lists to America

With my bundle on my shoulder
Sure there's no man could be bolder
I'm leaving dear old Ireland without warning
For I've lately took the notion
To cross the briny ocean
I'm bound for Philadelphia in the morning.

Compulsory emigration from Ireland due to poverty rose sharply following the Act of Union 1800. The truth of this is evinced by the sharply increased numbers leaving the modestly industrial province of Ulster in the opening decades of the nineteenth century. The loss of native parliament exposed weak home industry to excessive competition from English factories resulting in thousands having to seek a fresh livelihood in the New Word. Worse was to follow. The failure due to blight of the potatoe crop in successive years in the forties deprived the masses of their staple food and resulted in the population being cut from eight millions to four by starvation and emigration.

Once the decision to emigrate had been taken and frequently there was little choice a sailing ticket was procured from the local agent of the shipping line, usually a small shopkeeper in the nearest market town, and then came the long trek to the port of embarkation. Here delays of several weeks were not unusual while the would-be passenger sought a place on a ship. The cost of a steerage passage from Ireland to America for a family of eight in 1855 amounted to £24. Under the Emigration and Passenger Acts the master of each ship was required to provide certain daily rations of food and water but mess utensils and bedding had to be provided by the passenger. Voyages usually took from fifty to eighty days depending on weather conditions.

Not only individuals but also whole families and even groups of people from the same district made the perilous voyage together. In 1850 owing to the aftermath of the famine a Wexford priest took the greater part of his parishioners to New Orleans. He was Fr. Thomas Hore of the united parishes of Annacurra and Kilaveney in north County Wexford. In November 1850 Fr. Hore together with 462 of his flock sailed from Liverpool on the ship *Ticonderoga*. The passenger list of that ship headed by the name Thomas Hore is preserved in the Louisiana State Library at Baton Rouge.

The pressing problems of over population and poverty in 19th century Ireland caused the Government to initiate a number of state-aided emigration schemes. One of the better known of these was known as the Peter Robinson emigration scheme. Robinson, a Canadian, while on a visit to Ireland was struck by the number of persons who had no prospect of obtaining useful employment in their native land. Forthwith he arranged for the transport of several hundred families mainly from the upper Blackwater area of County Cork to Upper Canada where they were given grants of land by the Government. The names of the ships involved which sailed from Cobh at various dates between 1823 and 1825 were as follows – the *Star*, the *Fortitude*, the *Regulus*, the *Resolution*, the *Elizabeth*, the *Brunswick*, the *Hebe*, the *Stakesby*. The passenger lists of those ships discovered in an old locker about a hundred years later revealed that 415 families (over 2,000 persons) sailed to Upper Canada from County Cork in the mid 1825's. The ships' papers containing the original lists of emigrants' names are now preserved in the library of Peterboro, Ontario.

While no official register of passengers leaving Irish ports in the last century was kept shipping lines appear to have made carefully compiled lists of persons using their ships. The whereabouts of many of these lists is now a matter of conjecture but it is know that the Cunard Line records dating from 1840 were irregularly destroyed by the British Board of Trade in 1900. Some of the lists made their way to the British Museum in London and it is on a manuscript in that institution that many of the lists below are based. Quite a number of lists have been abstracted from records in the National Archives, Washington and from early U.S. papers and periodicals. The frequency with which passengers describe themselves as 'labourers' and 'farmers' is accounted for by the fact that there was a ban in force at the time against the emigration of skilled labour so desperately needed to power Britain's industrial revolution.

The emigration agent's office. — The passage money paid.

A List of Passengers who have sailed on board the Mars for America from Dublin, 29 March, 1803. Age given in most cases after the name.

Wm. Ford	gent
John Morris	servant
Wm. Sherlock	merchant
Hugh Jackson	"
Robert Gibson	American merchant
----- Teeling	clerk
James Murphy	labourer
John Hobleton	"

A List of Passengers on the Ship Portland for Charlestown, 29 March, 1803. Age given after the name.

Charles Adams 48, farmer of Limerick	
Margt.Adams his wife 39,	"
Ric O'Carroll 22, farmer of Bolinbroke	
Danl. O'Carroll 20,	"
Thos. Egan 29, writing clerk Limerick	
Martin Corry 58, labourer	"
John Connery 29, labourer	"
Mary Egan 60,	"
Eliza Corry 33,	"
Mary Connory 24,	"
Mary Egan junior, 27,	"
Betty Fitzpatrick 26,	"
Michl. Quillan 48, gent	"
Mary Quinlan 46,	"
Mary Quinlan junior, 13,	"
Thos. O'Duyer 22, gent	"
Michl. O'Donnovan 26, gent	"
John Mullins 26, labourer	"
James Meehan 26,	" Clare
Patk. Kernan 24,	" "
Terence Murray 18,	" "
Patrick Magrath 21,	" Caperas
Andrew Lee 26,	" Limerick
Ric Ennery 19, writing clerk Limerick	
Hugh Morgan 22, labourer	"
James Kerly 37, farmer	Ballyhoben
John Walsh 27, labourer	Limerick
Ann Considen 22,	"
John Cummins 21,	" Claraline Co. Tipperary
Wm. O'Brien 26,	" Thomas Town
Margaret Fehilly 24,	Limerick
Margt. Hayes 18,	"
Mary Callaghan 14,	"
Joseph Fihilly 7,	"
Michl. Fihilly 5,	"
John Fihilly 3,	"
Mary Fihilly 2,	"

A List of Passengers on the Ship Eagle for New York, 29 March, 1803.

Alex Radcliffe 23, farmer	Ballyroney
John Menter 28, labourer	Belfast
Wm. Calvert 33, "	Killeagh
Ann Calvert 24, spinster	"
James Bryson 27, farmer	Kilrock
Peter Leonard 28, "	Hillsboro
Wm. Logan 36, labourer	Dromore
Thos. Bain 18, farmer	Dounpatrick
Joseph Webb 25, labourer	Cockslem
Wm. Wilson 22, "	Derrylea
Margt. Wilson 20, spinster	"
Wm. Kineard 52, farmer	"
Robt. Kineard 18, labourer	"
Wm. Hancock 19, "	"
Thos. Wilson 23, "	Armagh
James Diennen 19, "	Dovehill
John English 40, "	Tynan
Isabella English 32, "	"
Wm. Kerr 18, "	"
James Lister 20, "	"
George Lister 25, "	"
John Graham 24, "	"
Thos. Spratt 50, farmer	Clough
John Browne 24, farmer	Saintfield
Saml. Campbell 18, labourer	Banbridge
Charles Martin 20, farmer	Ballymoney
Robert Halridge 16, clerk	"
Robt. Eakin 38, farmer	Coleraine
Wm. Rafield 23, farmer	Ballymena
Wm. Woods 27, labourer	Sea Patrick
Neha. Kidd 20, "	Keady
John Shields 20, farmer	"
John Cully 24, "	"
David Clement 22, "	"

Andrew Clement 20, farmer	Keady
Wm. McAlister 20, "	Ballycaste

A List of Passengers on the Ship SUSAN for New York from Dublin, 5 April, 1803.

John Dornan 43, bookseller	Dublin
Mrs. Mary Dornan 40,	"
Three small children	
Mrs. Annie Russel 38,	Louth
Three small children	
Mrs. Frances Russel 40, grocer	Dublin
John Midleton 29, merchant	Louth
James Erwin 28, physician	"
Wm. Erwin 26,	"
Chas. Rivington 25, merchant	New York
Robert Noble 60, "	"
Mrs. Nelly Welch 31, spinster	Wexford
Miss Mary Ann Finly 21, spinster	Meath
James Truer 22, farmer	County Meath
Thomas Fitzgerald 23, farmer	County Wexford
James Byrne 19, farmer	County Meath
John Byrne 21, "	" "
Wm. Finly 18, "	County Wexford
James Kelly 24, "	" "
John Riley 31, "	" "
James Kelly 25, "	" "

A List of Passengers to go on board the American Brig NEPTUNE, Seth Stevens,Master, for Newcastle and Philadelphia, burthen per admeasurement 117 tons, at Warren Point, Newry, 29 March, 1803.

John Grimes 28, labourer	
Agnes Grimes his wife, 26	
James Crummy 45, farmer	
Agnes Crummy his wife 30	
Mary " their daughter 15	
Sarah " ditto 12	
James " their son 6	
David ditto	
Susan Dene 18, spinster	
David Gallon 40, farmer	
John Henry 40, "	
Hanna Henry his wife 30	
Nancy " their daughter 13	
James " their son 11	
William Countes 26, labourer	
Mary Countes his wife 21	

List of Passengers to proceed by the American Ship RACHEL, Benjamin Hale, Master, to New York from Sligo, 15 April, 1803.

Robert Ormsby clerk	Owen McGowen labourer
James Gillan farmer	Fredk. Corry "
John Read clerk	Pat Gilmartin "
James Henderson clerk	Pat Gilan "
Peter McGowan schoolmaster	Pat Foley "
Chas. Armstrong clerk	Pat Feeny
Lauee. Christian labourer	Michl. Horan
Patt Christian "	John Farrel
James Donald "	John Commins
Wm. Corry "	Danl. Gilmartin
Danl. McGowan "	

List of passengers on board the Ship MARGARET, Thomas Marsh, Master, bound for New York, from Newry, 18 April, 1803.

Eliz Brothers 44	
Mary " 19	
Saml. " 12, laboure.	
James " 10	
William " 7	
M Ann Anderson 30	
Matu. Doubly 12	
James Farrell 3	
James Harkness 40, labourer	
Jane " his wife 36	
Thos. " his son 12	
Margt. " his daughter 10	
Sarah " " " 10	
Abigal " " " 8	
Robt. " his son 6	
James " " " 4	
Eliz Story 47	

Ben Story 18, farmer	
Ann Story 16	
Hugh Alexander 29, labourer	
Jane " his wife 22	
Jane " his daughter 3	
Sarah " " " 2	
Robert Goocy 20, farmer	
Samuel Douglas 18, "	
Thomas Haxten 19, labourer	
John Rolston 27, "	
Ann Beard 24	
Ann Beard 2	
James McClean 60, farmer	
Eliz McClean 60	
David McClean 24, labourer	
John " "	
George " "	
William Riddle 19, "	
Samuel Magil 21, " .	
Samuel Magil 39, "	
Biddy Enery 35	

List of passengers intending to go from Belfast to Philadelphia in the Ship EDWARD, from Belfast, 19 April 1803.

James Greg 46, farmer	
Thomas Greg 18, "	
John Greg 19, "	
Thomas Fleming 19, labourer	
Hugh Porter 24, "	
John Martin 21, "	
Alexr. McMeekin 21, "	
Adm. Dunn 30, farmer	
Thomas Monks 60, farmer	
Robert Monks 22, "	
Joseph Monks 20, "	
Thomas Monks 17 "	
John Smith 20, labourer	
Hu. McBride 26, "	
W. " 25, "	
W. Dawson 28, "	
Jno. Craven 25, "	
James Fox 40, "	
Ja. Mooney 16, "	
James Towel 22, "	
James Burns 20, "	
Robt. Labody 32, gent	
Hers McCullough 27, farmer	
Wm. Scott 22, "	
James Kirkman 40, "	
Wm. Bingham 14, "	
John Norris 16, labourer	
Hugh Murphy 18, "	
Edwd. Wilson 18, gent	
Ardsal Hanlay 22, labourer	
James Read 23, "	
Jos. Haddock 27, "	

A List of Passengers who intend going to Newcastle, Wilmington and Philadelphia in the Ship PENNSYLVANIA, Elhana Bray, Master, from Londonderry, 16 April, 1803.

Patrick Lealer 50, labourer of Shabane	
Robert Donaldson 46, " "	
Bell Donaldson 36, spinster	"
Mary " 24, "	"
Jane " 25, "	"
Mary " 20, "	Clanely
Nancy Maxwell 30, "	"
Robert " 10, labourer	"
Nash Donald 26, "	"
Patrick Donal 50, "	"
Margaret Steel 26, spinster	"
Peter Derin 56, labourer	"
James McGonagal 26, "	Tulerman
Charles Canney 28, " .	"
Richard Dougherty 36, " .	"
Margaret Heaton 28, spinster	"
Patrick McCallen 33, labourer	"
Hugh Breeson 40, "	"
Mary O'Donnell 25, spinster	Strabane
Samuel Gilmour 20, "	Sr. Johnston
Ann Gilmour 15, spinster	"
Jas. Elgin 10, labourer	"
James Boyd 26, "	"
William Oliver 26, "	Sr. Johnstown

Thomas Wilson 25, labourer Sr. Johnstown
Nancy Wilson 26, spinster "
Jas. Wilson 20, labourer Muff
Nancy Wilson junr. 24, spinster Sr. Johnstown
John Wilson 56, labourer Muff
Saml. " 45, " "
Eleanor " 36, spinster Newton Limavady
John Moore 22, farmer " "
Bridget Dever 55, spinster " "
John Lewis 33, labourer " "
Fanny Lewis 70, spinster " "
Fanny Lewis junr., 15, spinster " "
Andw. Lewis 20, labourer " "
Susan " 36, spinster " "
George " 33, labourer " "
James Stewart 25, " Dungiven
Jas. King 45, " "
Willm. McBride 50, " "
Will. Parker 50, " "
Alexr. Houston 45, " "
Francis " 20, " "
John Brigham 26, farmer "
Jane Brigham 25, spinster Ballyshannon
Eliz Brigham 26, " "
Ezekl. Brigham 25, labourer "
David Brigham 22, " "
Wm. White 18, " "
Jas. Mitchell 22, " Derry
Fras. Dormet 20, " "
Wm. Montgomery 22, " "
May " 41, spinster "
Saml. " 12, labourer "
Rebecca " 10, spinster Ballendreat
Robert Little 26, labourer "
John Little 24, " "
Mathw. Armstrong 23, " "
Jas. Todd 20, " "

A List of Passengers who intend going to
New York in the Ship CORNELIA of Portland,
sworn at Londonderry, 15 April, 1803.

Andrew Little 35, labourer
Jane " 26, spinster
John " 12, labourer
Margaret " 9, spinster
William " 6, a child
Eliza " 4, "
Jane " 2, "
Hugh McAvery 24, farmer
Jane McAvery 30, spinster
Jane McAvery 1, a child
Simon Neilson 25, labourer
Mary " 25, spinster
Archibald Armstrong 18, farmer
James Neilson 3, a child
Catherine Rodgers 18, spinster
Wm. Brown 20, labourer
James McCann 25, "
David Henderson 20, "
Cons. Dougherty 20, "
Thos. McDonagh 50, farmer
Catherine " 50, spinster
Catherine " 50, "
James " 15, farmer
Hugh McDonagh 13, "
Richard " 11, "
Thomas " 2, a child
Hugh Donnelly 32, labourer
Mary " 28, spinster
Hugh Kennen 51, labourer
Catherine Donnelly 4, a child
Hugh Kennen 3, a child
James Tracy 30, farmer
Rose Tracy 32, spinster
Margaret Tracy 2, a child
James McCarron 29, farmer
Jane McCarron 29, spinster
John McCarron 5, labourer
Fanny McCarron 3, a child
John McQuoid 20, labourer
Robert Leonard 22, "
Jane " 20, spinster
John Kelly 24, labourer
Eliz Bruce 26, spinster
Robert Harper 30, farmer
Jane Harper 24, spinster
Charles Harper 35, farmer
John Forster 24, labourer

Jane Little 21, spinster
James Harper 7, labourer
Anthony O'Donnell 19, labourer
Manus Brown 19, "
Edwd. Brown 20, "
Patrick Collin 22, "
John Gallougher 22, "
Chas. Dougherty 23, "
Rebecca Beatty 21, spinster
James Muldoon 24, labourer
James King 25, farmer
John Lenox 30, farmer
William Coldhoune 30, labourer
Patrick Caldwell 25, "
Jane " 20, spinster
Thomas McKennen 3, a child
John Beatty 28, farmer
Isabella Beatty 22, spinster
Stephen " 2, a child
Mary McIver 17, spinster
Judith " 19, "
Shane " 25, farmer

A List of Passengers who intend going to
New York on the Ship AMERICAN, 340 Tons burthen,
Alexander Thompson, Master, sworn at Londonderry,
9 April, 1803.

David Kerr 28, farmer Donegal
Hannah Kerr 25, spinster "
Robert Virtue 22, farmer "
Ann Virtue 25, spinster "
Alexander Thompson 21, farmer Fermanagh
L. Jenkin labourer "
Andw. Brander " "
L. Miller " "
James McCafferty " "
John Ward " "
Robert Fitzpatrick " "
Robert Stinson " "
William Taylor " Sligo
Elinor " spinster "
Mary " " "
John Longhead labourer Donegal
R. Longhead spinster "
Robt. Longhead labourer "
John Longhead " "
John Whiteside " "
Ann " spinster "
Arthur Johnston farmer "
Mary " spinster "
Thomas Longhead labourer "
Thomas " 28, " "
James McCrea 20, " Ballantra
John " 25 " "
Barbara Spence 24, spinster "
Catherine " 23, " "
John Coulter 23 labourer Petigo
Dennis Carr 22, " "
Catherine Carr 21, spinster "
James Tremble 26, farmer Donegal
Patk. McGeragh 22, farmer "
Alex McKee 27, farmer "
Fanny McKee 26, spinster "
Patrick McMullen 29, labourer "
Hugh Devarney 26, labourer Monaghan
Bryan Devine 28, " "
Ann " 25, spinster "
Mary McGinn 22, " Cavan
Thos. McGinn 27, labourer "
James Murphy 27, " "
Thomas Murphy 23, " "
Thomas McSurgan 26, " "
Mary " 23, spinster "
Mark O'Neill 25, labourer Drunguin
Jane " 23, spinster "
Henry " 17, labourer "

A List of Persons who intend going to Philadelphia
in the Ship MOHAWK of and for Philadelphia, burthen
500 tons, John Barry, Master, sworn at Londonderry,
23 April, 1803.

Neal Callaghan 19, labourer Ardmalin
Darby Dougherty 25, " "
John Thompson 35, " "
Charles Hethrington 40, labourer Dungannon
Christy Hethrington 36, labourer "

Susna. Hethrington 40, Dungannon
Josh. " 14, "
Eliza " 16, "
George " 10, "
James Walker 32, house servant Enniskillen
Ann Walker 30, "
Ralph " 36, labourer "
Anne " 22, "
Alexr. Wood 26, labourer Lisnaska -
Mary " 20, "
Wm. Alexander 32, " Donagheady
Jane " 30, "
James " 11, "
Martha " 10, "
William Bacon 28, labourer Taughbone
Elizabeth " 27, "
William " 12, "
John McGrenan 18, house servant "
Pat McGafferty 19, labourer "
Tho. Donan 23, " "
Anne Martin 20, " Enniskillen
Thomas Drum 36, " "
Nathl. Drum 34, " "
Francis Smyth 29, " "
William Drum 20, " "
Mary Drum 16, " "
Pat Lunny 20, " "
John Bates 21, " Donamanagh
James Murray 20, " "
Richd. Jones 24, house servant Strabane
Barry McAna 24, labourer "
William Glin 25, " Letterkenny
Owen McDade 28, " Carne
Robert Hopkins 21, " Bolea
Robert Graham 20, " "
Abraham Philips 35, " Urney
Robert McCrea 30, house servant Strabane
Pat Diven 24, " "
Henry Forrester 24, labourer Clonis
Saml. Faggart 30, " "
Margt. " 28, " "
Elizth. Niely 21, stewart Newton
John McCoy 20, labourer Clougher
John Hastings 21, " Stewartstown
John Simpson 25, " "
George Walker 20, " "
Samuel Thompson 28, " Dungannon
Anna " 30, "
Andw. " 25, " "
James " 6, "
Sarah " 22, "
James Campbell 28, " "
Mary " 20, "
Patk. Brodley 19, house servant Londonderry
Alexr. " 28, labourer Newtonstewart
Archd. Anderson 19, " Armagh
James Tait 36, " "
James McGonegall 25, " Buncrana
Ferrol McAward 21, " "
Patk. McDonnell 20, " "
Denis Lynchakin 20, " "
Neal Dougherty 20, " "
William Kelly 23, " "
John Carton 35, " Claggen
David McConaghy 10, " Ballyarton
Robert McQuistin 26, " Dungiven

List of Persons who have engaged their
Passage on board the ship Ardent, Burthen 350
tons, Richard Williams, Master, bound for
Baltimore, sworn at Londonderry, 23 Apl., 1803.

Thomas Ramsey 28, farmer Nr. Muff Co. Donegal.
Hugh Elliott 40, " Rancel
Mrs. " 54, " "
James " 20, " "
Hugh " 14, " "
Jean Elliott 18, " "
James Richey 58, " Donan
Mrs. " 52, " "
Wm. " 18, " "
Cath. " 16, " "
Ann " 14, " "
John " 20, " "
Andw. " 12, " "
Ellen " 10, " "
Andw. McKee 38, " "
Mrs. " 34, " "
Eliza Richey 9, "

Nancy McKee	16,		Donan Co. Donegal
Pat "	14,		"
Eliz Finlay	57,		" "
John "	22,	farmer	" "
James "	17,	"	" "
Pat Cunigan	60,	drover	Killaughter "
James Manilus	26,	"	Kilcar "
Hugh Clark	30,	farmer	Donan "
Mrs. Clark, Snr.	28,		" "
James "	17,	farmer	" "
Wm. "	26,	"	" "
Mrs. Clark Junr.	22,		" "
Alexr. "	8,		" "
Mrs. Richey	38,		" "
George "	9,		" "
Charles "	44,	"	" "
Andw. McCullough	40,	farmer	" "
Mrs. McCullough	34,		" "
Andw. "	16,		" "
Jean "	14,		" "
George "	12,		" "
Alexr. "	10,		" "
John Montgomery	24,	gentleman	Killybegs "
John Jones	20,	"	" "
Wm. Graham	22,	farmer	Tyrough "
Francis Graham	22,	"	" "
James Cunningham	17,	"	Glenery "
John Crawford	28,	"	Ballybofey "
John Erwin	56,	"	" "
George Crawford	32,	"	Doren "
Ann Boyle	14,	"	Mt. Charles "
David Graham	48,	"	Dergbridge Co. Tyrone
Sarah "	41,	"	" "

List of Passengers who intend to proceed on board the American Ship JEFFERSON to New York from Sligo, James Adams, Master, sworn at Sligo, 16 April, 1803.

Peter Gonagle	labourer		Pat Nelis	labourer
James Clenten	"		Edmd. Gilfeader	"
Edmd. Leyonard	"		Thomas Reily	"
Pat. Waterson	"		James McKey	"
John McGan	"		James Curry	"
Thos. Wymbs	dealer		Danl. Gilmartin	"
Michl. Wymbs	"		Thos. Farrel	"
Pat Hangdon	labourer		John Higgins	"
John Harken	"		William Kalens	"
Frans. Kelly	"			

The following duplicate of the foregoing, sworn 28 April, 1803, by James Adams, the Master, gives fuller information.

Peter Nangle	40,	labourer		Sligo
James Clenton	26,	"	Clurbagh	"
Edmd. Leynerk	20,	"	" "	"
Pat Waterson	55,	"	" "	"
John McGan	32,	"	Carns	"
Thos. Wymbs	36,	dealer	"	"
Michl. "	30,	"	"	"
Pat Haregdon	41,	labourer	Moneygold	"
John Harken	26,	"	Grange	"
Fras. Kelly	29,	"	Bunduff	"
Pat Nelis	27,	"	Creery	"
Edmd. Gilfeader	23,	"	Mt. Temple"	
Thos. Reilly	29,	"	" "	
Jas. McKey	36,	"	"	"
Jas. Curry	28,	"	"	"
Danl. Gilmartin	29,	"	"	"
Thos Farrell	23,	"	Clurbagh	"
Jno. Higgins	37,	"	" "	
Wm. Kalens	42,	"	" "	

A List of Passengers who intend going to Baltimore in the Ship SERPENT of Baltimore, Archd. McCockell, Master, sworn at Londonderry, 30 April, 1803.

Joseph Neilson	26,	farmer	Strabane
Margt. "	24,		"
Jane "	14,	spinster	"
Elizabeth "	12,	"	"
John "	10,		"
James "	10,		"

Saml. McCarthy	25,	labourer	Omagh
Davd. Falls	25,	"	"
Saml. Turner	30,	"	Strabane
Jno. Neilson	27,	"	"
Pat Mounigle	28,	"	Rosquill
Neal McPeak	30,	"	"
Michl. McCann	40,	farmer	"
Phelix McCann	35,	farmer	"
Patk. "	28,	"	"
Peter "	18,	"	"
Nelly "	37,		"
Susan "	40		"
Hannah "	16	spinster	"
Mary "	14,	"	"
James McBride	25,	farmer	"
Catherine McBride	24,		"
Peter Corbitt	25,	"	Rathmullen
Isabella Corbitt	23,		"
John Mundell	40,	"	Gortgarn
Margaret Mundell	39,		"
Sameul "	46,	"	"
Wm. Jno.	25,	"	"
Isabella "	20,	spinster	"
Jane "	16,	"	"
Mary "	14,	"	"
Elizh. "	12,	"	"
Margt. Craig	36,		"
Geo. Laird	25,	farmer	"
Saml. "	22,	"	"
Mary "	24,		"
Rachl. "	25,	spinster	"
Peter Kenedy	27,	farmer	"
Margaret Kenedy	25,		"
Emelia "	6,		"
James Reed	40,	farmer	Maghera
Agnes Reed	37,		"
Mary McCool	45,	spinster	"
James "	24	farmer	"
Jn. "	20,	"	"
Nelly Ross	35,		"
James Rolls	18,	labourer	"

Passengers List of the Ship STRAFFORD for Philadelphia, sworn at Londonderry, 14 May, 1803.

John McGan	34,	farmer	Coagh
Elizabeth McGan	30,	spinster	"
Sarah "	2,		"
Elinor "	infant		"
Wm. Walker	30,	farmer	"
Mary Anne Walker	20,	spinster	"
Eliz "	18,		"
Wm. Mitchel	20,	farmer	Cumber
Thos. Conigham	18,	"	Ballymony
Alexr. Stewart	20,	labourer	Ketreights
John Moore	19,	"	Loughgin
James Hamilton	23,	"	"
Wm. Smily	23,	"	Ketreights
Edw. Clarke	40,	farmer	Enniskillen
John Miley	45,	"	"
Wm. Loughridge	30,	"	Cookstown
Mg. "	24,		"
Jane "	7,		"
James "	5,		"
Eliza "	2,		"
Nancy Harkin	30,	seamstress	Birdstown
Nelly "	4,		"
Wm. "	6,		"
John Chamber	20,	farmer	Co. Tyrone
Wm. Gray	24,	"	" "
James Ralston	45,	"	" "
Mary "	40,		" "
James "	15,		" "
Mary "	12,		" "
Davd. "	9,		" "
Josh. "	5,		" "
Anne "	34,	seamstress	" "
Anne "	2,		" "
Robt. "	19,	labourer	" "
Davd. "	15,	"	" "
John "	11,		" "
Jane "	8,		" "
Anne "	5,		" "
Josh. "	2,		" "
John "	40,	farmer	" "
Sarah "	40,	seamstress	" "
Davd. "	9,		" "
Andw. "	7,		" "
Wm. "	3,		" "

James Ralston	5,		Co. Tyrone
Elinor Shean	60,		Co. Down
Mary Anderson	24,		" "
Mary "	2,		" "
John Wilson	22,	farmer	
Wm. Carr	20,	"	
James Moore	19,		Ballykelly

A List of Passengers to go on board the Ship PATTY, sworn at Newry, 5 May, 1803.

Wm. Griffis	34,	labourer	Down
Andrew Hurs	30,	"	"
John Kenedy	41,	"	"
Saml. McBride	28,	"	Tyrone
John Gibson	50,	farmer	"
Patk. Lynch	27,	labourer	"
David Hunter	28,	"	"
Edward "	34,	"	"
George "	14,	"	"
Alexr. Armstrong	29,	"	Armagh
Mary Harvey	45,	spinster	"
Eliza "	23,	"	"
Robt. "	48,	farmer	"
Biddy Brown	38,	spinster	Down
Henry Williams	28,	gentleman	Armagh
Saml. Patton	32,	labourer	Down
Joseph "	36,	"	"
George Tilforde	28,	"	"
John Blair	29,	"	"
John McDale	36,	"	"
Walter Potts	25,	"	"
William Roncy	19,	"	"
James Eakin	46,	farmer	"
Samuel "	50,	"	"
James Fitspatrick	37,	"	"
Mary "	32,	spinster	"
Edward Maugher	26,	labourer	Queens County
John Fleming	24,	"	" "
Thomas Dick	32,	farmer	Down
James Nelson	28,	"	"
John Armstrong	29,	"	"

List of Passengers on board the PRUDENCE, of Philadelphia, Sworn at Dublin, 9 March, 1804.

Thos. Maitland	22,		Baltinglass
Ann "	56,		"
and child	7,		"
Mary Ann Maitland	19,		"
James Barry	25,	Apothecary,	Dublin
John McDermott	26,	Clerk	"
James McCarty	25,	"	"
John Gitten	30,	"	"
and child	8,		"
Jane Hines	22,		Glasnevin

Additional List of Passengers taken on board since the above was sworn to:

John Nixon	26,	farmer	Manor Hamilton, Leitrim
John Trevin	27,	"	" " "
James Gore	24,	clerk,	Dublin

List of Passengers in the EAGLE, for New York, sworn at Belfast, 10 March, 1804.

Josiah Kerr 28, height 5-8 clerk, Loughbickyard. Thin faced and pretty fair

Joseph " 21, 5-10 farmer, Hillsborough. Smooth and fair faced

Hamilton " 17, 5-0 farmer, Hillsborough. Smooth and fair faced

John McMurdy 30, 5-7 farmer, Banbridge. Pitted with the small-pox

James McMullen 28, 5-6 farmer, Loughbrickland. Red haired, smooth faced, and lame of a knee

Robert Cavert 36, 5-2 labourer, Rathfyland. Smooth and fair faced

Jas. Fulton 22, 5-8 labourer, Maghrolin.

Arthur Walker 27, 5-9 labourer, Drumore. Yellow and smooth faced

Thos. Gordon 28, 5-5 labourer, Drumore. Yellow and pitted with small-pox

Robert Whany 28, height 5-7 farmer, Drumore. Ruddy, a little pitted
Robt. Smith 21, 5-6 labourer, Hillsborough. Sallow thin and smooth faced
Hu. Hanison 13, 5-11 farmer, Drumore. Ruddy Complexion and black eyed.
Paul Rogan 30, 5-8 labourer, Loughbuckland. Spare faced
Wm. McKee 26, 5-10 labourer, Mt. Stewart. Thin faced and ruddy
Archd. Williams 21, 5-8 farmer, Castle Dawson. Smooth faced, fair haired
John Benson 19, 5-3 labourer, Near Drumore. Little pitted, black hair
Robert Patterson 24, 5-11 farmer, Ballindeny. Black hair and ruddy
Adam Patterson 20 5-6 farmer, Ballindeny. Fair haired, a little pitted
John Dickson 33, 5-7 farmer, Banbridge. Smooth face, black hair
James Black 34, 5-11 linnen draper, Banbridge. Smooth faced, black hair
James Moones 21, 5-7 farmer, Ballendeny. Little pitted, fair hair
Anthy. McMordy 44, 6-0 farmer, Banbridge. Ruddy complexion
Eliz Kerr 49, 5-4 spinster, Loughbickland. Brown complexion
Eliz Kerr 30, 5-6 spinster, Hillsborough. Brown and smooth faced
Sarah Kerr 49, 5-4 spinster, Hillsborough. A little pitted with the small-
Marg Cavart pox
Marg. Cavart 28, 5-0 spinster, Rathpiland. Fair and smooth faced
Eliza Walker 24, 5-3 spinster, Dromon. Fair, a little pitted
Margaret Gordon 21, 5-4 spinster, Dromon. Fair and smooth faced
Margaret Walker 25, 6-0 spinster, Hillsboro'. Yellow and a little pitted
Jane Whany 35, 4-0 Dromon. . Tender eyed and fair
Nancy Williams 23, 5-6 spinster, Castle Dawson. Black haired, a little pitted
Jane Dickson 21, 5-3 spinster, Banbridge. Smooth and fair faced
Hamilton Brown 35, 5-4 farmer, Killnechy. Pale faced and pitted
Jane " 35, 5-4 spinster, Killnechy. Pale faced and pitted
Wm. Whaly a child 7.

List of Passengers to go on board the American Ship MARIA, of Wilmington, bound for Philadelphia, sworn at Londonderry, 10 March 1804.

Nancy McKeever	45	spinster
Robert Fulton	43	labourer
John Rice	38	"
Mary Ann Hammond	27	spinster
Nancy Fulton	31	"
Robert Millar	26	labourer
Arthur Murphy	49	"
James Dougherty	33	"
Jas. McKinley	23	"
Sarah Murphy	21	spinster
Mary McGomery	17	"
Margt. Pearson	52	"
Frans. Scott	47	labourer
James Dogherty	51	"
Saml. McKinley	33	"
Patt Karlin	42	"
John McConway	28	"
Mary McConway	26	spinster
Hugh Smith	44	labourer
Humphry Graham	50	"
Thos. Graham	36	"
Barny McCanna	43	"
Robert Leonard	21	"
Henry Rankin	17	"
Wm. Anderson	53	"
Wm. Edmond	41	"
John Anderson	28	"
Heny. Anderson	46	"
Wm. Harkin	25	"
Jos. Arskine	56	"
Jas. Waker	40	"
Saml. Bellman	33	"

John Bellman	35	labourer
Saml. Anderson	46	"
Margt. Anderson	36	spinster
Ann Walker	24	"

List of Passengers to New York on the CHARLES and HARRIOTT, sworn at Sligo, 29 March, 1804.

Martin Carney	labourer	Mogherow
Peter Carroll	"	"
Wm. Curry	"	Conought
Fras. McGowan	clerk	Mogherow
Roger Gill	labourer	Co. Fermanagh
Bryan McManus	"	" "
Philip Rogers	"	Sligo
Robert Muns	"	Drumclief
Alexr. Rutledge	"	Tyrecagh
Hugh Murray	clerk	Sligo
Wm. Moreton	labourer	Co. Fermanagh
Thos. McIntire	clerk	Sligo
Bryan Collen	labourer	Brenduff
John Flynn	"	Drumcliff
Michael Golden	"	"
John Elliott	"	Mulloghmore
Michl. Dunn	"	"
Peter McGarry	"	Colooney
Michl. O'Hara	"	Co. Sligo
James "	"	" "
Edwd. "	"	" "
Payton Farrell	"	Boyle
Patt Fox	"	Boyle
Mark McGowan	"	Carney
Thos. "	"	"
Con. Hart	"	Co. Fermanagh
James McMorrow	"	Sligo
Alexr. Martin	"	Sligo
Wm. Chambers	"	Leitrim
Edwd. Chambers	"	"

A List of passengers from Londonderry to New York, on the ship AMERICAN, sworn at Londonderry, 31 March, 1804.

Patk. McKay	40, farmer	Moghera
Alexr. "	21, "	"
Nancy "	40,	"
Thomas Bradley 20,	"	"
John Dougherty 20,	"	Ballyarlin
James Parks	28, gentleman	Rushbank
Thomas McGomeray 19, clerk		Londonderry
Captain Sterling 25, mariner		New York
James Bond	18, clerk	Londonderry
John Clyde	13, servant	Rushbank
Geo. Crawford 19,	farmer	Coningham
Robert Johnston 20,	farmer	Nn. Cumber
Thos. Ramsey	21, "	Ballyauret
Gerard Twine	23, "	Nn. Stewart
Owen McGlenhy 34,	labourer	Cumber
Mary McGlenhy 32		Cumber
John Donaghy 41,	labourer	Ennishowin
James Dougherty 39,	"	Nn. Limavady
Elenor Dougherty 38,		" "
James Patterson 25,	farmer	Desartmarten
Alexr. McDonald 19,	labourer	Moneymore
Hugh Ramsay 29,	"	"
Alexr. Ramsay 23,	"	"
James Dougherty 29,	tanner	"
William Donaghy 48,	farmer	"
John "	19, farmer	"
Alex. "	24, "	"
Sarah "	39,	"
William McLaughlin 50, farmer		Cain
John McLoughlin 28,	farmer	"
Alexr. "	25, "	"
Mary "	48, "	"
James Buchannon 35, labourer		"
William Miller	28, servant	Nn. Limavady
Alex Dougherty	35, labourer	Magilligan

A List of Passengers intending to go by the British Brig ALEXIS, of Greenock, to Wilmington, North Carolina, sworn 29 March, 1804.

Hu. McNight	40, farmer	Near Belfast
Jas. "	54, "	" "
Batty "	36, "	" "
Margt. age uncertain		" "
John McNight	child	" "

Batty McNight junr. child		Near Belfast
Eliza "		" "
James Flanagan age uncertain,	labourer,	Dundalk
James Gordon	" " farmer	" .
Hu. Wilson age uncertain	" "	"
Thos. Gormen	labourer	Creggans
Wm. Greyson	"	"
Oliver Plunket	"	"
Michael Mackay	"	Cullaville
Terence Murphy	"	Carrickmacross
Willm. Vance	"	"
Patrick Fenor	"	"
Indorsed from Newry.		

A List of Passengers from Sligo to New York, sworn 29 March, 1804.

Wm. Jeffers	farmer	Loghadill
Alex Griffith	"	"
John Hodman	"	"
Geo. Taylor	labourer	"
Robt. Griffith	"	"
Jno. Low	"	Moghean
Robt. Elliott	"	"
Archd. "	"	"
David Ellis	farmer	Tilton
Thos. Armstrong	"	"
Andw. Taylor	labourer	"
Geo. Young	"	"
Michl. Farrill	"	"
Jno. McMorrow	"	Cloghfin
Peter Brady	"	"
Jno. Carty	"	Ardnaston
Patt McDonogh	"	Ardnastran
Andw. McNossen	clerk	"
McDonogher	labourer	"
James McDonogher	"	"
" " junr.	"	"
Robt. Cracy	"	Loghfin
Edwd. Crawford	"	"
Edwd. Crawford	"	"
Ben Caffry	"	"
Jas. Caffuny	"	"
Wm. Vaugh	clerk	"
Henry Dowler	"	Barton
Jno. Duffy	labourer	"
Hugh Crawford	"	"
Thos. Pattinson	"	"
Hugh Davis	"	"

List of Passengers of the Ship SUSAN, of and for New York, sworn at Dublin, 28 March, 1804.

Patrick Glenning	22, fair, labourer, Monasterevan, Kildare
Mary "	24, fair, spinster, Monasterevan. Kildare
Michael Cawlin	23, Dark, labourer, Nober, Meath
Mary Kenny	36, " married, Dublin
Edward Donagan	21, fair, labourer, Connotwood, Queens County
Michael Branghill	30, Sallow, labourer, Bala Braughin, Kings County
Eliza Fullard	26, fair, spinster, Edenderry, Kings County
Frances Fullard	11, fair, spinster " Kings County
Jane Fullard	10, fair, spinster " Kings County
Nicholas Caffrey	21, light, farmer, Monasterevan, Kildare
Patrick Wogan	20, fair, gentleman, Dublin
Good Rhind	23, light, " "
Keeron Carrill	23, " servant "
Thomas Durm	28, Dark, labourer, Bala Braughan, Kings County
Michael Taylor	38, sandy, labourer, Dublin
Thomas Matland	21, light, labourer, Dunlavin, Wicklow
Anne Matland	56, dark, married, " Wicklow
Mary Ann Matland	20, fair, spinster " Wicklow
James Barry	23, fair, gentleman, Dublin
Edward McDermott	30, dark, " "
Robert Dyas	19, light, " Kings Court, Cavan

James Gore   26, sandy, gentleman, Dublin
James Yates 34,   "   "   Newry
Joseph Dempsey 18, fair, servant, Upper Wood,
　　　　　　　　　　Queens County
Judith Campbell 25, brown, married, Knockmack,
　　　　　　　　　　Meath
Jane Hyres   30, brown, married, Drogheda
Mark Kelly   30, "   farmer, Monasterevan,
　　　　　　　　　　Kildare
Mary Kelly   30, brown, married,   "
　　　　　　　　　　Kildare
John Foran   35, sandy, labourer,   "
　　　　　　　　　　Kildare
Simon Donnolly 22, dark,   "   Naas
Luke Toole   28, fair, clerk, Donnybrook,
　　　　　　　　　　Dublin
William Christian 21, fair, labourer, Dublin
Nicholas Hobart 30, dark,   " Mullingar,
　　　　　　　　　　Meath
Michael Murthe 25, labourer, Lurganlyseen, South

A List of Passengers to Philadelphia on board
the BROTHERS of Philadelphia, sworn at Londonderry, 14 April, 1804.

Margaret Osburn 27, spinster, Omagh, Tyrone
Thom Thompson   23, farmer, Castlefin, Donegal
Ann Hearney   35, spinster, Dungiven, Derry
Patk. "   12, child   "   "
John "   9, "   "   "
Biddy "   7, "   "   "
Nanny "   4, "   "   "
Noble Young   22, farmer, Pethgow, Fermanagh
Jas. "   21, labourer   "   "
Sarah "   50, spinster   "   "
J. Hibran   30, labourer, Castlefin, Donegal
Jos. "   22, "   "   "
Jane Himton   35, spinster   "   "
Jas. Boyd   26, farmer, Pettigo, Fermanagh
Margt. Wishart   21, spinster   "   "
Jas.   "   51, labourer, Dungannon, Tyrone
Chas. Kelly   21, "   Drunmore,   "
Hugh "   22, "   Dunmore   "
Margt. Osburne   27, spinster, Omagh   "
Jane "   6, child   "   "
Jas. "   4, "   "   "
Chas. Flanigan   34, labourer, Ballyshannon,
　　　　　　　　　　Donegal
Mary   "   28, spinster   "   Donegal
Jno.   "   6, child   "   "
Hu. Kelly   30, labourer   "   "
Jas. Boyle   40, "   "   "
Wm. Robinson   32, "   Coleraine, Derry
Ann "   22, spinster, Innishannon,
　　　　　　　　　　Donegal
John Doherty   30, labourer,   "   Donegal
Mary "   26, spinster   "   "
Pat McLoughlin   32, labourer,   "   "
R. McLoughlin   24, "   "   "
Wm. Doherty   23, "   "   "
Jas. "   28, farmer, Beet,   "
Jas. Dunn   24, "   "   "
Mary "   19, spinster   "   "
Jas. Porter   35, farmer   "   "

List of Persons who wish to go to Baltimore,
sworn 14 April, 1804.

Robert Gibson 28, farmer   Dromon, Down
Sarah "   27, "
Mary   "   60,   Hillsborough, Down
John   "   30, "   "   "
David "   28, "   "   "
Ann   "   20, "   "   "
Elizabeth "   18, "   "   "
Jane Taggart   40,   Dromon,   "
Ann "   14,   "   "
Jane "   12,   "   "
Wm. Cotter   28, labourer, Ballymona, Antrim
Ann Cotter   26, "   "   "
Felix Divine   38, dealer, Philadelphia, America
Robert Nesbit 40, "   Killinchy, Down
James McCausland 30, farmer, Cookstown, Tyrone
Susanna "   28, "   "   "
Alexander Richardson 28, dealer, Baltimore, America
Mary Ann   "   26, "   "   "
William Greer 25, dealer   "   "

James Cleland 24, dealer, Ballymillon, Down
George "   21, farmer   "   "
William Lindley 20, "   "   "
Robert Lowry   55, dealer, Killinchwood, "
Mary Lowry   55, "   "   "
Robert "   26, farmer   "   "
James   "   24, labourer "   "
Wm.   "   20, "   "   "
Jane "   18, "   "   "
George Hutton 21, farmer   "   "
Francis Delap 50, "   Comber   "
Alexander "   22, "   Comber   "
Jane   "   50, "   "   "
Jane   "   20, "   "   "
Christian "   18, "   "   "
Andrew Morrow 40, labourer, Ballyargin "
Jane   "   30, "   "   "
Mary Boyd   31,   Dromon   "
Daniel Boyd   34, farmer   "   "

A List of Passengers who intend going to New York
in the American Ship WILLIAM AND JANE from
Belfast, sworn at Belfast, 14 April, 1804.

John Eaton   30, farmer,   Tanlagh, Derry
Jas. "   28, "   "   "   "
Saml. "   29, "   "   "   "
Mary "   25, spinster "   "   "
Matw. Maxwell 25, gentleman, Ballooly,
　　　　　　　　　　Rathfryland, Down
Robt. Loughran 23, labourer, Near Cookstown,
　　　　　　　　　　Tyrone
Brizbr. "   25, spinster "   "
　　　　　　　　　　Tyrone
Wm. Henderson 21, farmer, Raloe near Larne,
　　　　　　　　　　Antrim
John Lundy   34, farmer, Near Tandragee,
　　　　　　　　　　Armagh
Philp. McKevy 25, farmer, Raloe near Larne,
　　　　　　　　　　Antrim
Alexr. Robb   24, labourer, Broadisland,
　　　　　　　　　　Antrim
Wm. Alexander 20, labourer,   "
　　　　　　　　　　Antrim
Widow Brown   60, spinster, Kelleleagh, Down
Margt. "   25, "   "   "
Barbara "   18, "   Killilegh   "
John McCulloh 21, labourer, Drumbo   "
Margt. Withers 25, spinster "   "
John Robinson 28, labourer, Near Porlavo
　　　　　　　　　　Archin, Down
John Steen   13, labourer, Near Coan, Antrim
John Burns   30, " Drumgolan near Rt.
　　　　　　　　　　Fayland, Down
Denis Doyle   34, labourer, Drumgolden nr. Rt.
　　　　　　　　　　Fayland, Down
Margt. "   34, spinster, Drumgolden nr. Rt.
　　　　　　　　　　Fayland, Down
Michl. "   27, labourer, Drumgolden, nr. Rt.
　　　　　　　　　　Fayland, Down
Eliza   "   27, spinster, Drumgolden nr. Rt.
　　　　　　　　　　Fayland, Down
Arthur O'Neal 23, farmer, near Castlereagh, Down
Saml. Morrison 27, "   Killinchy   "
Mary   "   25, spinster "   "
James Rusk   23, farmer, Derriaghy near Lisburne
George McCray 20, " Donerisk nr. Cookstown,
　　　　　　　　　　Tyrone

A List of Passengers in the American Ship JANE of
New Bedford for New York, sworn at Dublin,
17 April, 1804.

James Normidge 26, dark, surgeon, Britan Street,
Mary " his wife 19, dark, Britan Street, cabin
George Nalleran 24, dark, clerk, Britan Street,"
Jane   " his wife, 26, dark, Britan Street, "
Edward Dartnell 27, fair, clerk, Britan Street,
　　　　　　　　　single, cabin
Catherine Corish 32, married, James Street, cabin
Miss Corish   8,
Michael Smith 24, dark, farmer, single, Clighen,
　　　　　　　　　Cavan, steerage
John Mullahy   22, dark, farmer, single, Callan,
　　　　　　　　　Kilkenny, steerage
John Shilly   35, dark, farmer, single, Callan,
　　　　　　　　　Kilkenny, steerage
Denis Finning 25, fair, steerage

Thomas Mahir   24, dark, farmer, married, Callan,
　　　　　　　　　Kilkenny, steerage
Mary " his wife, 22, married, Callan, Kil-
　　　　　　　　　kenny, steerage
infant child
Patrick Cormack 17, dark, farmer, single,
　　　　　　　　　Callan, Kilkenny, steerage
William Carty 17, dark, farmer, married,
　　　　　　　　　Barton, A.N. steerage
Alice White   50, dark single, Callan,
　　　　　　　　　Kilkenny, steerage
May White   20, dark, single, Callan,
　　　　　　　　　Kilkenny, steerage
Catherine White 22, dark, single, Callan,
　　　　　　　　　Kilkenny, steerage
Eleanor White 18, dark, single, Callan,
　　　　　　　　　Kilkenny, steerage
Margt. Cormick 20, dark, single, Callan,
　　　　　　　　　Kilkenny, steerage
John Rossiter 22, dark, farmer, single,
　　　　　　　　　Wexford, steerage
Thomas Bahan   26, dark, clerk, single,
　　　　　　　　　Bride Street, steerage

List of Passengers of the American Ship MARY
of New Bedford to Philadelphia, sworn at
Dublin, 17 April, 1804.

Richard Fell   50, dark, merchant, married,
　　　　　　　　　Philadelphia, cabin
Patrick Kenney 39, dark, clergyman, single,
　　　　　　　　　Lusk, Dublin, cabin
James R. Bainbridge 20, fair, clerk, single,
　　　　　　　　　Bride Street, cabin
Lawrence Cafsidy 25, dark, clerk, single, Coombe,
　　　　　　　　　cabin
Oliver W. Stone 22, fair, clerk, single, Largan,
　　　　　　　　　Armagh, cabin
Elizabeth Hudson 22, fair, single, Grafton Street,
　　　　　　　　　cabin
Ann Mullhollan 17, fair, single, Ballycumber,
　　　　　　　　　Kings County, cabin
Miss Gordon   17, fair, single, Philadelphia,
　　　　　　　　　cabin
William Coogan 40, dark, farmer, married, Pen-
　　　　　　　　　sylvania, steerage
James Fagan   30, dark, farmer, single, Mount-
　　　　　　　　　rath, Queens County, steerage
James McCarty 25, dark, farmer, single, Wexford,
　　　　　　　　　steerage
Henry Byrne   30, dark, farmer, single, "
　　　　　　　　　steerage
Owen Garter   26, dark, farmer, single, Mount-
　　　　　　　　　rath, steerage
William Power 28, dark, farmer, single, Fitt-
　　　　　　　　　hind, Tipperary, steerage
Mathew Daily   25, dark, farmer, single, Kil-
　　　　　　　　　kullen, Kildare, steerage
Thomas Daily   23, dark, farmer, single, Kil-
　　　　　　　　　kullen, Kildare, steerage
Edward Gumen   35, dark, farmer, single, Ruihale,
　　　　　　　　　Queens County, steerage
Mathew Boyn   30, dark, labourer, single,
　　　　　　　　　Kildare, steerage
Catherine Daily 22, dark, single, Kilkullen,
　　　　　　　　　steerage
William Gathan 10, child, Dublin, steerage
Mary Fagan   25, married, Mountrath, steerage
Robert Dickinson 30, dark, farmer, married,
　　　　　　　　　Wickton, steerage
Rose Dickinson his wife 25, Wickton
Patrick Kogan 30, dark, farmer, single, Barris
　　　　　　　　　in Opary, steerage
Anthony Hagdon 25, dark, single, Barris in
　　　　　　　　　Opary, steerage
Ann Field Porter 20, dark, single, Barris in
　　　　　　　　　Opary, steerage

A List of Passengers on the American Ship
PRESIDENT of New Bedford from Newry for New
Castle in America, sworn 21 April, 1804.

Edward Lynch   22, labourer, Armagh
Robt. Frances 30, farmer, Cavan
Jane Frances   28,   "
Mary "   2,   "   "
Margt. Farley 20,   "

Wm. Gilmore 50, labourer Cavan
Jane " 50, "
Frances Gilmore 21, "
James " 19, labourer "
Rose Gilmore 17, "
Jourdan " 16, "
Bartley Hart 17, "
Andw. McQuillan 40, farmer "
Margt. McMullen 41, "
John McMullen 20, farmer "
Saml. " 13, "
Wm. Wright 40, labourer "
David Ferguson 54, " Armagh
Robt. " 25, farmer Down
Wm. " 21, " "
Hugh " 19, " "
Jas. " 16, " "
Eliza " 14, " "
Jas. McBride 37, " "
Wm. McBride 22, " "
Sarah " 10, " "
Jas. Lard 30, " Armagh
Margt. " 31, " "
Jane " 8, " "
Sarah " 2, " "
Jas. Murphy 36, " "
Mary " 30, " "
James " 5, "

A List of the Passengers for Philadelphia on the American Ship COMMERCE, sworn 28 April, 1804.

Hugh Jelly 35, labourer, Loughinisland, Down
Hugh Thomson 36, " Kilmore "
Joseph Lindsey 33, " Sea Patrick "
James Beck 30, farmer, Ashegarg "
John " 25, " " "
Margt. " 24, spinster " "
Thomas Kilpatrick 37, farmer, Kellead, Antrim
Patt Cunningham 30, " Loughinisland, Down
Sarah Mitchell 13, spinster " "
Wm. McGowan 35, farmer Dunmurray, Antrim
John Gordon 36, " Keddy, "
Willm. Dinwiddie 40, " Dunaghy, "
Geo. Logan 30, labourer Killinchy, Down
Geo. " 25, " "
Robt. McCaughty 25, farmer, Cammoney, Antrim
Jane " 20, spinster " "
Isaac Dickey 20, farmer, Magheragill, Down
Anne Stewart 18, spinster, Belfast, Antrim
Thos. Stevenson 21, farmer, Dunaghy, "
John Douglass 38, " Seaford, Down
Mary " 38, spinster " "
Agniss McAfee 20, " Belfast, Antrim
Geo. Martin 35 farmer, Blaris, Down
John Shery 34, " "
Patrick McCarroll 26, farmer, Augher, Tyrone
John Duross 21, farmer, Dublin
Francis O'Neill 27, labourer "
Emelia O'Neill 22, spinster "
Richd. Courtney 25, farmer, Clough, "
Margt. " 24, spinster " "
Mathew Bailie 48, farmer " "
Eliza " 46, spinster " "
Stewart " 20, farmer " "
Matty " 18, spinster " "
William Ferris 25, farmer Ballymena, Antrim
Ann " his wife 32, "

A List of Passengers in the American Ship DILIGENCE of New Bedford for New York, sworn at Dublin, 30 April, 1804.

Richard Despard 25, married, fair, merchant, New New York, an American, cabin
Mary his wife 28, fair, cabin
James McAnnally 47, married, fair, cabin
Thomas Taylor 25, single, light, farmer, Bally-water, Wexford, steerage
William Berford 19, single, dark, farmer, Bally-water, Wexford, steerage
Thomas Price 24, married, fair, labourer, Dublin, steerage
Hanoia his wife 17, married yellow, Dublin
Mary Doland 26, Single, dark, servant to

Mrs. Despard, Mountrath
Geo. Reynolds 50, married, fair, farmer, St. Margaret, Dublin, steerage
Mary his wife 40, dark, steerage
Jonathan son 8, fair, steerage
Thomas son 7, fair, steerage
Eliza their daughter 5, steerage
William Davison 28, married, sandy, farmer, Laiterbeag, Cavan, steerage
Mary his wife 28, brown, Laiterbeag, Cavan, steerage
William their son 5, fair, steerage
Edward " 4, " "
Easter Brown 20, single, fair, servant to Mr. Davison
Betsy McMullin 60, widow, dark, Caverhalman, Cavan, steerage
Jane her daughter 28, single, dark, Caverhalman, Cavan, steerage
Fany McMullin 18, single, fair, " Cavan, steerage
Henry Shields 30, married, dark, farmer, Kings Court, Cavan, steerage
Ann his wife 29, married, dark, Kings Court, Cavan, steerage
James Higgins 27, single, dark, farmer, Caverhalman, steerage
John Brady 27, single dark, farmer, Caverhalman, steerage
John McMullin 50, married, fair, farmer, Pattle, Cavan, steerage
Mary his wife 50, fair, steerage
Jonathan their son 20, single, fair, Pattle, Cavan, steerage
William " son, 18, single, fair, " " steerage
Thomas " 16, single, fair, " " steerage
Andrew " 13, fair " " steerage
Easter their daughter 9, fair, " " steerage
Alexandrew McMullin 22, married, fair, farmer, Pattle, Cavan, steerage
Barbara his wife, 22, fair, Pattle, Cavan, steerage
Patrick Redmond 47, married, dark, farmer, Baley, Wexford
Bridget his wife 35, dark, Baley, Wexford
Jonathan their son 12, fair " "
Nicholas " " 10, " " "
Eliz. daughter 7, " " "
Bridget " 5, " " "

Passengers on the Brig GEORGE of New Bedford, bound for New York, in addition to the list before the Privy Council, sworn at Dublin, 29 August, 1803, Jacob Taber, Master.

Peter Roe 45, merchant Ross
Stephen French 30, " Carrick-on-Suir
Hugh Madden 30, Clerk Dublin
Mats. Joyce 18, " "

Passengers engaged to sail on board the Brig GEORGE of New Bedford, Jacob Taber, Master, for New York, sworn at Dublin, 29 August, 1803.

John O'Brien 28, clerk Dublin
Michl. Bannon 23, farmer Mayo
John Lyons 30, " Tullamore
Mark Evans 30, " Queens County
Ann Evans his wife " "
James Hennessy 25, labourer Dublin
Patrick Doyle 20, farmer Mayo
Bernard Fitzpatrick 36, farmer Tullamore
His wife & child " "
Heny. O'Hara 23, farmer Clare
Peter Roe 30, merchant Ross
Shephard French 45, merchant Carrick-on-Suir
Mats. Joyce 18, clerk Dublin

Passengers of the American Ship SUSAN, John O'Connor, Master, from Dublin to New York, sworn 6 Sept., 1803.

Abraham Bell 28, merchant, cabin, New York
Robert Bleakly 26, linen merchant, cabin, Armagh
Davd. " 24, " " " "

Mrs. Mathew 45, cabin, Londonderry
Simon Felix Gallagher, 45, Catholic pastor, cabin, Londonderry
John Carbery 36, merchant, cabin, Danish Island
John Watters 27, clerk, steerage, Navan
James Hornidge 25, surveyor, steerage, New York
John Curtis 28, super cargo, steerage, Dublin
Thomas Roberts 25, farmer, steerage, England
John North 36, gentleman, steerage, America
Laurence Toole 22, labourer, steerage, Dublin
Walter Fleming 21, clerk, " New York
Hugh Maddin 23, " " Dublin
Roger Morris 28, " " " "
William Sedgwick 36, " " " "
Arthur Fulham 12, " " Edenderry
Jane Hughes 22, " " Down
Mary Kelly 40, " " Dublin
Mary Mathews 12, " " "
Mary O'Brien 9, " " "
Ann " 8, " "
Eliza Langley 22, " " Kilkenny
Margaret Nowlan 22, " " "
Biddy O'Connor 14, " " Wexford
Mary Larkin 16, " " "
Mary Ann Reilly 22, " " Dublin

List of Passengers on the FORTITUDE of New York, Hezekia Pinkham, Master, bound for New York, sworn at Cork, 1 September, 1803.

John Sullivan Scully 35, merchant Cork
Mary " " his wife 28, "
James Ryan 34, farmer Bantry
Mary " his wife 30, "
James Long 22, shop keeper, Bantry
Denis Sullivan 21, " " "
Corn " 17, farmer "
John Barry 25, " "
Mary Harte 40, sailors wife Cobh
Mary Hart her daughter 10, "
John Harte her son 5, "
Thos. Johnson 30, clerk Cork
Mary Stewart 55, "
Wm. Devayne 60 gentleman Exeter Devon
Harriott Devayne her daughter 24, " "
Charlotte " " " 22, " "
James Hughes 30, gentleman Richmond, America
Mary " his wife 28, Richmond, America

A List of Passengers of the ship AMERICAN of New York, from Londonderry to New York, sworn at Londonderry, 10 September, 1803.

John Patton 34, merchant New York
Robert Boreland 20, farmer Strabane
Mary " 19, spinster "
Hannah McGhee 45, " "
Edward McGowan 25, labourer Tamlaght, Derry
William Dunn 25, farmer, Gellygordon
Thomas Buchannon 22, " "
John Donahy 21, labourer Limavady
John Patterson 30, farmer Moneymore
Mathew " 27, " "
George " 26, " "
Eliza " 20, "
James Dougherty 23, labourer Ramullen
James Cormick 28, clerk Strabane
Rebecca " 20, spinster "
Alexander McKinley 23, farmer "
John Torbet 18, labourer Tyrone
Thomas Miller 28, farmer Coagh
David " 24, " "
Marth. " 50, "
Elizh. " 23, spinster "
Robert Foster 22, farmer "
Martha Foster 22, spinster "
William Browne 34, farmer "
Margaret Browne 26, spinster "
Philip McGowan 34, farmer Gleek Tamlaght
Grace " 27, spinster Gleek Tamlaght

Philip McGowan junr. 12,   Gleek Tamlaght
John McKenney   38, merchant   New York
David Birket   30, farmer   Castlefin
William Beatty   25, trader   New York
George Lindsey   32, farmer   Pettigo
William Cook   26,   "   "
Isaac Cockran   27, merchant   New York
James McFarland   24, farmer   Tyrone
Alex McIntire   29, farmer, Waterside, London-
                        derry
Edward McClary   21, farmer, Tamlaght, Derry
Mary McGhee   38, spinster   Cookstown

Additional list of Passengers intending to
proceed to New York on board the American Ship
SUSAN, from Dublin, sworn 13 September, 1803.

John Price   35, surgeon, New York, cabin
Thomas Dawdal   25, labourer, Dublin, steerage
John Gavan   30, attorney   "   "
Thos. Flood   20, clerk   "   "
Andrew Flynn   23,   "   "   "
Patrick Synnott   25, farmer   Wexford   "
Francis Murphy   50,   "   America   "
Owen   "   25,   "   Monaghan "
Andrew Connor   43, merchant   Dublin   "

Names of persons who wish to go to Philadelphia
in the Snow GEORGE of Philadelphia, indorsed
from Belfast, sworn 22 September, 1803.

Ephriam Lee   26, farmer, Killeshandra,
                        Co. Cavan
Edwd. Lee   23, farmer, Killeshandra,
                        Co. Cavan
Hugh Gably   18, labourer, Killinchy, Down
Robt. Walsh   22, dealer, Downpatrick,   "
Alexr. Fulton   34, farmer, Loughsill   "
Thos. Kelly   36,   ". Grange,   "
Edwd. Donnelly   27,   "   Lessan   Tyrone
Will. Lowry   29, labourer, Killinchy   Down
Thos. Service   18, labourer Brochan   Antrim
Sarah Dawson   17,   Connor   "
Marcus Toole   39, servant Belfast   "
Jane Toole   28,   "   "
John Dodds   30, farmer   Dromal   "
Henry Wilson   24, schoolmaster Belfast   "
John Thompson   28, dealer   Ballymony   "
Patrick Mullan   21,   "   Tynan   Armagh
James Strachan   20, farmer   Connor   Antrim
John Johnson   19,   "   "   "
Nathl. Byst   30, dealer   Gencany   "
Jane Develin   32,   Ballymow   Armagh
Roger   "   35, farmer   "   "
Patrick McKey   38,   "   Drumgoland   Down
Alexr. Stewart   21,   "   Tullylisk   "
James Ganet   30, dealer   Annalult   "
Mathew Timoly   28, labourer Ballymasaw   "
Thos. Armstrong   31, farmer   Clonfeech   Armagh
Mary   "   27,   "   "   "
Thos. Mathews   27, dealer   Belfast   Antrim
Eliza   "   25,   Belfast   Antrim
Joseph Wilson   22, dealer   "   "
John Pumphy   29, farmer   "   "

A List of Passengers on board the BETSY for New York,
sworn at Newry, 22 September, 1803.

James Kilheath   25, farmer   Kilkeel
Jane   "   26,   "
Pat Murray   28, labourer   Hillsborough
Sarah Murray   26,   "
Robert Smith   28, farmer   Clough
Jenny   "   26,   "   "
James Conwell   28,   "   Armagh
Catherine Conwell   27,   "   "
Anthony   "   26,   "   "
Bernard   "   25,   "   "
Jeremiah   "   24,   "   "
Mick Burns   25, labourer   "
George Tedford   28,   "   Down
Eliza   "   28,   "
Rachael Weston   20,   Charlestown, America
Pat McCullough   26, farmer   Armagh
Sally McCullough   27,   "   "
Pat Cassidy   17,   "   "

John Humphry   32, merchant   Lisburn
Owen McUraney   22, labourer   Carrickadrummond
James Moore   45,   "   Cranfield
Nelly Small   30,   Down
Saml. Patterson   21,   "   Grange

A List of Passengers who have engaged to go
in the Brig LADY WASHINGTON, John Luscombe,
Master, from Belfast to Charleston, sworn
22 September, 1803.

Jane McCance   54, Blackumigo, So. Carolina
William Craig   54, farmer, Mageradroll, Co. Down
Agnes Craig his wife, child and servant boy
Hugh McCance   55, farmer   Magerdroll
Elizh. " his wife 57,   "
Hugh   " his son 19,   "
Samul. "   "   " 22,   "
Jane   " his daughter 19,   "
John Blackwood   15, farmer   Clough
David Bell   26, merchant   Belfast, Antrim
Saml. Carson   36,   "   "   "
Arthur O'Neill   24, farmer Drumarra, Down
Saml. Leslie   22   "   Kilmore   "
Willm. "   20,   "   "   "
John Wilson and wife 43, 35, Ballycam
William Hoey   18, farmer Ballykill, Antrim
John Young   22, labourer Gleary   "
John Sherlock   23   "
Saml. Rabb   23, farmer, Ballinahurch Antrim
Thomas Caldwell   20, labourer,   Broad Island
William Caldwell   18,   "   "   "   "
Widow Lamont   Charleston, So. Carolina
John Lowry   35, farmer   Garvagh, Down

A List of Passengers of the Ship INDEPENDANCE
who have contracted to take their Passage to
New York in the said ship being of the burthen
of 300 Tons and upwards, Mathias Fleming,
Master, sworn at Londonderry, 31 Oct., 1803.

Edward McKelvy   35, farmer   Letterkenny
Mrs. McKelvy his wife 35,   "
Three children to the above
Luke Creyon   20, labourer   Sligo
Roger   "   18,   "   "
John C. Steward   24, farmer   "
Francis Wood   26, labourer   Letterkenny
Isabella " his wife and infant child
Thomas Leary   28, farmer   Raphoe
Michael "   20,   "   "
Rose Caffry   18, spinster   "
Thomas Laughlin   18, farmer   "
Thomas Caffry   20, labourer   "
John Hopkins   24,   "   Letterkenny
John Fisher   26,   "   "
Wm. Latemore   30,   "   "
Mary   "   28,   "
James Ward   25,   "   "
Henry Tory   28,   "   "
Joseph Robinson   20,   "   "
Margt. Miller   20, spinster   Derry
Mathew McDole   36, labourer   Carrickfergus
T. McDole   20, spinster   "

List of Passengers intending to go to Norfolk
in America with the Ship VENUS, Resolve Waldron,
Master, Burthen 246 Tons, sworn at Dublin,
14 November, 1803.

John Sherman   18, merchant, 13 Little Britten
                        Street, Dublin
Edward Rooney   30, merchant, 45 Smithfield
George McEntire   " physician, 17 Crampton Court
Mrs. McEntire   22,   "   "   "   "
Edward Dempsy   22, farmer Kilmbullock, Kings Co.
Thos.   "   18,   "   "   "   "   "
Mary   "   50,   "   "   "   "   "
Esther "   20,   "   "   "   "   "
Judy   "   19,   "   "   "   "   "
Catherine "   16,   "   "   "   "   "
Thos. Best   17, gentleman   Smithfield

List of Passengers on board the FORTITUDE
bound to New York, sworn at Cork, 18 February,
1804.

Margaret Mahony   30,   Dunmanaway
Anne   "   9, her daughter   "
Goody Burke   30,   Kilkenny
Ellen   "   12,   " "   "
Edward   "   9,   " son   "
Biddy   "   7,   " daughter   "
Denis   "   5,   " son   "
John Buen   55, farmer   Co. Waterford
Pierce Corbett   22,   " "   "
Saml. Grace   19,   "   Cork
Thos. Mackay   30,   "   "
Ellen   "   25, his wife   "
Ellen   "   2, their daughter "
Thos. Brien   23, farmer   Cork
Thos. Brook   36, gentleman   "
Denis Flanigan   28, farmer   Limerick

List of Passengers going to New York on the
GEORGE of New Bedford, sworn at Belfast,
25 February, 1804.

Andrew Smith   24, farmer   Down
James Sprowl   30,   "   "
Alexr. Cochran   36,   "   "
Agnes   "   28, wife and four children
                        from 1 to 8 years old
Elenor Martin   70, spinster   Down
Margt. Fleming   20,   "   "
Wm. Hinger   20, gentleman   Drumara
Peter O'Hamill   27, labourer   Antrim
Thomas Duncan   18,   "   "
John Johnston   50 farmer   "
John Crothers   44,   "   "
Wm.   "   34,   "   "
Rt.   "   30, wife and four children from
                        1 to 8 years old
Thos. Gray   30, farmer   Antrim
Jane   "   27, spinster   "
Hans Wilson   24, farmer   Bangor
Edw. Templeton   20,   "   Coleraine
Jane   "   18, spinster   "
John Dawson   18, farmer   Antrim
David Rea   24,   "   Down

List of Passengers who have contracted to
take their passage to Baltimore on board the
Ship SERPENT, burthen 280 tons,
Archd. McCorkell, Master, sworn at the
Custom House, Londonderry, 5 May, 1804.

Charles Cochran   24, farmer   Fermanagh
Elizh.   "   24, spinster   "
Henry   "   3, child   "
John Irvin   21, farmer   Drunhing
Charlotte Irvin   45, spinster   "
Andrew McGee   21, farmer,   Killygordon
William Brandon   21, labourer   Crumlin
Henry   "   20,   "   "
Gerard   "   18,   "   "
James   "   16, farmer   "
John   "   14 labourer   "
Mary   "   18, spinster   "
Edward   "   15, labourer   "
Isabella "   10, spinster   "
Christopher"   8, child   "
Mary   "   40, spinster   "
Thomas   " her son 4   "
Jane   " her daughter 6   "
Oliver McCausland   22, farmer   Omagh
Thomas Harvey   22,   "   "
James Davis   26,   "   Dungannon
Margt.   "   25, spinster   Dungannon
Samuel Scott   60, farmer   Cosquin
Ann Scott   69, spinster   "
Rebecca Scott   30,   "   "
Francis "   22,   "   "
Jane Carter   30, spinster   "
John Carter   35, farmer   "
Ann Scott   20, spinster   "
Samuel Scott   28, farmer   "
John Johnston   22,   "   Ardshaw
James McColley   19, labourer   Linamore
Stephen Johnston   21,   "   Adderny

John Ball	36, farmer	Higham
John Dogerty	21, farmer	Clonmany
Prudence Ball	30, spinster	Higham
Edward Hall	14, labourer	Higham
John Ball	12, "	"
George Doherty	21, farmer	Clonmany

A muster foll of Passengers to go on board the Brigantine SALLY, Timothy Clifton, Master, for New York, Burthen 156 tons, Port of Newry, sworn 9 May, 1804.

Wm. McBerney	35, farmer	Diamary, Down
Alice McBerney	32	" "
Three children under 5		
David Kelly	36, farmer	" "
Mary "	30,	" "
Six children under 10		
Eliza Martin	30,	Killevey, Armagh
James McCrum	30,	Tynan, "
Sarah "	30,	" "
Two children under 4		
Richard Stewart	labourer "	"
John Famister	30, farmer	"
Ann "	22,	"
Jane "	25,	"
Robt. Kinmar	25, labourer	Keady, Armagh

Roll of Passengers by the Brig. JEFFERSON of Newberry Port in the U.S.A. Barthen 138 tons, bound from Ballyshannon to New Castle and Philadelphia, Daniel Knight, Master, sworn 10 May, 1804.

Francis Maquire	38, sandy, labourer, Barony of Lurg, Fermanagh	
Bridget "	36, dark	" " "
Edward Thompson	34, fair, labourer	" " "
John "	24, dark "	" " "
Mary "	22, fair	" " "
Edward " junr.	8, "	" " "
Patt Conolly	33, dark	" Resinuer, Leitrim
Rose "	31, "	" " "
Charles Stephenson	29, farmer	Firehugh, Donegal
John Stephenson	27, "	" "
Margt. "	22, fair	" "
Thomas Diver	25, " Chapman, cabin " "
Robert Johnson	15, fair, clerk	Donegal
John Connor	dark, labourer, Drumcliffe, Sligo
Will. Stephenson	20, fair, farmer,	Donegal
Francis Cullin	16, sallow, labourer, Resinuer, Leitrim
Hugh McPartlan	23, dark, "	Ballyshannon
Mary "	22, fair,	"
Daniel Tiffany	24, "	" Resinuer, Leitrim

List of Passengers in the WILLIAM AND MARY of New York, burthen 420 tons, to sail from Londonderry to New York, sworn at Londonderry, 18 May, 1804.

James Crawford	45, farmer	Kinnaty
John Robinson	40, "	Omagh
Jane "	36,	"
Robt. "	20, "	"
Joseph "	18, labourer	"
James "	11, "	"
John Robinson	16, farmer	"
Mary "	7, spinster	"
Barbera "	5, "	"
Ann "	3, "	"
Henry Mills	35, farmer	Ballyogrey
James Fulton	30, farmer	Omagh
Patrick McNamee	25, labourer	Augher
Joseph Gray	40, farmer	"
Hugh Doherty, senr.	38, labourer	"
Hugh " junr.	16, "	"
John "	14, labourer	"
Unity "	32, spinster	"
Elinor Doherty	19, "	"
John Caldwell	30, farmer	"
Elizh. "	29, spinster	"
James "	9, farmer	"
Elizh. "	7, spinster	"
Jane "	17, "	"
Thomas "	30, farmer	"
John Crawford	28, "	"
Elizh. Caldwell	20, spinster	"

Isabella Caldwell	13, spinster	Augher
Joseph "	11, farmer	"
Joseph "	9, "	"
Isabella "	7, spinster	"
Alexr. "	10, farmer	"
Jane "	7, spinster	"
Joseph Watt	30, farmer	"
Patrick McCann	24, labourer	"
Joseph Lowther	24, "	"
Thomas Quin	25, "	Hollyhill
Edwd. Divin	24, "	"
James Hargan	25, "	"
John Mulheron	26, "	"
Sarah Gray	30, spinster	Strabane
Boshale Gray	28, labourer	N. Town Stewart
Neal Crosby	24, labourer	" "
John Rodgers	21, "	" "
Robert Rodgers	23, "	" "
James McDivitt	24, "	" "
William Trevine	27, "	" "
Saml. McMellan	24, "	" "
Robert Wilson	24, "	" "
Robert McCay	24, "	" "
John Read	25, "	Bollindret
Alexr. Hunter	21, "	"
Robt. "	19, "	"
John Ross	26, "	New York
John King	32, "	" "
Susanna Armstrong	38, spinster	Carns
Mary "	23, "	"
John "	18 labourer	"
James McGuire	30, "	"
John Getty	50, "	Loughinwale
Abigail Getty	45, spinster	"
James "	26, labourer	"
Robert Adams	45, "	"
Elizh. "	45, spinster	"
John Adams	15, labourer	"
Archebald Adams	12, "	"
Mary "	10, spinster	"
Elizh. "	8, "	"
Martha "	6, "	"

Roll of Passengers to be received on board the Ship CATHERINE of Dublin, 170 tons burthen as per Register, George Thomas, Master, now in the Port of Killybegs and bound for New Castle and Philadelphia. Sworn at Ballyshannon 9 June, 1804.

John Conyngham	55, dark, farmer, Monargin in Killybegs, Donegal, hold
Isabella "	49, dark, Monargin in Killybegs, Donegal, hold
William Conyngham	26, fair, Monargin " Donegal, hold
Isabella "	23, dark, " " Donegal, hold
Alexr. "	21, fair, labourer " Donegal, hold
Jas. "	18, fair, labourer " Donegal, hold
John "	15, fair, labourer " Donegal, hold
Catherine "	12, fair, " Donegal, hold
George "	49, dark, schoolmaster, " Donegal, hold
Andrew "	34, dark, farmer, Lochris in Mishue, Donegal
Elitia "	34, fair, " " " Mishue, Donegal, hold
John "	12, fair, Lochris in Mishue, hold
Andrew "	6, fair, " " "
Robt. Johnston	15, fair, Donegal, cabin
Robt. Henderson	45, dark, farmer, Lochris in Mishue, Donegal, hold
Elenor "	44, dark, Lochris in Mishue, Donegal, hold
Elenor "	18, dark, " " " Donegal, hold.
Jane Henderson	15, dark " " "
Prudence "	13, dark, Lochris in Mishue, hold
George "	11, dark " " "
Ann "	8, dark " " "
Alexr. "	6, fair " " "
Arthur Fawcet	19, fair, labourer " " "
John Porter	43, dark, farmer " " "
Elitia "	44, " " " "
Catherine Porter	22, " " " "

William Porter	20, fair, Lochris in Mishue, Donegal, hold
Alexr. "	18, fair " " "
William Harran black, 37, Carrick East, Drumhome, Donegal, hold
Elizh. "	37, dark, Carrick East, Drumhome, Donegal, hold
Ann Harran, 15, dark, Carrick East, Drumhome, hold
Jane "	13, dark " " " hold
John "	10, dark " " " hold
Alexr. "	7, fair " " " hold
Matthew Brown 18, dark, labourer, Carrick East, Drumhome, hold
William Harran 37, farmer, Carrick Breeny, Drumhome, hold
Jane "	32, fair, Carrick Breeny, Drumhome, hold
Barbera "	11, fair, Carrick Breeny, Drumhome, hold
Jane Harran	8, fair, Carrick Breeny, Drumhome, hold
Thos. Grier 30, dark, Big Park, Drumhome, hold
Jane " 23, fair, Big Park, Drumhome, hold
John McCrea 24, black, labourer, Lignanornan, Drumhome, hold
Cath. Fawcett 21, dark, Mt. Charles Inver, Drumhome, hold
Elinor Devenny 27, fair, Benro in Killartie, Donegal, hold
Archd. Scott 26, black, farmer, Tullymore in Misheel, Donegal, hold
Elinor Scott 20, dark, Tullymore in Misheel, hold
Wm. " 20, dark, labourer, Ardara in Killybegs, Donegal, hold
Jas. McDade 22, fair, labourer, Killarhel, in Misheel, Donegal, hold
Andw. Lamon 18, black, Ardegat in Misheel, hold
Patt Kennedy 52, dark, farmer, Meenhallu in Killymard, Donegal, hold
Susan " 52, dark, Meenhallu, hold
Edward " 24, dark, " "
John " 19, dark, labourer, Meenhallu, hold
James " 13, fair, labourer " hold
Patrick " 16, " " " "
Charles " 11, " " " "
Biddy McCafferty 20, dark, " "
Danl. Sheerin 24, dark, Ardara in Killybegs, Donegal, hold
Michl. Carlain 26, dark, Killybegs, Donegal, hold
Geo. Maxwell 24, dark, Raferty in Killartie, Donegal, hold
Jas. Syms 45, fair, farmer, Bractcla in Killartie, hold
Mary " 40, fair, Bractcla in Killartie, hold
Samuel " 6, fair, " " " hold
Elizh. " 4, " " " " "
Tera Allis 30, " Drimahy in Done, Donegal, hold
James Allis 14, fair, labourer, Drimahy in Done, hold
Owen McGloghlin 29, dark, farmer, Glen, Donegal, hold
Nelly McGloghlin 30, dark, Glen, Donegal, hold
---- McGloghlin 5, dark, " " hold
Patt Gillespy 35, fair, " " "
Pegy " 24, " " " "
John McClosky, 25, fair, Drimreny in Inver, Donegal, labourer, hold
Rose McClosky 19, fair, Drimreny in Inver, hold
John Syms 30, fair, Glen, Donegal, hold
Cath. " 21, fair, " " "

Passengers engaged to Sail on board the American Brig. ATLANTIC, Robert Askins, Master, burden 196 tons, for Boston. Sworn at Dublin 19, June, 1804.
Sydenham Davis, 20, height 5-2, dark, farmer, Summerhill, Kilkenny

Ralph Morgan   20, height 5-11, sallow, labourer, Raheen, Kilkenny

Michl. Ryan   22, 5-7, fair, labourer, Thomastown, Kilkenny

John O'Hara   31, 5-3, dark, labourer, Kilmurray, Kilkenny

Hugh Heffernan   22, 5-6, dark, labourer, Clonsart, Kings County

Walter Madigan   35, 6 ft. fair,   " Thomastown, Kilkenny

Cath.   " his wife 28,   "

Andw. Shortell   21, 5 ft. dark, labourer " Kilkenny

Danl. Nowlan   21, 5-10, dark, clerk, Tullow, Carlow

John Bolger   36, 5-5,   " labourer, Dublin

Cath.   " his wife 36,   "

Saml. Duke   21, 5-5, dark, labourer, Thomastown, Kilkenny

Martin Switzer   28, 5-10, fair, labourer, Navan, Meath

James Maxwell   20, 5-8, dark,   " Dublin

William Gorman   32, 5-10,   " clerk,   "

Additional Passengers engaged to sail on board the Brig. ATLANTIC, Robert Askins, Master, for Boston. Sworn 26 June, 1804.

Wm. O'Brien   20, 5-6, dark, clerk,   Dublin

Michl. Kane   25, 5-6, fair,   "   "

Michl. Mallon   33, 5-6, dark, brewer, Dungannon, Tyrone

Henry Bowerman   40, 5-8, fair, Lieut. Novascotia Infantry

Anthony Kearns   23, 5-7, dark, labourer, Dunleer, Louth

Andrew Melvin   25, 5-9, dark, clerk, Bray, Wicklow

Thomas Reynolds   22, 5-6, fair   " Klena, Longford

List of Passengers for New York on the ship EAGLE, Charles Thompson, Master, sworn at Belfast, 1 August, 1804.

Wm. Biggem farmer, Bushmills. His name was sent in by the High Sheriff, who does not know his age

Alex. Beggs   30, 5-9, pale faced, farmer, Ballyroban

Margt. " his wife 30, 5-9, fair faced, Ballyroban

Thos. Clyde   21, 5-9, fair faced, farmer, Ballyroban

Wm. McQueen   39, 5-8, pockpitted, farmer, Bangor

Jane   " his wife dark colored, 36, 5-2, Bangor

Jane Robinson 26, 5-5, fair faced, Belfast

John Searight 30, 5-9, fair faced, farmer, Banbridge

Jane   " 30, 5-5, fair faced, spinster, Banbridge

John Henry   18, 5-6, fair faced, farmer, Banbridge

Jas. Anderson   28, 5-6, fair faced,   " Banbridge

Tho. Norris   58, 5-10, sallow, farmer, Belfast

Jas. Warden   21, 5-9, brown, labourer, Randalstown

Robt. McCroy   30, 5-7, fair, labourer, Randalstown

Hu. Liddy   20, 5-6, brown,   " Randalstown

David Bell   47, 5-7, brown, farmer, Banbridge

Patience Bell   45, 5-5, his wife and their child

George   " 16, 5-3, brown.   Banbridge their son

Thos. Bell 14, 5-0, brown, their son   "

Alexr. Ellis 36, 5-8, farmer, pitted, Ballymena

Margt. " his wife 30, 5-6, fair faced   "

Jno. Crothers 44, 5-8, brown, farmer, Randalstown

Laifanny Crothers 32, 5-4, his wife, fair, Randalstown

Jenny Crothers 68, Randalstown

Nanny Acheson 21, 5-4, spinster, fair, Randalstown

Jane Wilson 30, 5-5, spinster, brown, servant to Lafanny Crothers, Randalstown

Joseph Warden 26, 5-8, farmer, brown, Randalstown

James Warden 22, 5-8, brown, farmer, Randalstown

Robt. Carrothers, 35, 5-8, brown, farmer, Randalstown

Willm.   " 29, 5-7, farmer, brown, Randalstown

Eliza Carrol, 22, 5-4, spinster, brown, servant to Jenny Crothers, Randalstown

Isiah Young   28, 5-6, farmer, fair, Monaghan

Henry Hose   25, 5-7, merchant, a citizen of the United States of America

---

A Report of Passengers on board the American Ship ACTIVE, whereof Robert McKown is Master, burden 138 tons, bound for Philadelphia, sworn at Newry, 6 May, 1803.

James Moore   21, clerk

James Rendles 40, labourer

John   " 38,   "

Eliza   " 16   "

Thomas   " 12,   "

John Barnett 38,   "

Margt.   " 34

Eliza Laverty 20

Andrew Barnett 24   "

Annabella   " 20

Martha Parnell 18

Robert Mills 40, labourer

Eliza Barnett 16

Jane   " 12

Wm. Stewart   50, labourer

Margt.   " 38

Ann   " 24

Agnes   " 20

Susannah " 18

A Report of Passengers on board the American Ship DIANA of New Bedford, burden 223 tons, whereof Henry Hurter is Master, bound for New York, sworn at Newry, 18 May, 1803.

Isabella Allen   32,   Market-hill

John Collins   36, labourer   "   "

Patk. Crowley   39,   "   "   "

Mary   "   39   "   "

Richd. Burden   28,   "   Fentona

James Farrel   40,   "   Stewartstown

Patrick Philips 24,   "   Strabane

Thomas Rooney   40,   "   Banbridge

Mary Martin   20,   "   "

Charlotte Brothers 26   "

Isaac Collins   30,   "   Monaghan

John Martin   36,   "   "

John Brothers   30,   "   "

Thomas Lewis   30,   "   "

John Michael   30,   "   Dundalk

Wm. Sleith   23,   "   "

Henry Ellis   30,   "   Newry

Thos. Fure   39,   "   "

Thos. Smith   37,   "   Bathfriland

Rebecca Brothers 45,   Newry

Benjamin Philips 30,   "   Dundalk

Hanna Mytrood   25,   Newry

James Downs   30,   "   Cootehill

Samuel Crawley   35,   "   "

John Burden   32,   "   Ballybery

Sarah Barder   31,   "

Rebecca Deblois 24,   Ballyconnell

Eliza Whithom   23,   Killyshandon

Mary Cahoone   22,   Cavan

Mary Overing   25,   "

A List of Passengers intended to go from this Port by the Ship HOPEWELL of and for New York, burden 125 tons, sworn at Newry, 6 June, 1803.

Peter Downey   22, labourer

William Thornbury 40,   "

Wm. Daly   35,   "

Geo. Ferrigan   32,   "

Wm. Martin   36,   "

Sam Smyley   35,   "

John McCeaverell 35,   "

Pat Cullager   20   "

David Humphries 52,   "

Joseph   " 26,   "

Robert   " 40,   "

Moses   " 17,   "

James Couser   18   "

Robt. Humphries 19,   "

James Reed   20,   "

Thos. McLeherry 21,   "

John Anderson 25,   "

A List of Passengers intending to go from Belfast to New York in the Ship WILMINGTON, Thomas Woodward, Master, 360 tons, sworn 9 July, 1803.

John Houston 30, farmer

Mrs.   " 27

---- Houston 5, children

"   7,   "

"   2,   "

Robert Stewart 27, farmer

Mrs.   " 24

----   " 2, child

James Galway 18, farmer

Thomas Allen 25, farmer

Willm. Erskin 32,   "

Isabella Dick 16,   "

John Cross   35,   "

Wm. Crozier 26,   "

Henry McHenry 40, gentleman

Hen. Read   30,   "

Jane Curry   36,

Mary   " 14,

Eliza   " 12,

John Curry   9,

Robt. Warwick 30, gentleman

Hen. Garrett 33, farmer

S. Ann   " 27,

Mary Maucally 23,

John Browne   45, gentleman

Robt. Jackson 30,   "

John Murphy 28,   "

John Thompson 26,   "

Thos. McCrellos 34, farmer

Thos. McConaghy 27,   "

John Cameron   39,   "

Lavinia   " 20

Agnes   " 17

Martha   " 14

Elinor   " 8

Saml. Chestnut 30, gentleman

Mary Cameron 36

List of Passengers engaged to sail on board the American Ship MARGARET, Wm. M. Boyd, Master, for Wiscasset in the United States, sworn (indorsed from Dublin) 12 July, 1803.

Edwd. Irwin   50, labourer   Wexford

Geo. Phillips   30,   "   "

Thos. Maguire   32,   "   "

Patrick Irwin   31,   "   "

Jos. Cavanagh   34,   "   "

Tho. Best   22,   "   "

Mary Irwin   40   "   "

Ann   " 9   "   "

A List of Passengers intending to go in the Brig. SALLY, Timy. Clifton, Master, for New York, burden 147 tons, now lying in the Harbour of Dublin, sworn 5 August, 1803.

Alice Flood   22, spinster   Dublin

Margt. Kelly   45,   "   "

Elizh. Flood   24   "   "

Alice Purfield 18,   "   "

Ann Eagle   10,   "   "

George Eagle   9   "   "

Mary Bennett 30,   "   "

Nich. Campbell 24, labourer   "

Nancy Fallis 20, spinster   "

James Grant 17, Scotch labourer   ----

Hugh Kelly   24, labourer   Dublin

Bernard Fitzpatrick 38, farmer Tullamore

Ellen Fitzpatrick 28, his wife   "

Mary   " their daughter   "

John Lyons   30, farmer   "

& infant

A List of Passengers engaged to sail on board the Brig. GEORGE of New Bedford, burden 172 tons, Jacob Taber, Master, for New York, sworn 16 August, 1803.

John O'Brien   28, clerk   Dublin

Michael Brannon   23, farmer   Mayo
John Lyons   30, farmer   Tullamore
Mark Evans   30,   "   Queens Co.
Mary   " his wife
James Henney   25, farmer   Dublin County
Patk. Doyle   20,   "   Mayo
Bernd. Fitzpatrick 36,   "   Tullamore
his wife & child
Henry O'Hara   23,   "   Clare

A List of persons who have engaged their passage
in the Ship EAGLE, Andrew Riker, Master, of and
for New York, sworn 27 August, 1803.

Robert Small   27, height 5-5 labourer,
                          Ballymony
Wm. Conroy   40, 5-10, farmer, Pensylvania
Alexr. McKeown   18, 5-5, labourer, Belfast
Wm. Williamson   25, 6-1, "   Killinchy
Owen Miskelly   25, 5-10 "
Killy   "   spinster   "
Wm. Magill   23, 5-11, labourer   "
Roger Welsh   24, 6-1, "   "
James Reid   22, 5-7, "   Saintfield
Thomas Armstrong 31, 5-9, farmer Clonfeakle
Mary ------   spinster
John Treanor   25, 5-9, farmer Killinchy
John Murphy   24, 5-9 labourer   "
Alexr. Orr   21, 5-9, gentleman Ballymony
Jas. Boyd   30, 5-9, merchant, Nr. Ballameane
Saml. B. Wiley   30, 5-10, clergyman, Philadelphia
John Moorhead   24, 5-7½ merchant   Antrim
Marcus Heyland   22, 5-3, "   Coleraine
Wm. Freeland   20, 5-8, farmer   Co. Armagh
Wm. Deyrman   25, 5-10, labourer Drumbo
Jas. Mild   25, 5-10, farmer   Aughaloo
Jos. Caldwell   22, 5-8, merchant Ballymony
Mrs. Orr   Tobermore
John Breen   15, 5-7, farmer   Killenely
Saml. McNeill   20, 5-8, grocer   Ballymena
Jas. Campbell   30, 5-5, labourer Carmoney
Saml. Miniss   21, 5-7   "   Saintfield
James Macauley   22, 5-11   "   "
Wm. Dixon   22, 5-7   "
Saml. Moore   18, 6 ft. gentleman Portglenone
Alexr. Graham   34, 5-8, M.D. last residence Glasgow
Thos. Neilson   24, 5-5 merchant   Ballinderry
Saml.   "   11, 5-8
Robt.   "   28, 5-7,   "
James Grant   28, 5-7   Armahilt

List of Passengers on board the American Ship
MECHANIC of Baltimore, Peter Thorn, Master, from
Dublin to Baltimore, Navigated with ten men, 203
tons burden, sworn 28 May, 1804.

Benjamin Clegg   22, single, fair, gent. Stradbally,
                           Queens County, cabin
George Clegg   26, single, dark, gent. Stradbally,
                           Queens County, cabin
Rev. Matthew Ryan 60, single, fair, clergyman, Dublin,
                           steerage
James Carney   35, married, dark, farmer, Athy,
                           Co. Kildare, steerage
Mary   "   50, married, fair, Athy, steerage
Thomas   "   30, single   " farmer, Athy,
                           steerage
John   "   20, single, fair, farmer, Athy,
                           steerage
Nicholas Carney   19, single, fair, farmer, Athy,
                           steerage
Martin Carney   11, single, fair, farmer, "
                           steerage
Ellen Dobbyn   20, single, "   " Queens Co.,
                           steerage
William Rogers   30, single, brown, gent. St. Mar-
                           garets, Dublin, steerage
John Hay,   23, single, fair, gent., Newry,
                           Down, steerage
George Reynolds   42, married, brown, gent. St. Mar-
                           garets, steerage
Mary   "   --- married, fair, St. Margarets,
                           steerage
Matthew Christian 22, single, brown, labourer, Borris,
                           Queens County, steerage

List of Passengers who have contracted to take
their passage on board the ship DUNCAN of
Whitehaven, burden 238 tons, Abraham Sebson,
Master, for New York, sworn at Londonderry,
26 May, 1804.

George Cuthbert 35, labourer,   Coleraine
James Alcorn   40,   "   Glenvenogh, Donegal
Michl.   16,   "   "   "
John   "   17,   "   "   "
Mary Gallagher   35, spinster   "   "
Ann Cuthbert   13,   "   "   "
Fanny   "   12,   "   "   "
John Coyle   20, farmer   "   "
James McCaran   20,   "   "   "
Edward McCaran   22,   "   "   "
James Todd   19, labourer, Largilly   "
John Gibson   19,   "   Ballycloy   "
Thomas Paul   20,   "   County Down   "
George Elliot   24, farmer   "   "
James Gamble   25,   "   Donaghady, Co. Tyrone
Samuel Patterson 26, labourer   "   "
George Watson   29,   "   "   "
William Sanderson 35, "   Langfield   "
Margt.   "   18, spinster   "   "
Sidney   "   28, farmer   "   "
James Davitt   24, farmer   Astraw   "
Patrick McGawly 26, labourer, Urney   "
John Ginn   28,   "   Drumceeran   "
Margt.   "   26, spinster   "   "
Jane   "   20,   "   "   "
Anne   "   50,   "   "   "
Matthew Gibson   38, farmer   "   "
Eliza   "   28, spinster   "   "
Fanny   "   18,   "   "   "
Charles Johnston 38, labourer   Co. Fermanagh
Ann Johnston   26, spinster   "   "
Thomas Keys   24, farmer   Magheranny   "
Eliza Keys   20, spinster   "   "
Francis Crow   22, labourer   "   "
Richard Guthrie 34,   "   "   "
James Crozier   22,   "   Dromash   "
James Brisland   26, farmer   Co. Tyrone   "
Margaret Woods   28, spinster, Lissenderry   "

A List of Passengers intending to go by the American
Brig. Ceres of New York, Herbert Forrester, Master,
from Newry for New York, sworn 31 May, 1804.

Robert Tronson   17, gentleman   Newtown, Hamilton
Thomas Hanlon   26, farmer   Armagh
Judith   "   26,   "
Joseph Love   23, labourer   "
Rose Love   18,   "
John Pebbes   43, gentleman   Hamiltonsbawn
Ann   "   37,   "
Margt.   "   14,   "
Sarah   9,   "
Annebella Pebbes 5,   "
Mary Jane "   infant   "
Ann Murray   26,   Fivemiletown
Betsy   "   23,   "
Mary Patterson   34,   Lisdromore
Patt McConell   24, labourer   Moy
Kitty   "   22,   Moy

A List of Passengers intended to be taken on board the
Ship LIVE OAK of Scarboro, Christopher Dyer, Master,
burden 400 tons, bound to New York in America, sworn
at Londonderry, 23 June, 1804.

Henry Wilson   24, farmer   Dungannon
Jane   "   20, his wife   "
Mary   "   2 month old child   "
Mark McQuillan   21, farmer   Nughnacloy
William Pedin   22, labourer   Nughadown, Derry
William Davidson 20,   "   "   "
Susan Greer   40, married   Cookstown
Sarah   "   20, spinster   "
Susan   "   15,   "   "
Mary   "   14,   "   "
Hannah   "   12,   "   "
Anna   "   7,   "
Joseph   "   4,   "
Sarah Dougal   20, servant girl   "
John Webb   50, farmer   "
John Webb   19,   "   "

Susan Webb   16, spinster   Cookstown
Janet   "   44, married   "
Thomas   "   15, farmer   "
Maria   "   10, spinster   "
Jane   "   5,   "
Alice   "   8,
William Hannah   22, labourer   Armagh
John   "   20,   "   Newtown
                                        Stewart
William Patrick   19, farmer   "   " .
Samuel Steel   16,   "   "   " .
Jane Patrick   18, spinster   "   " .
Nancy   "   4 month old child "   " .
Alexr. McKeever   21, labourer   Gortin,
                                   N. Stewart
David Anderson   20,   "   "   "
Alex. Irvine   21,   "   "   "
James Russell   22,   "   Dunnamany
Elizh.   "   22, married   "
Isabella "   5 month old child   "
James Sands   26, labourer, Cranah,
                                    Moneymore
Mary   "   26, married   "   "
Robert   "   7, child   "   "
John   "   5,   "   "   "
Ellen   "   1,   "   "   "
Mary   "   22, spinster   "   "
Jo. Hunter   45, farmer   Gortmurry,
                                    Moneymore
William McKeon   23, " Lisabany,   "
Ann   "   24, spinster   "
William Blair   20, farmer   N. Limavady
John Murdock   20, " Glass Lough,
                                    Monaghan
Patrick Gallagher 21, labourer, Furmeny,
                                    Omagh
John   "   22,   "   "   "
John McQuin   15,   "   Cookstown
Ann   "   17, spinster   "
Ostin Allen   19, farmer   "
James Crooks   30,   "   "
Jane Crooks   50, married   "
Mary Crooks   20, spinster   "
Margt.   "   18,   "   "
John   "   17, farmer   "
Sarah   "   14, spinster   "
James   "   12, farmer   "
Benjam "   11,   "   "
James   "   6, child   "
Alexr. McKeon   20, labourer, Lisabany,
John McCue   20,   "   Ternamenter,
                                    Tyrone
James Walker   54,   "   Dromagalagh
Wm. Dick   30,   " Kilane Ceepeyt,
                             Near Ballymena
Samuel Gault   30,   " Kilane   "
Samuel Reed   30, farmer, Castledaunt,
                             nr. N. Stewart
Alex.   "   28, farmer, Castledaunt
Wm.   "   23,   "   "

The following extracts are from 'The
Shamrock'; or 'Hibernian Chronicle', a
weekly newspaper published in New York,
1810-1817.
(From the issue of December 29th, 1810)
A List of Passengers by the ship ERIN,
Murphy, from Dublin:

Miss W. Larkin   Co. Wexford
Miss F. Walsh   "   "
John Barry   Co. Louth
Edward Furlong   Co. Wexford
Michael Butler   "   "
Mary Butler   "   "
Bridget Rigan   "   "
Bridget Byrnes   Co. Louth
John Byrnes   "   "
Nicholas Byrnes   "   "
C. Byrnes, junior   "   "
Francis Duffy   Co. Monaghan
Fargus Duffy   "   "
Mary Walsh   Co. Galway
John Walsh (child)   "   "
William Ray   Co. Cavan
Mrs. H. Bowles   Co. Sligo
James McNally   Co. Meath
Patrick Ryan   Co. Wexford

William Malvin, wife, 5 sons & 4 daughters,	Co. Cavan
Owen Duffy	Co. Monaghan
Ann Weapher	Rathfarnham
James Murphy	Co. Louth
John Giles	Bailieborough
Andrew Waters	Co. Wexford
William Stewart	Belfast
John Bishop and wife	Co. Dublin
Patrick McCabe	" "
James O'Brien	Co. Meath
Terence Farley	Co. Cavan
Isabella Plaus	Co. Longford
Joseph Manly	New York
Emanuel Toole	Dublin
William Bleakly	"
John Fitzgerald	"
John Roberts	"
Darby Kelly	Co. Meath
Mathew Neall, and wife	" "
Edw. McGuinness	" "
Patrick Keally	Dublin
John Thomas	Ballyhayes
Thomas Hales	Glasstown
Francis Leonard	"
James West	"
John McBrien	"
Simon Horan	Mullicash
Thomas Hearn	New York
J. Cunningham	Sligo
Christian Wogan	Co. Dublin
James Diffy	Co. Cavan
Wm. Floughsby	Dublin
Mart Ryan	New Ross, Co. Wexford

(Issue of Jan. 12, 1811)
List of Passengers per THE HARVEY HIDE, from
Belfast

Name	Parish	County
William Simpson	Lochgall	Armagh
Mrs. John Speirs	Donegoare	Antrim
William Davis	Blairis	Down
Robert Harvey	"	"
Mrs. R. Harvey	"	"
Leonard Dobbin	Killeman	"
Mrs. Dobbin	"	"
Isaac Jenkinson	Lochgall	Armagh
Mrs. Jenkinson	"	"
James "	"	"
Elizh. "	"	"
Isaac "	"	"
Ann "	"	"
Mrs. Wm. Miller	Ahahill	Antrim
William Davis	Hillsboro	Down
James Coal	Drumboa	"
Alley Coal	"	"
J. Montgomery	Counmoney	Antrim
Mrs. J. Kennedy	Douaghmore	Tyrone
William Law	Kalmchie	Down
John Aslein	Belfast	Antrim
James Couples	Aughderg	Down
Elizh. Couples	"	"
Alex. McMurray	Kelmore	Armagh
Hannah McMurray	"	"
James Spiers	Donegoare	Antrim
James McCance	Newtonards	Down
Samuel Anderson	"	"
John Welsh	"	"
Louisa Welsh	"	"
John McKenzie	"	"
H. Mubrea	"	"
James Moore	Donaghmore	Tyrone
John Brown	Lochgall	Antrim
Francis Brown	Kelbroghts	"
David Bell	Lochgall	Armagh
John Davidson	"	"
Mrs. W. Campbell	Blairis	Down
Wm. Frances	Drumall	Antrim
Martha Frances	"	"
James Auld	Grange	"
Mary "	"	"
Robert Grendle	Kellmore	Armagh
Sarah Grendle	"	"
William Coil	Daryluren	Tyrone
Peter Coil	"	"
Sarah Coil	"	"
Rosa Coil	"	"
John McLanna	"	"
Thomas Lictson	Larne	Antrim

Mary Lictson	Larne	Antrim
Mary Harrison	Aughdary	Down
John "	"	"
John Liston	Kellmore	Armagh
Eliza "	"	"
T. Anderson	Newtonards	Down
George Anderson	"	"
Jennet "	"	"
Alex. McKenzie	Lochgall	Armagh
Philip "	"	"
Ralph "	"	"

List of Passengers by the ship RADIUS, Clark,
from Cork.
As published in "The Shamrock", New York,
May 11, 1811.

Hugh Parker	Cork
Hugh Sadler	"
Frances "	"
Samuel Freeman	Waterford
David McKardy	Dungannon
John Bull	Kilkenny
Jane Hannah	London
Mary Connor	Cork
Jeremiah Connor	"
Eliza Kirby	"
Cornelius Kirby	"
Mary Ann "	"
Margt. Keane	"
Richard Carey	"
Thomas Rice	"
Thomas Fowey	Castlelions
Timothy Murphy	"
Robin Pigott	Castlehyde
James Barry	Youghal
Thomas McKey	Fermoy
Ellen McKey	"
Henry Bullen	Clonakilty
Mary "	"
John Leaky	Glanmire
James Sanders	"
John Ranihan	Cork
James Barry	Watergrasshill
Jerry Maloney	Aglis
John "	"
Edmund Murray	"
Margt. Maloney	"
John Gunn	Castlereagh
Stephen Cronin	Castlemartyr
James Fogarty	Dungarvin
Bridget Gallivan	Cappaquin
John Cunningham	"
Frances "	"
Michael Cavanagh	"
Peter Slattery	"
Margt. "	"
John Slattery	Lismore
William Devine	Tallow
Redmond Kent	Lismore
John Kearceay	"
Margt. "	"
Patrick Foley	"
John Callihan	Tallow
Luke Linnen	Cappaquin
Henry O'Brien	Clonmel
Massy Hassett	Borris O'Kane
Richard "	" "
Michael Kearney	" "
Thomas Rian	" "
James Guess	" "
Thomas Dunnahough	Narragh
John Lane	Clonmel
Mary Lane	"
Catherine Buckley	"
Ellen Lane	"
John Blake	Emily
John Casey	"
Francis Kearney	Birr

'We were led into error by the daily papers
stating that the HANIBAL was last from Cork;
she never touched at Cork after leaving Belfast,
on the 2nd January - we now annex a list of her
passengers, furnished us by one of themselves"

Napshall Fendlay	Lesburn
Joseph Knox	Balleybay
Peter Hughes	"

Robt. McElwrath, wife and one child	
	Hollowood
Nathaniel Alsop and wife	Sanfield
Geo. Brown, wife and seven children	
	Banbridge
John Carr	Hellsborro
Henry Cochrane	Co. Mayo
Wm. "	" "
Robt. "	" "
Henry Drain	Co. Antrim
John "	"
John McFall	Portglenone
Owen McPeak	Portglenone
Jas. Hughes	Dublin
James Connor	Lisburn
Patrick Garvin	"
Charles Davis	Armagh
Charles Ferris	"
Patrick Mollin, wife and four	
children	"
Robert English	Scotland
Wm. Ross, wife and four children	Verners-bridge

List of Passengers per the PERSEVERANCE,
Capt. Crawford, from Belfast to New York,
6 April, 1811.

Andrew Stewart, wife and one child	
	Stewartstown
George Wallace	Town of Antrim
Hugh McMullan	Co. Down
Moses Montgomery, wife and three	
children	Killele
Alexander White	Dromore
Elizh. Nielson and one child	"
James Martin	Bangor
Alex. Ritchie	"
Stephen Stewart	England
Stephen "	"
Thomas Donaldson, Cooper in Fife, Scotland	
Henry Scott	" "
Daniel Aiken	Glasgow "
William Donnelly	Belfast
John Danwoody	"
Wm. Danwoody	"
David Park	"
Mathew McMurrey	"
William Stewart	Dunsmurry
Alexan. "	"
Jane " sen.	"
Jane " junr.	"
Andrew Kenmaer	Broom-Hedy
Samuel Piper	Menneyre
Robert Wilson, wife and three	
children	Dunmuny
Elizabeth Wilson	"

Amongst those passengers, are 10 weavers,
1 miller, 1 bricklayer, 1 saddler, 1 hosier,
1 cooper, and 1 gardener. Three of the
first are Cotton Weavers.

List of passengers by the ship PROTECTION,
Bearns, from Belfast to New York 27 April,
1811.

Patrick McCartney	Banbridge
Eliza McCartney	"
Ellen "	"
Catherine Parker	"
Mary Sinclaire	"
James Ferris	"
William Gordon	"
Easter "	"
Sarah Bryans	Moy
John Gamble	Ballybay
Eliza "	"
James "	"
Wm. "	"
Joseph "	"
George "	"
Bell "	"
John Morron	"
Wm. Clement	"
John Smyth	Downpatric
James Glass	Belfast
Nevin See	Ballybay
Owen Maron	Ballytrea
Christopher Banecan	"

Samuel Magell	Banbridge
Ellen "	"
John "	"
Robert Forsyth	"
Valentine Forsyth	"
Mary "	"
Robert "	"
John "	"
Sarah "	"
George Irwine	Waringstown
George "	"
Rachael "	"
Robert McCracken	Ballymacaret
John Henry	Rathfreland
Wm. Carse	Killinchy
Robert Hamilton	Cumber
James Taylor	Armagh
James Bell	Lisburn
Louisa Taylor	Armagh
Jane McWherter	Newry
David Bell	Lisburn
Mgt. "	"
Henry Brown	"
Rachael "	"
James Ross	Killinchy
Thomas McKee	Newtownards
Margt. "	"
Robert "	"
Samuel McCartney	Banbridge
Hannah "	"
John Sinclaire	"
Anne "	"
Eliza McMullen	Larne
Patrick McKee	Armagh
Easter Teas	Belfast
Margt. Watt	Banbridge
Henry McComb	Keady
Ann "	"
Margt. "	"
Thomas "	"
John McWhatey	Armagh
Jane "	"
Alexander McKenny	Bangor
James Pinkerton	Killinchy
Thomas Hamilton	Antrim
John Conaghy	"
Robert Douglas	Ballymena
Ann Bunham	Newry
Wm. Patterson	Bangor
Eliza. "	"
John Andrews	Combers
Hugh McCawley	Crumlin
Mathew McCully	"
Robert Sterling	Doagh
James "	"
James Watt	Lisburn

Of the above passengers there are
2 between 5 and 10 years old
16 " 10 " 20 inclusive
43 " 20 " 30 "
12 " 30 " 40 "
— " 40 " 50 none
3 " 50 " 60 inclusive
1 of 70
1 of 72
79, chiefly farmers, and some with considerable property in guineas."

Passengers per THE ALGERNON, Clark, from Belfast to New York, 18 May, 1811.

Robert Lowry and family	Charlemont
Alex. Beally " "	Hillsborough
Wm. and Eliza Armstrong	Co. Down
John Neilson and family	" "
James Tate	Maze
Robert Hasby	Maze
James Kennedy	Halls Mill
John and Mary Hamilton	Hillsborough
James Amberson	Halls Mill
John Gurley and family	Co. Down
Hamilton McCullough	Co. Tyrone
Edward Pepper and family	Moyallon
James and Sarah McConnell	Hill Hall
Richard Hinds and family	Dromore
Wm. Copeland and family	Co. Down
James Morrison and family	Armagh
Ellen Tetterton	Banford
Robert Tetterton and family	"

John Bonnel	Queen's County
John Morrow	Banford
Edward Dail and family	Rathfreland
Robert and Rachel Kennedy	Banford
Wm. Orr and family	Hill Hall$
John Orr " "	" "
Mary Nixon, George Nixon and family	Kill Warlin
Ann Coin and children	Belfast
Hobert Hall and family	"
Wm. Cobora " "	Kill Warlin
Henry McCurry	Hillsborough
Mary Curry	"
A Carlton	"
John Wall and family, Easter Wall,	Banbridge
Samuel Gelison and family	Co. Down
Samuel Burns	Halls Mills
Mary Sinton and family	Moyallon
James Gamble	Ballynahinch
James Deek	"
Agnus Deek	"
John Smith	"
Susan Smith	"
George Thompson	Belfast
John Maguinis	Co. Down
Isabella "	"
John Morrison	Magheragel
Sally Green	Lurgan
John Lamb	Maze
James Maharg	Co. Down
Sarah McMahon	Dromore
Joseph Mark	"

Of these passengers there are
42 under 10 years of age
38 between 10 and 20 years of age
36 " 20 " 30 " " "
19 " 30 " 40 " " "
8 " 40 " 50 " " "
5 " 50 " 60 " " "
————
148"

Passengers per the WESTPOINT, from Londonderry to New York 25 May, 1811.

John Lambert	John Hamilton
Henry Lenon	Benjamin McLary
John Dougherty	Samuel Gilmer
Edward Rice	John Madden
Margt. Christie	Margt. Hanlan
and her child	and family
John O'Neill	James Grey
Philip McLaughlin	Catherine Kerr and family
Ann McLaughlin	Benj. McLaughlin
Martha Sloane	Conell Curry
Robt. Thompson	Geo. McCaughall
Thomas Russell	Corn. McGinley
James Russel	W. Marshall and family
Joseph Marshall	Thos. McMenamy
Eliza Marshall	Jos. McMenamy
George "	Robt. McElkeney
John McCready	James Brown
Nath. McCaghy and family	Mgt. McMenamy
James Steel	Wm. . "
Michael Hamard	Michael Denvant
Math. Kirpatrick	James Ward
John McKinlay	Connel Sweeny
George McKinlay	Peter Lyons
Edw. Hamilton	Cornelius Lyons
Jane Donnell	Isaac Vance
Dennis Hanagan	William Brown
James Dougherty	D. Vance
James Piden	Charles Logan
Thomas Freeborn and family	Rebecca Crawford
Patrick Kearny	Hugh Strong
James Carrigan	Chr. Strong
Wm. "	Cath. Graham and family
Henry Scott	John Smiley
Alexander Scott	Wm. Thompson
Andrew Funston	Susan McCafferty
Ar. Donaghy	William Porter
Roger McGuire	John Hutton
Patterson Jolly	John Campbell
John Hamill	A. Witherington
Mary McGohey	Elizabeth Miligan

Passengers per the JUPITER, William H. Hutchins, Master, from Belfast to New York, 1 June, 1811.

Hugh Johnson	Hillsborough
Elizabeth Johnson	"
Matthew Murdough	Moira
William Harshaw	Down
John McCoskery	"
John Boyd	"
John McKee	Magradill
Jane "	"
Hugh Perry	Cullsallag
Margt. "	"
David Evart	"
Arthur Deolin	"
Joseph Camble	Dungannon
John Turkenton	"
James "	"
Jane "	"
Thomas Dixon	"
Joanna "	""
John Clark	Lurgan
Thomas McDowl	Saintclaire
John "	"
Alexander McDowl	"
Elizabeth "	"
Rachael "	"
Mary Ann "	"
Thomas Fair	"
Ann "	"
James "	"
Patrick Sweeny	Ballinahinch
William "	"
Prudence "	"
Edward Patton	Grable
John Glass	"
John Johnson	Antrim
Elnor "	"
David "	"
Elizh. "	"
Wm. Chaley	"
James McAlpin	Molany
Jane "	"
Hugh "	"
Conway Hamilton	"
Margt. "	"
Elizh. "	"
James Gallery	Moreyrea
Eliza "	"
Wm. McKelery	"
Jane "	"
John Ewart	"
James Kearns	Aghadie
Elizh. "	"
Andrew George	Killead
Wm. "	"
Martha "	"
Mark McAtter	Blares
Betty "	"
Alexander Mention	"
Agnes "	"
William Reid	Cumber
James Gelston	"
Thomas Stephans	"
Elnor "	"
David McMagan	Banbridge
Sarah "	"
Agnes "	"
William Anderson	"
Cath. "	"
Samuel Jamison	Killinchie
Agnes "	"
Bernard Conaghy	Banbridge
John McKee	Ballinahinch
Charles McCarton	"
James McCalton	"
Samuel Gamble	"
Robert Patrick	Belfast
Daniel Deolin	Banbridge
Geroge Best	"
Seragh "	"
Alexander McDowl	Llandery
Ezibella "	"
Thomas Harrison	Cairn
Jane "	"
James McAttur	Killead
Ann "	"
John Mitchon	"
Seragh Rhea	"
David Rhea	"
Samuel Stephenson	"

Thomas McKey — Dunleery
Samuel Cleland — "
Henry Cook — Armagh
John Stephanson — "
Thomas Phillips — Glenary
Eliza " — "
James McMullen — Tyrone
Eliza " — "
Robert " — "

Passengers by the Brig. ORLANDO, Josiah Cromwell, Master, arrived in New York, 19 May, 18111.

John Davison and family — James Thompson
Thomas Kennedy — Margt. "
James Frasier — Henry Johnston and family
Robert " — Felix McAllisted
Mary Russell — James "
Jas. Morrow and family — John Quin and family
Wm. Maxwell — Henry McMahon
Ann Patterson — James Ker.
Mary Logan — Thomas Sherran
James Little — James Henderson and family
Henry Drake — James Anderson
Thos. W. Ray — John Cannon
Richard Hughes and family — James Brady and family
William Burns — Elizabeth Burns
Robert McCard — John Owens
Thomas Stark — James Johnson
William Munn and family — Martha Little
Rachael Hun — Jane Morrow
— Anah Dreison

Passengers by the Ship AFRICA, John E. Scott, Master, from Belfast to New York, arrived 9 June, 1811.

George Roberts — Armagh
Samuel McCammar — "
William Murphy — Monagher
Mary " — "
John Hawthorn — Bellikiel
Agnes " — "
David Scott — "
Margt. " — "
John Logan — "
Jacob Pierson — Armagh
Jane " — "
Margt. Moffit — "
James Rock — "
Mary " — "
Joseph Bridget and family — Belleck
JohnMcCullaugh " " — Carmery
William Heson — "
William Spratt — "
Mary " — "
William Shaw — Billamegary
Margt. " — "
John Porter — "
Eliz Fullan — Lisburn
Sealton Fullan — "
Andrew Martin — Kilmore
Jane Morrow — Monaghan
Ellen " — "
Jane " — "
John Finlay — "
James Cowser — "
William McCaird — "
Sophia Cowser — Armagh
Eliza " — "
Jane Clagher — "
Hugh O'Ray — Belfast
John Gruir and family — "
Robert Moore — Dungannon
Eliza " — "
Thomas Moore and family — Rathfriland
Thomas Calvin — "
William Forcade and family — Belfast
Henry Moore — Rathfriland
Mary " — "
John Patterson — Belly Keell
Arthur Shee — Rathfriland
William Willis — Dungannon
Felix Farren — "
Margt. Willis — "

Sally Farren — Dungannon
James " — "
Thomas Kelly — "
Molly " — "
Hugh Cunningham — Rathfriland
Michael McAnorney — "
Patrick Maney — "
Jane McFade — Hillsborough
John Buchanon — Carrickfergus
Samuel Irvine and family — Dungannon
William Gatt — "
John McCartney — Loughbrickland
Nancy " — "
James Bodd — "
James McCurtney — "
Martha Heran — "
James Herker — Belfast
William Quail and family — Downpatrick
William Stockdale — "
Jane " — "
Jane Warren — Belfast
Hugh " — "
Ann Aiken — Dromore
Jane Aiken — "
John Cleland — Lisburn
Wm. Armstrong — Down
Arabella Armstrong — "
Wm. " — "
Eleanor Blany — "
Joseph Patterson — "
David " and family — "
Mary " — "
Wm. Willis — "
James White — "
Robert Burke — "
Edward Hazleton — "
James Morgan and family — "
George Patterson — "
Eliza Thompson — "
Maria " — "
Sarah " — "
John " — "
James " — "
George " — "
Joseph " — "
John Hodgsdon — "
John Lockat — "
John Fulton — Lisburn

Passengers by the Ship AEOLUS, from Newry, Charles Henry, Master, arrived in New York, 23 May, 1811.

John Fulton and family — Abraham Keating
Moore McDonald — Thomas Seeman
Samuel Hunter and family — Luke Morgan
William Clark — John Hunter
John Seave and family — Peter Grabbin
Joseph Fleman — Edward De Hart
William Boyd and family — Samuel McMurray and family
Francis Henrietta — John Harshaw and family
John Kell — Frances Henrietta
Betsey Fleman — John Hughes
Jane Sleeman — James Copeland
James McCabe — Thomas Copeland
Betsey McCabe — John Sewere
John Walker and family — Francis Devan
F. McLaughlin and family — Eliza Lister and child
George Lemman — John McGurrah and family
Mary Lemman — James Bell
John Thompson and family — Joseph Douglass
Betsey Hetherton — Elizabeth Smith and family
James Moore — William Ballah
Samuel Crary — James McSleeve
Margt. Armstrong and child — Isaac Armstrong Margaret Moore

Passengers by the GOLCONDA, from Londonderry to New York.
(Published by 'The Shamrock', 15 June, 1811.)

Robert Philson — John McFaden

John Fletcher — John McCauley
John Duffey — Danl. M'Guiness
Alex. Smiley — William Crome
James " — Michael Donald
Daniel Kirr — Eleanor "
James Shawkling — Mary Atkins
Dudly Dougherty — John Mollony
Dennis Boyle — Darby Burns
John Cannon — Peter Haughey
John Caldwell and family — John Burns and family
Dan. Cunningham — John Rodgers
Margt. Alexander — Alex. Glass
Isabella Glass — David Stewart
Francis Minetes — William Henry
Biddy Minetes — Jacob Giller
Mary Haggerty — John Kerr
Barney Donald — Benjamin Haughey
James Burns — John McColley
Murphy Burns — Henry Burns
John White — John Fanan
Thomas Burns — Catherine Burns
Thomas Faren — James Burns
Coudy Cunningham — Margt. McGrave
Mary Rodgers — William Pollock
Patrick Barney — Samuel Pollock
Michael Manely — John McMannyman
Henry Manely — Philip Carling
William Hickings — Edward McGanty
Patrick " — Samuel Johnson
Michael Hagerty — Dominick Golley
Daniel " — Thomas Scott
John Burns and family — C. Cunningham
Timothy Timons — J. Cunningham
Jeremiah Starr — Issabelly Timons
Ralph Waddel — Robert Lyons
Rodger Murray — Bany Traner
John Hazelton — Thomas Burns and family
John Rudder — Jacob Bell
Patrick Rudder — Mary Bell
John McGreedy — John Fanen
Edw. McConway — James Taylor

List of Passengers by the Ship MARY, Wallington, from Londonderry, arrived at Philadelphia, 17 June, 1811.

Thos. McGrath — Adam Woods
Margt. McGrath — David Harvey
James McGrath — Thos. Dougherty
Martha Smith — Abigal "
Wm. Key — Patrick Flanagan
Wm. Craig — William Ross
Elizabeth Morrison — Andrew Gibson
Martha " — Barnard Davis
John Moorhead (drowned) — Joseph Magis
Samuel Wallace — Sarah Wishat
Wm. Ceyrin — Mary "
Wm. Williams — Ruth "
John Cummings — Sarah "
Z. Bennett — Margaret Duncan
Nathan Rogers — George Williams
Wm. Beatty — Charles Hamilton
Jane " — Daniel "
George " — Robert Wishat
William Clark — David McKnight
Ann Clark — Mary "
Eleanor Ross — Andrew "
Joseph " — Jane "
David Clark — Thomas "
Wm. Hamilton — Daniel "
James Edmondon — Francis Monegan
James Gillaspie — Jane McBrine
Terrence McLorten — Ann Brown
Cather. McLorten — Patrick Connelly
Harvey Roulstone — Pat. McGellaghan
Martha " — Alex. Larkie
James " — Mary "
Archer Wason — Robert Norris
Jane " — Mary "
Sarah Curragan — Cornelius Crossen
James Fife — Catherine Doyle
Joseph Douglass — Abrm. McIntire
Laurin Folhall — John Rein
Mary Genagal — John Clary
William McCurdy — John Thorne
Morgan " — Arch. Raulstone
James Hunter — James Fee
Wm. Hunter — Antho. Campbell

117

Eleanor Hunter	Gabriel Andrews
Samuel Glen	Andrew Mills
James Thompson	Francis Maze
Patrick Crosson	Patrick Fee
James Woods	Anthony Mulden
Joseph Tagart	James Laverty
Patrick McLeon	Jane Lurkie

Passengers by the BELISARIUS, from Dublin to New York, 6 July, 1811.

Richard King	William Turner
Jane King	William Morgan
James "	Lawrence Current
Mary "	Peter Courtney
Jane King and	Michael McHolland
five children	Thomas Bird
Benjamin Tuckerbury	Richard Langer
and family	Mary Bird
Peter Folly	Valient Needham
William Phelan	Catherine Needham
Patrick "	Eliza "
James Graham	Mathew Murphy
Bartlett Turner	Joseph Gilbert
John Gilbert	Ann "
Mary Ann Gilbert	Ally Burton
John Birk	Patrick Pierce
Eliza "	Michael Murphy
Thomas Walsh	and family
Thomas Newan	William Sutton
James Costagan	Edward Lacy
Edward Dove	John Dunn
James Charowell	Martin Baimbrick
Rev. Mr. Ryan	and family
Denis Menieur	William McDonald
Robert Hughes	Stephen Mathews
and family	and wife
Wm. Nailor	Henry Stanhope
and family	and wife
Jane Connor	William Harding
and family	and wife

Passengers by the Ship HUNTRESS, Thomas Ronson, Master, from Dublin to New York, arrived 24 June, 1811.

John Field	Dublin
Peter Kenney	"
Cath. "	"
Jos. Craig and family	"
Chas. " " "	"
John "	"
George Echard	"
Peter Toole	"
John Armitage	Tipperary
John Horan	Kings County
John "	Tipperary
T. Kinch and family	Wexford
James Kinch	"
John Stout	"
John Keating	Dublin
Mary "	"
M. Gregory and family	Meath
John Gregory	Co. Louth
Bridget Harman	" "
Thomas Branigan	" "
Michael Devine	" "
Susan Gunea	Dublin
James Byrne	Wicklow
Patrick Meeghan	Tipperary
M. Flanery and family	"
N. Carden " "	"
Margaret Phelan	"
John Cullin	Kilkenny
Patrick Cancannon	"
Patrick Lawler	Wexford
John Doyle	"
John Murphy	"
Michael Doyle	"
Patrick Finney	"
Matthew Finney	"
John Dealy	"
Thomas McCormick	Longford
George Lanigan	"
Patrick Forley	Cavan
William Ryan	Tipperary
Thomas Davis	Wicklow
Edward Clark	Cavan

Owen Gerighaty	Meath
Martin Justin	Queen's County
Henry Sutliff	" "
Edward "	" "
Betsey Lucus	" "

Passengers by the Ship SHAMROCK, McKeon, from Dublin to New York, 6 July, 1811.

Edward Caffray	Queen's County
Morris Fitzgerald	Dublin
Mark Pigott	Carlow
Matthew Ketly	Kilkenny
William Walsh	"
John Scully	Borris a Kane
Timothy Murphy	King's County
John Stockdale	Dublin
Miles Byrne and family	"
Matthew Murphy	"
Wm. Fitzpatrick	Queen's County
G. Edwards and family	Dublin
John Laplin	Kilkenny
James Ryan	Queen's County
J. Shinluig and family	Antrim
Richard Hallugan	Co. Louth
Henry Colin	" "
Andrew Daye	Queen's County
James Trenar	" "
Patrick "	" "
James Durham	Dublin
Margaret Durham	"
Henry Stephenson	"
T. Fitzpatrick and family	Cavan
Thomas Phelan	Kilkenny
John Platt	Youghal
Thomas Ryan	Tipperary
David Ryan	"
Thomas Delany	Wexford
Nicholas Sinnot	Wicklow
James McKey	Tipperary
Wm. Reynolds	King's County
John Carrall	Tipperary
Thomas Murtagh	Drogheda
Michael Kelly	"
Brian Reilly	Castle Pollard
William Moran	Dublin
M. Erraty and family	Kilkenn7
John McEvory	Dublin
Benjamin Wilson	New York, U.S.A.
Wm. Thompson	Philadelphia U.S.A.
Mary McClane	Cavan
John Bradley	Tipperary
Henry Withers	Dublin
Michael Alchorn	Philadelphia U.S.A.
Patrick Rorke	Tipperary
Patrick Sherlock	Dublin
John Wright	"
Elize Wright	"
James Kerwan	Castle Pollard
Wm. McGrath	Drogheda
Thomas Corcoran	Dublin
Wm. Corcoran	"
Michael Leary	Castle Pollard
John McClane	Co. Cavan
Mary "	" " "
Peter Philar	Queen's County
James Ryan	Dublin
Catherine Wright	Cavan
Wm. Stanley and family	Dublin

List of Passengers on board the Ship MARGARET, of which Thomas Marsh is Master, burden 300 tons, bound for New York, 18 April, 1803.

Eliz. Brothers	44	Hugh Alexander	29
Mary "	19	Jane "	22
Samuel "	12	Jane "	3
James "	10	Sarah "	2
William "	7	Robert Gooey	20
M. Ann Anderson	30	Saml. Douglas	18
Mathew Doubly	12	Thomas Harten	19
James Farrell	30	John Rolston	27
Eliz. "	22	Ann Beard	24
Wm. "	3	Ann Beard	2
James Harkness	40	James McClean	60
Jane "	36	Eliz. "	60
Thos. "	12	David "	24
Margt. "	10	John "	22

Abigail Harkness	8	George McClean	28
Sarah "	10	Wm. Riddle	19
Robt "	6	Samuel Magil	21
James "	4	Samuel "	39
Eliz. Story	47	Biddy Enery	35
Ben "	18		
Ann "	16		

List of Passengers intending to go from Belfast to Philadelphia in the Ship EDWARD, burden 231-86/95 tons per Register.

James Greg	46	James Fox	40
Thomas "	18	Patk. Mooney	16
John "	19	James Tower	22
Thomas Fleming	19	James Burns	20
Hugh Porter	24	Robert Labody	32
John Martin	21	Hers. McCullough	27
Alex. McMeikin	21	Wm. Scott	22
Wm. Dunn	30	James Kirkman	40
Thos. Monks	60	Wm. Bingham	40
Robt. "	22	James "	14
Joseph "	20	John Norris	16
Thomas "	17	Hugh Murphy	18
John Smith	20	Edwd. Wilson	18
Hu. McBride	26	Ardsal Hanlay	24
W. "	25	James Read	23
W. Dawson	28	Jos. Haddock	27
Jn. Craven	25		

List of Passengers who intend going to Newcastle and Philadelphia on board the ship BRUTUS of Philadelphia, George Craig, Master, burden 500 tons, 19 April, 1805.

Thomas Kennan	25	Stewartstown
Patrick Curley	20	"
Bennet Boles	22	"
John Wilkinson	23	Nn. Stewart
Michael Kelley	25	Omagh
Thomas Callaughan	23	Strabane
John Wilson	19	Nn. Conningham
James Clendining	18	"
Patrick Cue	22	Aughnacloy
James Wilson	20	Nn. Conningham
Wm. Stewart	25	Coleraine
Alexr. Eakin	28	"
James Thompson	25	Donegal
Isaac Cochran	27	Ballynoconey
James Ferrier	24	Bushmills
George Morrow	28	"
John MacCad	29	"
James Peoples	23	Letterkenny
Darby Bayle	24	"
Alexander Thompson	30	"
Stephen Alley	24	Derry
John Ewing	20	"
James Smily	27	"
Thomas Murphy	26	"
Patrick "	30	"
John Hasson	24	Cumber
Jean Bayle	21	"
John Johnston	23	"
David King	29	"

A List of Passengers who intend going to New York on Board the Ship Rover of New York, George Bray, Master, burden 287 65/95 tons.

Michael Muldoon	27	gentleman	Co. Meath
Mrs. Muldoon	24	"	" "
John Jamison	21	merchant	Dublin
Robt. Greer	38	chapman	Dungannon
Fras. Ennis	24	gentleman	Queen's Co.
Henry Herron	28	merchant	Dublin
Elinor Neilson	22	spinster	Clones
Francis Evatt	21	labourer	Co. Cavan
Jno. MacNeill	19	"	"
Mich. Connor	21	"	Wexford
Ben. Hood	30	"	King's Co.
Morris MacNeill	19	"	" " "
Hugh Brady	18	clerk	Dublin
Stephen Flynn	24	"	"
Pat. Cranning	30	"	Drogheda
Wm. Armstrong	22	apothecary	Co. Meath

Peter Donnolly	18 clerk	Dublin
David Jones	29 clerk	"
Margt. Hawthorne	34 spinster, Britain St.,	
		Dublin
Jas.	"	8	"
Kitty	"	5	"
Sally (servant girl)	19	"
Patt Fegan	30 labourer	Co. Kildare
James Heeran	32 clerk	" "
James Wyland	20 "	King's Co.
Patk. Lansdown	21 farmer	Co. Meath
Thos. Fitzgerald	35 farmer	Co. Dublin
Patt MacNaughly	27 labourer	Co. Longford
Matt. Mickson	20 clerk	Dublin
Peter Smith	12 "	Co. Cavan
Andrew Murphy	21 labourer	Co. Cavan

List of Passengers on board the Ship AKIN ALEX-
ANDER, Captain Howland, from Londonderry to
New York, 14 September, 1811.

William Crow	John & Margt. Vale
Jane "	James Eakins
Margt. "	Rosannah Eakins
Mathew Orr	Margt. "
Alex. Armstrong	Margt. " junr.
Jane Campbell	Sarah Eakins
John Grey	Rebecca McMahin
H. Welch	John McFarland
P. Kirk	wife & family
John Jackson	Margt. Farland
William Orr	William Buchanan
John Johnston	George Wason
Margt. Wason	Arm. Armstrong
14 children	

List of Passengers per Ship FAME, Captain,
William Pollock, arrived at Philadelphia, from
Derry, 31 August, 1811, in 63 days.

Samuel Torrers	George Crocket
John Rutherford	Samuel "
Mary "	Moses Hunter
Sarah "	John Kerr
George Crockett	Robert Hector
John "	James Grimes
Robt. "	Robert McArthur
George Smyth	John "
Arch. McElroy	Mrs. McTogart
and family	and family
James Alcorn	Joseph Alcorn
John Alcorn	Elizabeth Cross
and family	Francis Alcorn
Jane Simon	and wife
Martha Martin	Charles Quin
Rose Carolan	Samuel Dickey
Martha Quigley	Nathaniel Dickey
H. McLaughlin	John Wilson
James Reed	Matthew Kerr
James Arthur	James Dickey
Samuel Martin	John George
James Martin	Esther Bailey
Robert Orr	James McCloskey
James Neilson	Ruth Torrers
James Anderson	Samuel "
James McConnell	Ann "
Hugh McKinley	Samuel Rodgers
George Culbert	Joshua Orr

List of Passengers per the Ship MARIA DUPLEX,
from Belfast to New York, 21 September, 1811.

James Gray	Antrim
James Bennett	Armagh
Dennis Carroll	Tyronw
James McBride	
wife and family	Down
Andrew Morran and wife	Down
John Walsh " "	Dublin
Mrs. Bryson	Belfast
John Barr and family	Ballinahinch
Miss Mary Rodgers	Belfast
Miss Susanna Bowen	Belfast
William Quale	Downpatrick
Patrick Kelly	Dublin

List of Passengers per the Ship PROTECTION to
New York, 28 September, 1811.

William Boyd	Killybegs
Robert Campbell	Killinchy
Henry Atkinson	Dromore
Eliza Atkinson	"
James "	"
Henry "	"
Jane "	"
Samuel Blair	Cullybackey
Eliza "	"
William Gray	Armagh
Jane "	"
Walter "	"
George "	"
Samuel "	"
John "	"
Elizabeth Gray	"
Jane "	"
Thomas Davis	"
Thomas Preston	"
John Wattsher	Tyrone
Anna Martin	Antrim
Nancy Martin	"
James Luke	"
Jane Martin	Charlemont
Isaac Cubbert	Armagh
John Syllyman	Kellywaller
Billy "	"
John P. Barron	New York
Effy Tweedy	Dromore
John Robinson	Willsborough
Jane "	"
Thomas "	"
Mary "	"
Hugh Neil	Crumlin
John Wallace	Bangor
Thomas Harris	Banbridge
Mary Ann Willis	Stewartstown
Thomas Knox	Brougshane
William "	"
Jane "	"
Henry Williamson	Saintfield
Elizh. "	"
Jane "	"
Robert McDonald	Portoferry
Jane Knox	Brougshane
Mathew Willis	Stewartstown
Joseph Verty	Penreth
Joseph "	"
Anthony Clothard	Kellenchy
Thomas Hamilton	Connors
Thomas McClure	Saintfield
Robert J. Walker	Galway
Robert McGaw	Stewartstown
Thomas "	"
Anthony Bridge	Bedford, State of
	Pennsylvania
Mary Campbell	Belfast
Jeremiah Campbell	"
Samuel Boony	Greencastle
Sarah "	"
Harriet "	"
John Quin	Antrim
Margt. "	"
Jane "	"
Henry "	"
James Thomson	Lisburn
Jane "	"
John Hughes	Bangor
Jane Sloan	Doagh
Jane Watt	Castlewilliam
Hugh Laverty	Newtownards
Jane "	

Passengers by the WHITE OAK, from Dublin to
New York, 5 October, 1811.

James Hannah and family	---- coe and sister
John Bacon " "	Dennis O'Brien
---- Martin " "	James Mulony
---- Moran " "	Mary McManus
---- Cannon " "	John Burke
William Kennedy	near Mullingar
and Wife	Edward Smith
	near Drogheda

Passengers by the Ship MARINER, from Londonderry, arrived at New-London, 21 Dec., 1811,
in 48 days.

James Mulloy and family	James Corrins
Wm. McFarland " "	John McColgin
David Virtue " "	John Moffit
Archibald Elliott	William West
and family	David West
Edw. Dever and family	Dennis Dogherty
Thomas Long " "	Bernard Arenner
Charles Kane " "	John Boyle
Robert McKnott	James Knox
and family	and family
John Scanlon	Wm. Reynolds
Widow McPharland	Hugh Atcheson
and 2 children	and wife
James Bryan	M. Murphy
and wife	and wife
Anne Bryan	Mary Ross
S. Henderson	John Rafferty
Alexander Carr	Edward Timmony
John Henderson	Henry Williams
William Scott	Alexander Hall
James "	Robert "
Richard Crozier	John McEwen
Elizh. "	Hugh Reed
P. McPharland	John Boyd
Oliver Beatty	Patrick Mathew
Aily Rice	Patrick McGrath
Maurice Ferry	David Lindsay
John Alges	James "
John McAskin	Torry Monaghan
Thomas Hunter	

List of Passengers per Ship HARMONY, Capt.
Hobkirk, from Londonderry, arrived at
Philadelphia, 31 October, 1811, in 70 days.

Edward Loughead	Eliza Blair
Cath. Loughead	James Blair
Robert Rankin	Hugh Gallen
Manus McFaddin	Mary Gallen
Eleanor "	Margt. "
Mathew Nanson	Owen "
Hugh Anderson	Sally "
Ann "	Biddy "
James "	Mary "
Mary Bull	James "
Thomas McShane	Cath. "
Michael McCue	John Colvin
Daniel McCue	John Hamill
John Gordon	Robert Thompson
Robert Hamilton	Roger McNeal
Andrew Irvine	Mary Norris
John Irvine	John Coyle
Bernard Size	Daniel Coyle
Hannah "	James Logue
William Moore	Thomas Devilt
Adam George	James Cullen
John Rea	Mary Logan
John Young	Philip McGowan
Mary "	Fran. McLaughlin
John Manson	Biddy McLaughlin
Wm. Kirpatrick	James Blair
John "	John Devilt
Joseph Steel	Allen Kerr
Elizabeth Steel	Patrick Browne
Sally Steel	Bridget Browne
Samuel Patterson	Charles McKay
Wm. Knox	Mary Browne
Gerard Hunter	Wm. "
Martha "	Samuel Boyd
John "	Ellen "
Mary "	Mary Ann "
John Smiley	John Gilmour
Henry Dougherty	John Cochran
Cath. Dougherty	James Kavanagh
Anthy. "	Elea. McLaughlin
Thomas Stirling	Rose Griffeth
Martha "	Biddy "
Edw. McCafferty	Wm. McFarland
George Blair	Mary Logue
Jane "	Biddy "
Cath. "	Michael Rodder
Wm. "	Chas. Gallagher
Mary Gallagher	Charles McCoun
Cath. "	Bryan Cooney
Patk. "	Samuel Chestnut

Michl. Gallagher   John Hanlan
Hugh   "   Jane Colvin

List of Passengers per the Ship ERIN from Dublin to New York, 10 November, 1811.

Mr. Thomas and Mrs. Robinson   Queens County
Mr. Cornelius Smith   Manoch, County --------
John Lynch   Navan
John Androhan   Wexford
William Gibbons   of Ohio
Thomas Neil   Dublin
James Harrold   "
David and Dennis Doyle   "
Mrs. Cooper   "
Mrs. Riley   Co. Wexford

Passengers by the Ship WESTPOINT, T. Holden, Master, from Londonderry to New York, 23 November, 1811.

Robert Hunter   New York
James White   N. Limavady
Bernard McCosker   Omagh
John Hemphill and family   Dugh Budge
John Wawb   Castlefin
David Doak   Fannit
Susana McDermot and family   Derry
Francis Gillespie   Ballyshannon
Daw Griffin   Fannit
William Rafferty   Gawagh
Patrick McVeagh   Campsey
William Thompson   Carrick
Robert Henry   Coleraine
James Martin   N. Limavady
John   "   "
Patrick Cartau and family   Claudy
Alex. Thompson   "   "   Leuck
Alex. Brown   "   "   Aughanwerry
Robert O'Neill   "   "   Co. Antrim
John Crampsier   Magilligar
Donaldson Black   "   "   Co. Tyrone
Elinor McCready   Gortward
Wm.   "   "
John Graham   Kilrea
Thomas Hutchinson   "
Joseph Douglas   "
Thomas Martin   "
Daw. Kelley   Ballintrea
Ann Coulter   Co. Derry
Sarah Coulter   "
Patrick Divin   Ballyshannon
Hugh Coulter   Pettigo
Hugh Stevenson   Donegal
Mr. Cochran   Ballymoney
Joseph McCoy and family   Florinscourt
Cath. Kelley   Fannit
Edward McMennomy   Ballybofey
John Kelley   "
John Hilton   Gawagh
Edward Dogherty   Cauakeel
Robert Johnston   Pettigo
Francis Johnston   "
Alex. McAlvin and family   Co. Antrim
Samuel Moorhead   "   "
John Jack   "   "
James O'Donnell   Rushey
Ann Donaghey   Roeman
John   "   Rushey
Patrick Froster   Straban
George Kirk   Mountcharles
George McKee   "
James Love   Donagheda
Robert Love   "
George McEliver   "
Nancey Wason   Ray
David Hunter   Omagh
James C. Sproul   Stranorla
Eliza Paul   Omagh
John Hunter   N. Limavady
Farguis McGaughrin   Donegal
John Cummings   Ballymoney
Paul Boggs   New York
Luke Flyn   Co. Cavan
John O'Neill   "   "
Ann Masterson   "   "
Elizh. Wardlaw   "   "
Edward Masterson   "   "

Elizabeth Hasting   Co. Cavan
Edward McMinimin   Castlefin
Nancy McKagh   "
Hugh McElwin   Dromore
Hugh Catherwood   Coleraine
Neal Janga   Castlefin

Passengers by the Ship HIBERNIA, Graham, from Belfast to New York, 30 November, 1811.

David McClean and family   Wm. Stewart
Mary Willikin   "   "   Eliz. Armstrong
Cath. Coal   "   "   Luke Jackson
Edward McKever   "   "   Wm. Thompson
Thomas Mathews   "   "   Mary Reilly
Polly Connolly   "   Margt. Auld
L. Barklie   "   James Getty
Richard Blair, Ann Blair   Alex. McCullough
H. Stewart   Bernard Doorish
P. Quin   Ann Wright
Nicholas Lapsy   Wm. Freeland
John McGaw and family   R. Armstrong
James Leman   Margt. Leman
John McNeily   James Gaffin
James Shephard   George Roberts
Robert Peadon   Thomas Reilly
Daniel Quin   John Jones
Hugh Quin   Benj. Stewart

Passengers by the Ship AEOLUS, from Newry to New York, 14 December, 1811.

John Brown and family   John Murphy
Robert McIndoo and wife   James Harpur
Wm. Burns and family   Lucy Fuller
John Davidson and family   John McConnell
Margt. Ferris and family   Samuel Evans
Daniel McKey   "   "   Alice McKenney
John George   "   "   John Moore
John Class   "   "   George Black
John McMullen   "   "   James Kerr
Robert Cunningham   "   Mary Orr
George Grady and niece   Wm. Bell
David Hawthorn and family   Mary Roark
James Ryers and wife   Edward McQuaid
Henry Holland and family   John Flanigan
Hannah Couden and family   Patrick   "
John Triven and wife   Peter Casey
Samuel Kirk and family   George Wilkins
John Jeffrys   "   "   Hugh Crothers

Passengers by the Ship ALEXANDER, Captain Fanning, from Londonderry to New York, 21 December, 1811.

James Wright and wife   Eliz. Ritchie
William Rea and family   Joseph Caldwell
Tully Sieven   "   "   Francis Bradley
Thomas Rogers and family   Thomas Swan
Francis McManus and wife   Hugh Wallace
Patrick Campbell   "   "   Percival Kain
James Buden and family   John Thompson
Alexander Child   Dean Knox
Anne McClure   Wm. McMalin
Wm. Maitland   Eliza McKinney
John Givun   Anne Miller
Wm. Thompson   Cath. Bradley
George McKinney   Phillip Kelley
Robert Moore   James Collins
P. McDevill   Sally Devlin

List of Emigrants from the Parish of Magilligan for the years 1833-1834. Particulars given in the following order: Name, Age, Religion, Townland and Destination.

Name	Age	Religion	Townland	Destination
John Quinn	19	R.C.	Ballymagolane	Quebec
James Melon	23	"	Oughtymore	Phila.
Nancy Melon	25	"	"	Quebec
Jane Doherty	18	"	"	N. York
Wm. Kelly	20	E.C.	Ballyscullion	Phila.
Wm. Doherty	22	R.C.	"	"
Edw. "	25	R.C.	"	"
Michael Doherty	24	R.C.	Ballyscullion	Phila.
Cath. McLaughlin	20	"	Ballycarton	Quebec
Pat. McCormick	25	"	Duncrun	Phila
Wm. McCormick	23	"	"	"
Jas. Kennedy	20	"	"	N. York
John Doherty	22	"	"	Quebec
Wm. Rudden	24	"	Ballycarton	"
Cath. McLaughlin	26	"	"	"
Abraham Kilmary	30	"	"	"
Hugh Lane	23	"	Claggan	Phila.
Robt. Smith	23	"	Ballyscullion	"
Mark McLaughlin	30	"	Ballyleighery	Quebec
Wm. Ferson	24	P	Ballymultimber	Phila
Wm. Doherty	24	"	"	"
Mary A. Snell	28	E.C.	Servant at Bellarena	Quebec
John Bleakley				
Samuel Tate	28	P.	Woodtown	Quebec
Thos. Tate	20	"	"	"
Thos. Paterson	35	E.C.	"	"
Jas. McNally	30	R.C.	Aughill	"
Margt. McNally	21	"	"	"
Geo. Redgate	25	"	"	N. York
Wm. McFeely	24	"	"	"
Jas. Farren	25	"	"	Quebec
Ellen Doherty	20	"	Tirreeven	"
Wm. Gilchrist	40	"	Ballymaclary	"
Sara "	41	"	"	"
John "	10	"	"	"
Wm. " junr.	8	"	"	"
Patrick "	12	"	"	"
Holland O'Brien	25	"	"	"
Margt. "	35	"	"	"
Margt. Tonner	7	"	"	"
Margt. McCague	24	"	Clooney	"
Ellen O'Kane	20	"	"	St. Johns
Margt. "	18	"	"	"
Margt. "	18	"	"	"
Margt. "	18	"	"	"
Nancy McCague	22	"	"	"
Geo. Doherty	26	"	Upr. Drumons	N. York
Nancy "	22	"	" "	Phila
Hugh McTyre	22	"	"	Quebec
Betty McTyre	25	"	"	"
Robert Smith	24	"	"	Phila
John Bleakley				

Emigrants from Aghadowey in the year 1834.

Name	Age	Religion	Townland	Destination
Margt. Wallace	22	P.	Bough	Quebec
James Orr	30	"	Cullycapple	Phila.
Jane "	32	"	"	"
Margt. "	11	"	"	"
Elizh. "	9	"	"	"
Elizh. "	9	"	"	"
Ann "	5	"	"	"
Isabella Orr	7	"	"	"
Hannah "	3	"	"	"
Thomas Mullen	25	R.C.	Mullaghmore	"
John "	30	"	"	"
Bernard "	23	"	"	"
Cath. "	22	"	"	"
John "	20	"	Glassgort	"
John McFetridge	24	P.	Lands Agivey	Phila.
Margt. McGonigle	5	"	"	"
John "	3	"	"	"
Jonathan Tracey	20	R.C.	Cahery	Quebec
Margt. "	21	P.	"	"
Mary Canning	30	"	"	"
Soba Mairs	40	"	Ballylough	Phila.
Margt. Mairs	18	"	"	"
Ann "	43	"	"	"
Sara "	12	"	"	"
Jane "	10	"	"	"
Matilda Mairs	3	"	"	"
John Moon	25	"	Clarkhill	"
Jonathan Moon	24	"	"	"
Edward "	20	"	"	"
Daniel Thompson	20	"	Ballywillan	N. York
William Young	25	"	Shanloughead	Phila.
John Smith	20	"	Moneycarris	"
Jane Jamison	19	"	Aghadowey	"
Andrew McAlister	40	"	Keely	Quebec
Ann "	16	"	"	"
Ann "	38	"	"	"
Thos. McAlister	14	"	"	"
James "	12	"	"	"
Margt. "	10	"	"	"
Robert "	8	"	"	"

Name	Age	Religion	Place	Destination
Susan McAlister	6	P.	Keely	Quebec
Mary "	4	"	"	"
Andrew "	2	"	"	"
Michael McAfee	24	R.C.	"	"
Martha "	22	"	"	"
Martha McAlister	50	P.	Dirnagrove	"
Rebecca "	18	"	"	"
Olive "	14	"	"	"
James Neil	20	P.	Drumacrow	N. York
John Fleming	21	"	"	"
James Moore	22	"	Ballincallymore	"
Isabella Moore	21	"	"	"
Wm. Workman	70	"	Mullan	Quebec
Mary "	60	"	"	"
John "	20	"	"	"
Richard "	16	"	"	"
Margt. "	18	"	"	"
James McKeemins	25	"	"	"
Edward Quinn	20	R.C.	Mullaghinch	N. York
Mary Gillon	45	"	Meanougher	Quebec
Patrick Logue	16	"	"	"
Ann Logue	14	"	"	"
Sam. Patterson	33	P.	Clintagh	Phila
Elizh. Patterson	25	"	"	"
Joseph "	62	"	"	"
Richard "	43	"	"	"
Mary "	26	"	"	"
Margt. Stewart	30	"	"	"
James Morrison	20	"	Crossmakeever	Quebec
Hugh Kennedy	20	"	"	"
John Adams	28	"	Carnroe	"
Elizh. McClurg	40	E.C.	Lisnamuck	N. York
Jane "	16	"	"	"
Arch. "	14	"	"	"
Jackson "	10	"	"	"
Hugh Hemphill	27	P.	Ballybritain	Phila.
Robt. Henery	22	"	Lisboy	"
Jas. McFarrell	30	"	Ballymacallaghan	Quebec
John Boyd	20	"	"	N. York
Mary Jane Fream	18	"	"	"
William Hill	25	"	Bovagh	"
Cath. Boyd	20	"	Ballymacallaghan	"
Hanah Doherty	25	"	Bovagh	Quebec
Eliz. Adams	22	R.C.	Mullaghmore	"
Michael McAlice	24	"	"	"
Elizh. "	22	"	"	"
Jas. Jameson	40	E.C.	"	"
Jane "	30	"	"	"
Robert Reid	60	P.	Margagher	Phila.
Ann "	55	"	"	"
John "	21	"	"	"
Miss "	16	"	"	"
Esther "	10	"	"	"
Sarah "	52	"	"	"
Levy "	16	"	"	"
Jas. Anderson	30	"	Margoher	"
Sam. Fulton	44	"	Ballinclough	"
Mary Ann Fulton	42	"	.	"
Robert "	20	"	"	"
Thos. Boyd	23	"	Ballygauley	"
Esther "	20	"	"	"
Robert McNeil	24	"	Aghadowey	"
Andrew Harkin	18	"	"	"
Robert Blair	50	"	"	"
Rosey "	48	"	"	"
Joseph "	20	"	"	"
James "	18	"	"	"
Robert Riddells	64	"	Lisnamuck	Phila.
Mary Ann "	60	"	"	"
Mary Ann "	12	"	"	"
Charles "	20	"	"	"
Elizh. "	41	"	"	"
Matty "	22	"	"	"
Charles "	40	"	"	"
William "	12	"	"	"
Matilda "	10	"	"	"
Samuel "	8	"	"	"
Margt. "	6	"	"	"
Robert "	4	"	"	"
Hugh "	2	"	"	"
James Boyes	40	"	"	"
Ann "	38	"	"	"
John "	18	"	"	"
James "	16	"	"	"
David "	12	"	"	"
Leslie "	10	"	"	"
Ann Creiten	22	"	"	"
Fanny "	24	"	"	"
John Rosburg	17	"	"	"
Margt. Fulton	18	"	Ballyclough	"
Samuel "	14	"	"	"
James Fulton	12	P.	Ballyclough	Phila.
Mary Ann "	10	"	"	"
Thomas "	8	"	"	"
James Fisher	17	"	"	"
Samuel "	19	"	"	"
Jas. Stewart	19	"	Crevolea	"
David Torrens	20	"	"	Quebec
Robert McEntire	28	"	Collins	Phila.
Wm. McFetridge	22	"	"	"
David Canning	24	"	"	"
Thomas Sanderson	22	"	"	"
Andrew Cochrane	24	"	Ballinlees	"
Samuel Barr	28	"	Leggury	St. John
Francis Burke	40	R.C.	Cornamuckla	Phila.
Mary "	30	"	"	"

List of Emigrants from the Parish of Balteagh to New York for the years 1833-1834.

Name	Age	Religion	Place	Destination
Alex. George	21	P.	Terrydremond	Phila
Sally Thompson	30	"	"	"
Alex. Eakin	26	"	"	"
Mary McManus	20	"	"	"
Mary "	20	"	"	"
Cath. "	18	"	"	"
Mary A. Diamond	6	"	"	"
John "	4	"	"	"
Joseph McCool	21	"	"	"
Henry McGowen	22	R.C.	Ballyquin	St. John
Thos. Lafferty	18	"	"	"
Joseph Smith	18	P.	Carnet	N. York
Ann Lynn	16	"	Derry Little	"
twins				
Jane Lynn	16	"	"	"
James Scullion	18	R.C.	Ardmore	Quebec
Wm. McNamara	20	E.C.	"	"
James Ceahy	20	P.	"	Phila.
Margt. Adams	23	"	Edenmore	N. York
Eleanor Boyle	30	R.C.	Ballymulty	"
Sally "	1	"	"	"
Susanna "	1	"	"	"
(twins)				
Mary Ann "	4	"	"	"
John "	7	"	"	"
Joseph "	5	"	"	"
John Woods	20	E.C.	Drumagosker	Quebec
Robt. Hutcheson	22	P.	Lislane	Phila.
David Ross	24	"	"	"
Jane "	26	"	"	"
Jas. Cunningham	19	"	"	N. York
Michael O'Kane	50	R.C.	"	"
Robert McCauley	30	P.	Ballyleighery,	Phila.
Jane O'Kane	48	R.C.	Lislane	N. York
Thos. Colwell	30	P.	Cloghan	Quebec
Eliza Colwell	32	"	"	"
Eliza "	25	R.C.	"	"
Ann Bradley	22	"	"	"
Mary "	18	"	"	"
Patrick McDaid	30	"	"	"
Edward Mullen	25	P.	Maine	"
Mary Lagan	20	R.C.	Drumsurn	"
John Long	18	P.	"	"
David Ross	24	"	Gortnarny	Phila.
John Scott	30	"	Aghansillagh	"
Robert Scott	32	"	"	"
John Clyne	21	"	Terrydoo Clyde	"
John Doons	22	"	Terrydoo Walker	N. York
Robt. McCausland	20	"	"	"
Joseph Kennedy	30	"	Ballyvelin	Phila.
Bell Ollover	18	"	Drumgesh	"
Eliza Ollover	20	"	"	"
Mary Logan	20	R.C.	Killoyle	St. John
Bernard Log	15	"	"	Phila.
John Logue	18	"	"	"

List of Emigrants from the Parish of Bovevagh to New York for the Years 1833-1834.

Name	Age	Religion	Place	Destination
Wm. McClenaghan	17	R.C.	Drumadreen	N. York
Alex. Smith	18	P.	"	"
William Dale	40	"	"	"
Eliza "	38	"	"	"
John "	5	"	"	"
James Lowden	40	"	Drumneechy	Phila.
Jane "	36	"	"	"
Mary "	3	"	"	"
John Lowden	1	P.	Drumneechy	Phila.
Neil Begley	20	R.C.	"	"
Jane Sterling	50	P	Gorticlare	N. York
Ann "	25	"	"	"
Sally "	20	"	"	"
Joseph Hamilton	40	"	"	"
Ann "	38	"	"	"
Daniel Haran	20	R.C.	Inisconagher	Quebec
James McBeath	25	"	Camnish	"
Marcus Dogherty	18	"	"	"
John Boyle	24	E.C.	Dirnaflaw	N. York
John Ferguson	23	P.	"	"
Patrick McCloskey	18	R.C.	"	Quebec
Andrew McCully	50	P.	"	Phila.
Cath. "	24	"	"	"
Letitia Guy	30	P.	Leeke	N. York
Samuel Hamilton	20	P.	"	Quebec
Mary Ann Guy	20	"	"	"
Mary Devlin	40	R.C.	"	"
Margt. "	35	"	"	"
Eliza Connor	48	E.C.	"	"
Alex. McEntin	18	P.	"	"
Margt. Connor	20	E.C.	"	"
Dennis Devlin	40	R.C.	"	"
Peter "	42	"	"	"
James "	40	"	"	"
Dennis "	26	"	"	"
Ann "	28	"	"	"
Molly "	64	"	"	"
John Moore	20	P.	Killybleught	Phila
Samuel McFadden	22	"	Bovevagh	Quebec
Robert Taylor	20	"	"	"
Wm. O'Kane	24	"	"	"
Margt. "	22	"	"	"
Kyle Quigley	20	E.C.	"	"
Gordon Meehan	20	P.	"	"
Jas. McManamin	30	R.C.	"	"
Bryan O'Kane	20	"	Ardanarn	"
Eleanor McCloskey	22	R.C.	"	"
Mary A. "	20	"	"	N. York
James Craford	18	P.	"	"
James Douglis	18	"	"	"
Robt. Stewart	20	"	Templemoyle	"
Thos. Forrest	25	"	"	Quebec
John Forrest	46	"	Carnet	N. York
John Mullen	30	R.C.	Formal	"
Alex. Anderson	26	P.	Ballymoney	"
Patrick Farrell	23	R.C.	"	"
Jas. McCloskey	25	R.C.	Farkland	"
Eliza "	30	"	"	"
Bernd. McLaughlin	30	R.C.	Muldony	"
Michael Deehan	24	R.C.	"	"
Pat Brawley	32	"	"	"
Neill Deehan	24	"	"	"
Henry Hasson	24	"	"	"
Ann "	22	"	"	"
Mary Deehan	20	"	"	"
Ann Dogherty	20	"	"	"
Jas. McFeely	35	"	"	"
Bernd. "	20	"	"	"
Jas. "	40	"	"	"
Mgt. McCloskey	14	R.C.	Drum	"
James Hutton	32	P.	Ballyharigan	St. John
John Stinson	20	"	Glenconway	Phila.
John Rea	20	"	"	"
Alex. Nutt	18	"	"	"
Grace McCloskey	25	R.C.	Gortnahey Beg	Quebec
Jas. O'Neill	18	"	Derryland	St. John
Ann Coughlin	26	"	"	"
Bell Boyle	20	P.	"	"
Wm. Donaldson	20	"	Flanders	N. York
Ann Heaney	22	R.C.	Derryard	Quebec
John McEntee	20	"	"	"
Jane "	6	"	"	"
Mary McCay	20	E.C.	"	"
Ann "	18	"	"	"

List of Emigrants from Drumachose and Limavady in 1833 and 1834 to New York.

Name	Age	Religion	Place	Destination
Jas. McCloud	30	P.	Drummond	St. John
Pat. Gallaher	22	R.C.	"	"
David Lynn	20	P.	"	"
Ollover Martin	40	"	"	"
Jas. Hagerty	28	"	"	"
Wm. McConaghy	16	"	"	"
Jas. Cook	40	"	"	"
Jane "	38	"	"	"
Dan. "	20	"	"	"
Ann "	18	"	"	"

Name	Age		Place	Destination
Jane Cook	14	P.	Drummond	St. John
Kitty Ann Cook	8	"	"	"
Bell Cook	10	"	"	"
Jas. Cook	6	"	"	"
Molly Mullen	30	R.C.	"	"
Marcus "	10	"	"	"
Edward "	6	"	"	"
Patrick "	4	"	"	"
Robert "	2	"	"	"
John "	8	"	"	"
Elenor Grey	30	"	"	"
Mary McCay	26	"	"	"
John Brawley	24	"	"	"
John McMackin	22	"	"	"
Jas. Dogherty	17	"	"	Phila.
Docia Mullen	22	"	"	St. John
Wm. Conway	10	"	"	"
Hugh Right	64	P.	Bovalley	"
Wm. Connor	24	R.C.	Ardgarvin	"
Wm. Brown	30	P.	Limavady	Phila.
Hugh McClary	22	E.C.	"	N. York
Robert McAllister	18	E.C.	"	"
John Taggart	16	E.C.	"	"
Jas. Scott	24	"	"	Quebec
Wm. Greer	24	"	"	St. John
Jas. Flanigan	28	"	"	Quebec
Eliza "	26	"	"	"
Alice "	4	"	"	"
Mary A. Miller	18	P.	"	"
Daniel McFaull	23	E.C.	"	St. John
Pat. McLaughlin	26	R.C.	"	"
Mary A. "	24	"	"	"
John McElvan	19	"	"	"
Wm. McLaughlin	18	"	"	"
Daniel Lynn	19	"	"	"
Wm. Hunter	23	P.	"	Quebec
Jos. Callaghan	20	"	"	Van Dia. Land
Jas. "	20	"	"	N.S.Wales
Matw. Nodwell	30	"	Glenkeen	St. John
Cath. "	28	"	"	"
Mary Ann "	5	"	"	"
Eliza "	26	"	"	"
Thos. Rankin	30	"	Termaquin	N. York
John Johnston	18	"	"	Phila.
Molly Heney	40	"	"	"
Rachel Kennedy	50	"	Ballyavelin	"
Joseph "	30	"	"	"
Jane "	28	"	"	"
Mary "	7	"	"	"
Geo. "	5	"	"	"
Fullerton "	3	"	"	"
Kennedy (male)	1	"	"	"
Pat. Garven	20	R.C.	Drumramer	St. John
Arch. McSparran	40	P.	"	Phila.
M.H.McSparran	35	"	"	"
Jas. Richey	50	"	Ballycrum	St. John
Molly "	48	"	"	"
Samuel "	20	"	"	"
Jas. "	18	"	"	"
Geo. Douglass	20	"	Leck	"
Matthew Douglass	21	P.	Largyreagh	Phila.
John Canning	20	P.	"	"
Marcus "	18	"	"	"
Annyan "	11	"	"	"
Matilda Sterling	22	"	"	"
John Conn	25	"	Gortgarn	N. York
Jas. Flanagan	1	E.C.	"	"
Mary A. "	3	"	Limavady	Quebec
Conoly Dogherty	18	R.C.	"	N. York
Wm. Given	18	E.C.	"	"
Jas. McLaughlin	24	R.C.	"	"
Cath. "	18	"	"	"
Elenor Murray	35	"	"	"
Mary Ann "	18	"	"	"
Edward "	46	"	"	"
Daniel "	18	"	"	"
Edward "	17	"	"	"
Wm. Hunter "	24	P.	"	"
Edward Mullan	17	"	Derrybeg	"
Sara Linsey	20	"	Derrymore	Phila.
Eliza "	18	"	"	"
Jas. "	20	"	"	"
Jas. McCloskey	26	"	Bolea	"
Samuel Smith	20	"	"	"
Wm. Campbell	20	"	"	"
Jane McCloskey	28	"	"	"
Martin Wisely	18	"	"	"
Margt. "	45	"	"	"
Chas. Mullen	24	R.C.	Dunbeg	"
Wm. Wisely	16	P.	Bolea	"
Geo. Allen	26	"	Ballyriskmore	"

Name	Age		Place	Destination
Robert McFetridge	28	P.	Ballyriskmore	Phila.
Michael Langey	26	R.C.	Collessan	Quebec
Mary Eaton	22	P.	"	"

List of Emigrants from Tamlaghtfinlagan in 1833 and 1834.

Name	Age		Place	Destination
Sally McClane	22	P.	Ballymore	N. York
David Wark	20	"	"	"
Jas. Baird	58	"	"	Phila.
Wm. "	28	"	"	"
James Baird jr.	23	"	"	"
Robt. "	18	"	"	"
John "	9	"	"	"
Ann "	30	"	"	"
Elenor "	17	"	"	"
Mary Ann Baird	14	"	"	"
Martha Baird	7	"	"	"
John McCanlis	25	"	"	"
John Stewart	40	"	"	"
Jane "	40	"	"	"
Wm. "	16	"	"	"
John "	14	"	"	"
Robt. "	12	"	"	"
Hugh "	1	"	"	"
Elizh. "	8	"	"	"
Mary Ann Stewart	6	"	"	"
Andrew Morrison	22	"	Moy	"
Joseph McCracken	21	"	"	Quebec
James Neilly	25	"	"	"
Joseph Neilly	23	"	"	Phila.
Robert Busby	52	"	Ballynary	N. York
Robert " jr.	24	"	"	Phila.
Elizh. "	50	"	"	N. York
Ann "	18	"	"	"
Rachel "	16	"	"	"
David "	12	"	"	"
William Neely	55	"	"	Phila.
Jane "	40	"	"	"
James "	20	"	"	"
William "	15	"	"	"
John "	25	"	"	"
Mary Ann "	22	"	"	"
Andrew Alcorn	20	"	"	"
Martha "	20	"	"	"
Joseph Getty	20	"	Largy	"
John McCash	60	"	"	"
Jane "	56	"	"	"
William "	30	"	"	"
Joseph "	24	"	"	"
Hugh "	22	"	"	"
Eacy Neily	20	"	"	"
James Beer	22	"	"	Quebec
Elizh. "	24	"	"	"
Samuel "	26	"	"	"
Jane "	20	"	"	"
Mary Jackson	20	"	"	"
John Campbell	46	"	Maghermore	St. Johns
Mary "	44	"	"	"
Mary A. "	9	"	"	"
Wm. Gilderson	40	R.C.	"	"
Thos. "	8	"	"	"
Wm. "	4	"	"	"
John "	2	"	"	"
Mary "	6	"	"	"
John Lowry	32	P.	"	Phila.
Mary "	30	"	"	"
Jas. Mullen	40	R.C.	Drumreighlin	"
Sarah "	40	"	"	"
Ann Mullen	10	"	"	"
Margt. Mullen	8	"	"	"
Jane "	6	"	"	"
Sally "	4	"	"	"
Jas. McDonnell	35	P.	"	Quebec
Andrew "	30	"	"	"
William "	24	"	"	"
Eliza "	32	"	"	"
Edward McLaughlin	24	R.C.	"	St. Johns
William Pedin	19	E.C.	Tamlaght	N. York
Mary Pedin	16	"	"	"
John Keer	22	P.	"	Phila.
James McCook	22	"	"	"
John "	20	"	"	"
John Hutchenson	22	"	"	N. York
James "	23	"	"	"
Patrick McCay	30	R.C	"	"
John Thompson	30	P.	Drumcarney	"
Henry "	26	"	"	"
Scott Hunter	26	"	Tarnakelly	Phila.

Name	Age		Place	Destination
Mary Ann Cartin	28	R.C.	Tarnakelly	Phila.
Michael "	28	"	"	"
John O'Kane	26	"	"	St. Johns
T. White Morrison	20	P.	Drummore	Phila.
J. "	18	"	"	"
John Stewart	18	"	"	"
Sam. Caskey	50	"	"	"
Ann "	47	"	"	"
John "	22	"	"	"
Mary "	24	"	"	"
Eliza "	22	"	"	"
Ann "	20	"	"	"
Milly "	18	"	"	"
Margt. Jane Caskey	16	"	"	"
Jos. Crawford	26	"	Culmore	"
John Wilson	20	"	Clagan	"
John Devine	30	R.C.	Glack	"
John Craig	20	"	Sistrokeel	"
Mary "	18	P.	Glasvenagh	St.Johns
Robt. McCauly	30	"	"	"
George Gordon	18	"	"	"
Neil Healy	28	R.C.	Ballyking	"
Margt. "	26	"	"	"
Mary Ann Healy	4	"	"	"
Eliza Healy	2	"	"	"
John Healy infant		"	"	"
John White	19	P.	"	"
Jas. McCauly	30	"	"	"
Ann "	28	"	"	"
Girl, name forgotten	4	P.	"	"
Girl, name forgotten	2	"	"	"
Margt. Entiney	18	P.	Drummond	"
Ann Littlewood	24	R.C.	"	"
Chris. Stewart	24	E.C.	Ballykelly	N. York
James Campbell	28	P.	"	"
John Diamond	28	"	"	"
Daniel "	26	"	"	"
Thos. Meine	22	"	"	Quebec
Matilda Connor	22	E.C.	"	St. John
Andrew Dearmott	40	P.	"	Quebec
Ann "	25	"	"	"
Sara Ann "	7	"	"	"
Fanny "	3	"	"	"
Girl, name forgotten	1,	P.	"	"
Owen McCloskey	30	R.C.	"	"
Patrick "	28	"	"	"
John McLaughlin	50	P.	"	St. John
Ann "	50	"	"	"
Martha "	22	"	"	"
Cath. "	24	"	"	"
Ann McGarry	50	R.C.	"	"
Margt. McGee	45	E.C.	"	"
Eliza "	1	"	"	"
Matty "	32	"	"	"
A. McMilne	18	P.	Walworth	"
Margt. "	18	E.C.	Finlagan	"
John Latten	20	"	Drumdonaghy	N. York
Solomon Mitchell	35	R.C.	"	"
Susanna "	36	"	"	"
Thos. "	12	"	"	"
John "	10	"	"	"
Joseph "	8	"	"	"
Mary Ann "	6	"	"	"
Rosey "	4	"	"	"
Susanna "	O.L.		"	"
Daniel Martin	22	P.	Ardnargle	Phila.
Wm. Piper	22	"	Corndale	"
Wm. Lagan	22	"	Burnally	"
Mary O'Kane	22	R.C.	Lomond	Quebec
Wm. "	20	"	"	"
Thos. Stewart	50	P.	"	"
Jane "	46	"	"	"
John "	22	"	"	"
James "	17	"	"	"
Thomas "	15	"	"	"
Alex. "	13	"	"	"
Barton "	11	"	"	"
Jane "	9	"	"	"
Robert Main	20	"	Culmore	"
Alex. Peery	22	"	"	N. York
Ann Smith	50	"	"	"
John "	24	"	"	"
Eliza "	18	"	"	"
Sam. Crother	24	"	Carrymuckle	"
Mat "	20	"	"	"
Eliza "	3	"	"	"
Jane "	6	"	"	"
Mary Ann Crother	1	"	"	"
Wm. Kinney	60	"	"	"
Jane "	34	"	"	"
Joseph Miller	25	"	"	"

Cath. Miller	24	P.	Carrymuddle	N. York
Elenor "	2	"	"	"
Wm. Gault	18	E.C.	Broglasgow	"
Robert McLaughlin	24	P.	"	St. Johns
Wm. Sloan	20	"	"	"
David "	24	"	"	"
Wm. Wark	18	"	Broheris	N. York
Mary Jane Wark	20	"	"	"
Mary Torrens	26	"	Carnreagh	"
Mgt. J. McLaughlin	20	P.	Carrowclare	"
Sam Wark	20	P.	Farlow	"
Jacob Wark	18	"	"	"
John Simpson	24	"	"	"
Eliza "	22	"	"	"
Wm. Dogherty	30	R.C.	"	"
Margt. "	28	"	"	"
John "	7	"	"	"
Robt. "	5	"	"	"
Saly "	3	"	"	"
Ann "	1	"	"	"
John Moore	28	P.	Moneyhanna	Quebec
Margt. McMine	26	"	"	"
Mary A. "	20	"	"	"
Joseph White	22	"	"	"
John Johnston	22	R.C.	"	"
Wm. "	20	"	"	"

List of Emigrants from Coleraine to New York in the years 1833-1834. Particulars given in the following order: Name, Age, Religion, Townland, and Destination.

John McClean	5	P.	North Brook	Quebec
Ann "	2	"	"	"
Sam Ramsay	38	"	New Row	St. John
Jane "	22	"	"	"
Cath. "	7	"	"	"
Eliza "	one month	"	"	"
John "	5	"	"	"
Sam "	3	"	"	"
Thos. Duffy	21	R.C.	"	Quebec
John McCrotty	21	"	"	"
John Dunlop	24	E.C.	Blindgate St.	"
Mary Hurley	19	R.C.	Ferryquay St.	Phila.
Wm. Taylor	24	E.C.	Millbrook St.	Quebec
Mary "	20	"	"	"
Wm. "	18 months"	"	"	"
Andrew Douglas	22	"	"	"
John Miller	21	P.	Church St.	Phila.
Mgt. McCauley	20	"	"	N. York
Dorothea Linigam	23	"	Diamond	Quebec
Sibby Black	45	Sec.	Blindgate St.	St. John
James "	17	"	"	"
Mary A. "	4	"	"	"
Mathy "	1½	"	"	"
Eliza "	3	"	"	"
Stewart "	14	"	"	"
Joseph "	10	"	"	"
Robert "	3	"	"	"
Archibald Hill	30	P.	Long Commons	"
Margt. "	31	"	"	"
John Hughes	25	"	Gaol Lane	N. York
Thomas McLaughlin	21	R.C.	"	"
John Cassidy	24	"	"	Quebec
Henry McLaughlin	27	"	"	N. York
Thos. Sheils	24	"	Ferryquay St.	"
John Hughes	22	"	"	"
Wm. McLaughlin	35	"	New Row	Van De L.
Hester "	20	"	"	"
Chas. "	20	"	"	"
Thos. Bell	36	P.	Long Common	Liverpool
Chas. McLaughlin	10	R.C.	Bellhouse lane, Van De L.	
John McIntyre	10	"	"	"
Wm. Baxter	28	E.C.	Meeting Lane	Quebec
Jas. Rodgers	23	"	"	"
John Hinds	40	P.	Society S. Ho.	London
Hariot "	40	"	"	"
John " jr.	12	"	"	"
Hariot " "	10	"	"	"
Mary Hinds	9	"	"	"
Wm. "	8	"	"	"
Frederick Hinds	6	"	"	"
Chas. Hinds	5	"	"	"
Jas. "	4	"	"	"
Arthur "	2	"	"	"
John McIntyre	50	Sec.	Shamble St.	Quebec
Wm. Creighton	25	P.	Society St.	N. York
Elizh. "	30	"	"	"
Chas. Williamson	25	"	Rampart	Quebec
Margt. "	30	"	"	"

Jane Williamson	1	P.	Rampart	Quebec
Hugh Rankin	16	"	Blagh	Phila.
Wm. "	18	"	"	"
John McAtyre	25	"	Ballysally	St. John
Wm. McKee	19	"	"	"
Ann "	23	"	"	"
John McClane	25	"	"	Quebec
Jane "	25	"	"	"
Wm. Kennedy	18	"	Cross Glebe	"
Martha Hannah	52	"	Dundooan	N. York
John "	29	"	"	"
Eliza "	24	"	"	"
Martha "	22	"	"	"
Lydia "	20	"	"	"
Robt. "	18	"	"	"
Mary "	16	"	"	"
Henry "	14	"	"	"
Alex. Dunlop	22	"	Spittle Hill	Quebec
Jas. Dunlop	17	"	"	"
John McClelland	50	"	Loguestown	"
Neal "	46	"	"	"
Susan "	45	"	"	"
Rachel "	19	"	"	"
Mary A. "	21	"	"	"
Neal "	17	"	"	"
John "	14	"	"	"
James "	9	"	"	"
Hugh "	14	"	"	"
Wm. "	3	"	"	"
Susan "	5	"	"	"
John "	infant 1, P.		"	"
Jas. Reilly	21	P.	Millburn	"
Wm. Little	74	E.C.		Scotland
Mary Ann Little	35	"	"	"
Andrew "	19	"	"	"
George "	17	"	"	"
John "	15	"	"	"
Wm. Little Jr.	4	"	"	"
Hendrick Little	9	"	"	"
Mary Ann "	6	"	"	"
Jas. Parkhill Servt.	14	E.C.	Millburn	Scotland
Wm. Reilly	30	E.C.	Tullans	Quebec
Hester Wilson	35	P.		N. York
John Westley	24	"		Phila.
John Parke	35	"		Quebec
Hannah "	28	"	"	"
Geo. McCann	21	R.C.	"	"
Wm. Steel	25	P.	"	"
Henry Boyd	40	"		Phila.
John Miller	21	"	"	"
Margt. "	18	"	"	"
Thos. Shiel	30	"	"	"
Hugh Brian	28	"	"	"
Mary Steel	24	"		Quebec
John Brook	24	"	Windy Hall	"
Alex. McKee	38	"	Knockanturn	"
Jane "	30	"	"	"
Wm. "	12	"	"	"
James "	10	"	"	"
Margt. Jane McKee	8, P.		"	"
Alex. McKee Junr.	5	"	"	"
John Usher	20	P.	"	"
John Lyons	20	"	"	"
Hugh McAlister	26	"	Boghill	Phila.
Jas. Wright	24	"	"	"

Returned in 1834

Robert Girvin	20	E.C.	Spittlehill	N. York
Thos. Hegerty	21	P.	Danes Hill	"
Henry Caulfield	16	"	Bridge Street, New Orlean	
Sam McCay	16	"	"	"
Jas. Gilmour	19	Sec.	"	N. York

Returned in 1835

Wm. Orr	20	"	"	Quebec
John Kane	35	P.	Diamond	"
John Streen	50	E.C.	Nth. Brook St.	N. York
Isabella "	48	"	"	"
Wm. Steen	18	"	"	"
Saml. "	7	"	"	"
Anne "	20	"	"	"
Isabella Steen Jun.	9	E.C.	"	"
Patrick Gannon	17	P.	"	Quebec
Anne McClean	35	"	"	"
James "	7	"	"	"

Emigrants from Dunboe - 1833

Nancy Donaghy	25	Pres.	Articlave	St. John
Francis McGawney	30	E.C.	"	"

James McGawney	22	E.C.	Articlave	St. John
Mary Smith	22	Pres.	"	Quebec
Robert "	4 mths.	"	"	St. John
Cochran Colman	18	E.C.	"	"
Mary Colman	30	"	"	"
Stephen Thorpe	18	"	"	"
William Paul	50	Pres.	"	"
Sarah "	16	"	"	"
Elizh. "	45	"	"	"
Alex. Proctor	40	"	Knocknober	Phila.
Cochran Sterling	28	"	Knockmult	St. John
Gilbert Smith	22	"	Benarees	Quebec
Elizh. "	22	"	"	"
Robert Fulgrave	22	"	Fermoyle	St. John
Allen Black	22	"	"	Quebec
George Lestly	30	"	Beatwell	Phila.
John Clarke	21	"	"	Quebec
Nancy "	30	"	"	"
Jane "	2	"	"	"
Mary Ross	22	"	Sconce	"
Thomas "	36	"	"	"
Jane "	24	"	"	"
Robert " Jnr.	6	"	"	"
Thomas "	4	"	"	"
George McLaughlin	33	R.C.	Mullanhead	"
William Smith .	22	Pres.	Fermullen	St. John
Wm. Devenny	20	E.C.	Farnlester	Quebec
John Smith	22	Pres.	Ballyhacket Glenahoy	"
Ellen "	32	"	"	"
John McLaughlin	1	"	"	"
James Blair, Sen.	26	"	Ballywildrick	Phila.
Mary "	20	"	"	"
John Clarke	20	"	"	"
Thomas Brosters	20	"	Glebe	"
Mary "	18	"	"	"
Jane "	20	"	"	"
Isaac McMillan	20	"	Ardina	"
Charles Hazlett	35	"	Bogtown	"

Emigrants 1834

Hugh Evans	20	Pres.	Articlave	St. John
John Beatty	28	"	"	N. York
Robert Ray	18	"	Knocknogher	Penn.
Margt. Hindman	22	"	Killyveaty	Quebec
Chas. Wilson	25	"	Pottagh	Phila.
John Bond	32	"	Bratwell	"
Anne "	27	"	"	"
Mary "	5	"	"	"
Margt. "	2½	"	"	"
Barbara Bond	3	"	"	"
John McLaughlin	25	R.C.	Bellany	"
Jane Dunlop	23	Pres.	Drumgully	N. York
Thos. Johnston	26	"	"	St. John
Robt. McClement	19	"	"	"
Wm. McLaughlin	29	"	Ballyhacket Glenaboy	Quebec
Mary McLaughlin	25	"	"	"
James Blair	22	"	Ballywildrick	Phila.
Isaac Wark	20	"	Ballywoodstock	"
John Alexander	20	"	"	"
Jas. Williams	18	"	Articlave	N. York

List of Passengers
on Ship TORONTO
from London to
New York,
21 July, 1845.

William Moore
Tim McCarty
John Whaling

List of Passengers
on Ship WARSAW
from Glasgow to
New York,
1 August, 1845.

Joseph Donnelly
Peter Diven
James Dortherky
Nancy   "
Jane   "
Ruth Caldwell
George Ballantine
Elizabeth Grogan
John Hamilton

List of Passengers
on Ship STEPHEN
WHITNEY from
Liverpool to New
York, 1 August,
1845.

Margaret O'Connor
Mary Beaty
Rebecca Church
Mary Gleeson
Elias Dudley
Mary Shaw
Francis Shaw
Agnes Gilmore
Sarah   "
Philip Conlin
Susan Falkner
James Campbell
Catherine Wilson
Isabella   "
Hugh Hays
John McLoughlin
Edward Evans
Thomas Develin
Alexander McMullin
Margaret   "
Elisha   "
Mary   "
Daniel   "
Alexander   "
John Murphy
Mary Murphy
Mary Brady
James Allen
Margaret Rourke
Mary McBride
John   "
Elizabeth Allen
William   "
Mary Quinlan
Michael Crawford
Sally McQuade
John Fullerton
Ellen   "
James Whiteford

Passengers on Ship
CLYDE from
Liverpool to New
York, 2 August,
1845.

James Cassidy
Mary Hunt
Francis McNulty
Timothy Daly
Anne   "
Patrick   "
Margaret Keeffe

James Keady
Maria   "
Michael Rochford
Catherine Hackett
Thomas Bourke
Mary Walker
Pat   "
Ann   "
Eliza   "
Michael   "
James Kelly
William Kelly
Mary Kelly
Patrick Smith
Andrew   "
William   "
Mary   "
Jane   "
Francis   "

Passengers on Ship
ST. GEORGE from
Liverpool to New
York, 29 September,
1845.

John Russell
Michael Russell
Marsella Russell
Thomas McManus
Jane Young
Susan Young
John McNally
Ann   "
Biddy   "
Mary   "
Margaret   "
Eliza   "
Ann   "
Patrick   "
Daniel   "
Hugh   "
Arthur O'Neil
James Hare
Sally Dougherty
Thomas Clancy
Mary Clancy
Ellen Wall
Eliza Drennan
John   "
William   "
Sarah   "
William Barrington
Margaret   "
Francis Shaw
Mary Shaw
John Mallon
William Black
Catherine Dougherty
Samuel Wallace
George Abrahm
Fredrick McGee
John Boylan
Eliza Wallace
Ellenor Martin
Mary E. Divine
Isabella Gascoyne
Margaret Patterson

Passengers on Ship
OHIO from Liverpool
to New York,
29 September, 1845.

John Richie
Margrate Richie
Francis Pollard
Joseph McCoy
John   "
Fanny   "
Joseph   "
Ann Kinney
Bridget Gibney
Elizabeth McCan
Ellen McCan
Sarah Linch
Rose Galloway
Rose Beaty

Mary Hurst
Bridget Hacket
Margrate   "
Patrick   "
Edmond   "
Susan   "
John   "
Elizabeth Mathews
Bridget Mathews
Anne Mathews
Catherine Mulany
Catherine Sullivan
Mary Brown
Andrew Sanderson
Mary Donovan
Thomas Hughes
Patrick   "
John   "

List of Passengers
on Ship SHARON
from Liverpool to
New York,
4 October, 1845.

Helena Nagle
Mary Charlot Nagle
Richard Tyler
Catherine Ohara
John McNight
Ann Weeks
Susannah FitsSimmon
Catherine Corr
Alexander Robinson
Jane McClusky
Susan   "
Thomas Woods
Ann Brena
Mary Cochrane

List of Passengers
on Ship NEW YORK
from Liverpool to
New York,
3 November, 1845.

William Maxwell
Mary Shanley
Ann   "
George Dickse
Jane   "
Thomas Manning
Bridget Gaynor
Judy   "
Mary Sweeny
Charles McKeon
Mary Patterson
Mary A. Reynolds
Mr. Corcoran
Mrs.   "
Mary   "
Ann   "
John Boyle
Owen Philben
John Henry
Honora Clifford
Mary Mead
Bridget Carr
Mary Mulligan
Peter Ennis
Ann Fitzpatrick

Passengers on Ship
ST. PATRICK from
Liverpool to New
York, 3 December,
1845.

Thomas McCarty
Margaret   "
Julia   "
Mary   "
Margaret   "
Catherine Kelly
Ann Reilly
Edward Byrne

Mary Freel
Sarah   "
Martha Lewis
Christopher Delany
Rachel   "
John Richardson
Mrs. Elizabeth
Richardson
Christopher Lawless
Bridget   "
Mary   "
Patrick   "
Bridget Carlin
Mary A. Fitzpatrick
James McMahon
Mary McDermott
John Riggs
Mrs. Riggs
Mary Reilly
Mathew Kirby
Ellen   "
Bridget   "
John   "
William Byrne

List of Passengers
on Ship STEPHEN
WHITNEY from
Liverpool to New
York, 6 April, 1846.

James Mahon
Ann   "
John   "
Joseph   "
James   "
Margaret   "
Madge   "
Mary Leary
Catherine Magan
Catherine Hannigan
Anne Harrison
Thomas Finnan
Anne Doyle
Mary Connor
Anne Sheridan
Thomas Donohoe
Patrick Reynolds
Mary Murray
Rose Boylan
Rose Smith
Margaret Shanky
Thomas   "
Mary Malone
Margaret Good

Passengers on Ship
JUNIUS from Liverpool
to New York, 1 May,
1846.

Dennis Lyons
Marcilla Lyons
James Doyle
Sally Noble
John Mourne
Christopher McCormack
Ann   "
Christian   "
Helen   "
Margaret   "
Patt Farrell
Margaret Farrell
Patt Farrell
Ann Casey
Catherine Casey
Mary   "
Biddy   "
Mary Hanlon
Mary   "
Ann McCormack
Dennis Sullivan
Dennis   "
Jeremiah   "
Dennis Farrell
Michael Connor
Jeremiah Casey
Mary McMahon

Florence Sullivan
William White
Dorothy Reilly
William Ryan
Lawrence Coopey
William Butler
Walter Madden
Mary   "
Richard   "
Alice   "
John Walsh
Johanna Walsh
Mary   "
Patt   "

List of Passengers
on Ship ALHAMBRA
from Dublin to New York,
1 June, 1846.

Patt Costigan
Cathrine Conway
Bridget Quinn
Michael Whelan
Julia Cuff
Bridget Madden
Thomas   "
John   "
Julia   "
Ellen   "
Mary   "
Susan   "
Michael   "
Sarah Leonard
Hugh   "
Bridget Carey
Michael Dunne
Catharine Lyons
Mary Donelly
Julia O'Neal
Bridget Farrelly
Thomas Fallon
Michael McDonal
Ann Lynch
Bridget Hely
James Lawless
James McLaughlin
Mary   "
Patt   "
Patt McCaffry
Mary Treacy
Malachy Treacy
Richard Scot
John Brenan
Miles McNulty
Patt Flanagan
Bridget Flanagan

List of Passengers on
Ship MILICETE from
Liverpool to New York,
13 July, 1846.

Thomas McDonnell
Mrs.   "
Mary   "
Pat Maher
Julia Maher
Julia Doorly
Margaret Brophy
Patrick Moore
Pat Maloney
Mrs.   "
George Slack
George Hall
M. Cunningham
Mary Collins
Michael Dooley
Mary   "
Mary Wise
Martin Sullivan
Mrs.   "
William Martin
William Stephen
George Dalzel
Patrick McDon...
Mrs.   "
Mary   "

Pat Whelan
John Hennessy
Mrs.   "
Michael Cosgrove
Mrs.   "
Abraham Thomas
James McNulty
Mrs.   "
Frederick ".
Henry   "
Emily   "

List of Passengers
on Ship ST. GEORGE
from Liverpool to
New York, 3 August,
1846.

Edward Moriarty
Bridget   "
Ellen   "
Catherine   "
Henry   "
James   "
Thomas Brennan
Mary   "
Margaret   "
Sarah   "
Patrick Curren
Michael Kelly
Michael Brannigan
Catherine Madden
Michael   "
Patrick Lavell
James Garrity
Anne   "
Daniel Ennis
Hugh White
Bernard McCullen
Patrick Quinn

List of Passengers
on Ship SARACEN
from Glasgow to
New York,
1 September, 1846.

Michael Benny
M. Fleury-Cash
James Lee
Agnes Lee
Elizabeth Lee
Thomas   "
James   "
Mary   "
Agnes   "
Charles Melone
Agnes   "
Cathrine Denny
Harriet McGlocken
Margaret Colwell
Benjamin Guthrie
Martha   "
Mary   "
Ann   "
Jane   "
Elizabeth   "

Passengers on Ship
PANAMA from
Liverpool to New
York, 12 October,
1846.

Christopher Carroll
Hohn Naughton
Catharine Naughton
Bridget McCauley
Mary Noon
John Nally
Mrs.   "
Patrick Nally
Mary Anne Nally
Mary Langan
Mary Smith
Jane Mitchell

Patrick Heslin
Maria   "
Margaret   "
Pat Lynch
William McNamara
Catherine Burns
Brien Golding
Eliza Brien
Andrew Brien
Cormick McGarry
Ellen   "
Catherine Brennan
Dennis Ryan
Margaret Lynch
Mary   "

Passengers on Ship
JOHN R. SKIDDY from
Liverpool to New
York, 4 November,
1846.

Bridget Mathews
James   "
Patrick   "
Margaret   "
Margaret McKeone
Patrick   "
Catherine McGuire
Ann Gray
Mary Gray
Catherine Gunning
Ann Hickey
Michael Shanley
Mary Ann   "
Maurice Connor
Ellen   "
Ellen Driscoll
Catherine McGuire
Ann Bohan
Thomas Searles
William Buckley
Dominick Brady

Passengers on Ship
WESTMINSTER from
London to New York,
4 December, 1846.

Edward Graham
Mary Fitzgerald
Joseph Cavena
William Nappier
Mary Ann Tallon
William   "

Passengers on Ship
AMERICAN from
Liverpool to New
York, 4 December,
1846.

Mary Waters
Patrick Waters
Edward Hollywood
Pat Clarke
Cathrine Oates
Bridget Tracy
Ailis   "
Mary Morris
Mary McLean
Mary Curley
Michael Madden
Thomas Donlen
John Hoban
Mary Connell
Peggy Fahee
Jude Quinlon
Margarett Quinlon

List of Passengers
on Ship SARDINIA
from Liverpool to
New York, 6 February,
1847.

Ann Cannon
Bridget Cannon
Peter   "
Nellie   "
Anna   "
Patrick Sheehan
John Lyons
Mary   "
Mary   "
Catherine Lyons
Andrew   "
Biddy   "
John   "
William Brown
Mary   "
A. Davis
Michael Lundy
Margrate Lundy
John   "
Thomas McNicholas
Margrate   "
John   "
Charles O'Dougherty
John Glynn
Eliza   "
Eliza   "
Mary Ann Glynn
Henry Marman
Margaret Plunkett
Julia   "
Mary Brady
Terence Molloy
Catherine Molloy

List of Passengers
on Ship ST. GEORGE
from Liverpool to
New York, 8 April,
1847.

Charles Gildea
Phillip   "
William Bishop
David Hogan
Ann   "
Morris Whittey
Margaret Whittey
Bessy McDonald
Theresa McDonald
Mary McGafney
James Curren
Honora Drew
Honora Dundon
Richard Wall
Mary   "
Abby   "
Margaret Parker
Mary Casey
Laurence Casey
Owen McCarthy
Briget Cummins
Patrick Early
Bridget   "
Thomas Flanery
John Kelly
Michael Hanley
Patrick King
Michael Nelan
Martin Fetherston
Bridget Smith
Catherine Mileagh
Letty Corrigan
Peter Cormick
John Carroll
Thomas Riley
Bridget Monaghan
Martin Crane
Thomas Collyer

Passengers on Ship
FREE TRADER from
Cork to New York,
25 June, 1847.

Thomas Bass
Margaret Bass
Mary Bigley
Catherine Sullivan
John   "
Michael Roche
Johanna Foley
John Munday
Maurice Munday
Thomas Kenedy
Bridget Kirby
Daniel Sweeney
John Brian
Arthur McGuire
Hermione Harris
Timothy Murphy
Hannah Connell
Thomas Good
William Deane
Mary Desmond
Dennis Callaghan
Maria Townley
William Flynn
Bridget Scannell

List of Passengers
on Ship EMMA PRESCOTT
from Galway to New
York, 10 August,
1847.

Michael Burke
Pat Grady
Susan Tierney
Thomas Tiernan
Pat Joyce
Mary Lyons
Peter Rooney
Pat Hegarty
Austin Carrigg
Biddy   "
Mary Leyden
Bridgit Ahern
Mary McDonagh
Thomas Conroy
Martin Cosgriffe
Pat Crow
Mary   "
Edward Folan
Mary   "
Dominick Spelman
Anne Edwards
Mary Ready
James Connole
Mary O'Brien
Hanna   "

List of Passengers
on Ship YORKSHIRE
from Liverpool to
New York,
27 October, 1847.

John Irving
Ann Leonard
Mary Spencer
Ellen Carrol
Johannah Scanlan
Mary McCarty
William Longhead
Francis Farrel
Peter McHugh
Pat Dailey
Michael Gillooly
Mary Black
Mary Griffin
Thomas Brady
Bess Flinn
Catharine McGowan
Thomas McMahan
John Wall
John Griffin
Edmond Quin

Joseph Brown
Catharine Coile
Catharine Coleman
Ann Morrison

Passengers on Ship
LANCASHIRE from
Liverpool to New York,
13 December, 1847.

Mrs. O'Brien
Elizabeth O'Brien
John   "
Thomas   "
Mary Mahaffy
Anna   "
John   "
Sally McGarty
Mary Doyle
Michael Welch
William Clarey
John Purcell
John Moore
Ellen   "
Mary   "
James   "
John McGough
Michael Donnely
Alice Deary
Ann   "
Dan Darcy

Passengers on Ship
SARAH SANDS from
Liverpool to New York,
10 February, 1848.

Archibald Montgomery
James. B. Gamble
John McBride
James Ross
Mary Flannagan
John Thompson
Henry Quinn
Mary Ann Quinn
William H. Culloston
John Myers
William Russill
James Murphy
Pat Malony
James Smith
Jane   "
Martin Lardner
Bernard Murty
Ann   "
John Johnston
John Prentice
Andrew McKinny
John Davies
John Wilson
Owen O'Connor
Peter Smith

List of Passengers on
Ship SIR ROBERT PEEL
from Liverpool to New
York, 30 March, 1848.

Catherine Hughes
Mary   "
Ann   "
Dennis Driscoll
Jane   "
Bernard Brady
John   "
Ann   "
Edward Reilly
John McGowan
Susan   "
Richard Hickey
David O'Keefe
John Thompson
John Flannery
Patrick Kearney
James Cavanagh
Michael Duane

125

Bridget Duane
John Quin
Timothy Collins
Hugh McGrinnis
Bridget Connaughton
James Barret

List of Passengers
on Ship CONSTITUTION
from Belfast to New
York, 8 May, 1848.

John Blake
Catherine Blake
George   "
Jane   "
James   "
William   "
John   "
Henry   "
Thomas   "
William McBride
Ann   "
Thomas   "
Mary   "
Jane   "
Anne   "
William   "
John   "
George   "
Joseph   "
Eliza Smith
Isabella Crozier
Arabella Ferguson
Mary   "
Hugh   "
George   "
Sophie   "
Anne Johnston
Eliza Richardson
John Simpson
William Campbell
James Robinson
John Mullen
Eliza Love
Jane   "
James Donaldson
David Reed
Jane Todd
Robert Toben

List of Passengers
on Ship AGENORA
from Liverpool to
New York, 10 July,
1848.

William Laing
Mrs.   "
William   "
Margaret   "
Robert   "
Andrew   "
Walter   "
Charles   "
Emphemia   "
Elizabeth   "
Isabella   "
Andrew Haggart
Margaret Davis
Walter   "
Josee Scott
Helen Moore
William Clarke
Robert Lamb
George Kennedy
Henry Spencer
Mary Corcoran
William Graham
John Nowlan
Mathew Stokes
James Lavelle
Catharine Dowling
Pat Murtagh
Thomas Halpin
Pat Conway

List of Passengers
on Ship NICHOLAS
BIDDLE from
Liverpool to New
York, 7 September,
1848.

Peter Scott
Michael O'Connor
Miss Carroll
Patrick Hickey
Richard Barrington
Mrs.   "
Henry   "
Mr. Cassidy
John Lahy
William Allen
Ann Tansey
Mary Keane
Patrick Johnston

Passengers on Ship
INTRINSIC from
Liverpool to New
York, 6 November,
1848.

John Rian
John Toban
Mary McPartan
Mary McDermott
Judith Coffee
Honora Flin
David Platt
Martin Tain
Edward Fullerton
Patrick McPartin
James Brady
James McBrian
Daniel Barr
Morgan Brean
Richard Hamphrey
Michael Gallacher
Jeremiah Sulivan
William Morgan
Mary   "
Bridget Higgins
James Rice
Patrick Collins
James Gibbon
Stephen Duggan
James Hunter
Laurie Ward
John Biggly
Catherine Hay
Thomas Mangan
Robert Evans
Bridget Cane
James Flemin
Patrick Clifford
John Scully

List of Passengers
on Ship GLENMORE
from Belfast to New
York, 29 January,
1849.

Mary Donaldson
William Donaldson
Charles Stars
Andrew Largoon
Molly Tatton
Mary Steel
Mary Morton
Andrew Batty
George Scarlett
James McDonald
Thomas Bell
Ann   "
Margaret Elliott
Bridget Frazier
Robert Doran
John Whitelock
Biddy Malley
Ellen Rodgers
Ann McVeagh
Thomas Milliga
John English

Richard Shephard
William Munroe

Passengers on Ship
WEST POINT from
Liverpool to New
York, 6 March, 1849.

Richard Reid
Thomas   "
Julia   "
Marcella McCormick
Francis Whelan
Thomas Mahon
Charles Reilly
Mary   "
Edward Mannin
Edward Daily
Pat Cunningham
Jane Sheil
John Graham
Bernard Banks
Luke Kearney
Mary Taite
Bernard Kennedy
Catherine Donlan
Peter Scully
Pat McCsee
Ann Lynch
James Dimond
Richard Butler
Peter Minhin
Mark Lenehan
John Mansfield
James Heathers

Passengers on Ship
ANN HARLEY from
Glasgow to New
York, 29 May, 1849.

Duncan McVean
Anne Hescans
George McMurray
Peter Bird
John Kells
Briget Conroy
Bernard Quinn
Thomas Callihan
John McTaggart
Andrew Haggarty
Batty Creely
Samuel Ross
James Baxter Boyd
James Mooney
Samuel Jones

Passengers on Ship
W. H. HARBECK from
Liverpool to New
York, 3 July, 1849.

Denis McMahon
Mary Hogan
Michael Close
Thomas Gannon
Martin Oakley
Mary Ann Armstrong
Niall Battle
Patrick Finn
Arthur Henry
Patrick Gray
Thomas Igo
Mary Ann Wallace
Ellen Reeves
John Cummins
John Neary
Phillip Carberry
Daniel Rack
Thomas Gough
Thomas Penbroke
Garrett Stack
James Downes
Richard Clancy
Patrick Ireland
William Hill
James Mealy

Passengers on Ship
ST. PATRICK from
Liverpool to New
York, 3 September,
1849.

Catharine McGarry
Julia Lynch
Mary Cullen
Mary Murray
Eliza Jenkins
Martha Flanagan
Hugh Dyott
Catharine Monaghan
Michael McAuliff
Mary O'Hara
William Tierney
Ann Drury
Patrick Tighe
Joseph Clarke
Catharine Farley
Matilda Hoggs
Thomas Cox
Mary Devlin
Catherine Rock
Ann Ellen McCann
John Hammond
James Creswell
John Noble

List of Passengers
on Ship SWAN from
Cork to New York,
4 September, 1849.

Elizabeth Ahern
Mary   "
John   "
Patrick Hallihan
Mary   "
Thomas   "
Patrick   "
John   "
Bridget   "
Mary   "
Nany   "
Michael   "
James Kennedy
Maurice Stanton
Johannah Conroy
John Colbert
David   "
Timothy Magillacuddy
Thomas Dorgan
Margaret Dorgan
Maurice Dargan
Thomas   "
Margaret   "
Johanna   "
Thomas Cantillion
Bridget   "
Mary   "
John   "
Michael Connor
Patrick Quirk
Pat Crowley
Michael Murphy

List of Passengers
on Ship MARIA from
Belfast to New York,
5 November, 1849.

John Jenkins
Nancy Young
Pat Morgan
John Bole
William Harrington
Sarah   "
Mary   "
Isabella   "
Mary Farrell
Thomas Farrell
Isabella Nugent
Biddy Rogers
Eliza McGlone
William McGlone
Gregg   "
Joseph   "

Margaret Waters
James Ritchie
Mary   "
Biddy Graham
Thomas Wilson
Nano Wood
Thomas Phillips
James Bole
Thomas Andrews
John Sampson

List of Passengers
on Ship NEW WORLD from
Liverpool to New York,
15 January, 1850.

William Morris
Peter McMahon
Ann   "
Margaret   "
Bridgett   "
Catharine   "
Anthony   "
Bessy   "
Mick Riley
Catharine Ginty
John Dickson
Pat Kelly
Thomas Kelly
Owen Dunne
Mary Kelly
Ann   "
Bridget   "
Michael   "
John Jennings
Margaret Armstrong
Farrell Dugan
John Delaney
Michael Kelly
Elizabeth Kelly
Pat McGaw
Margaret McGaw
Peter Whelan
John Kelly
John Donaldson
Catharine Hogan
Maria   "
Catherine Gibney

List of Passengers
on Ship BRYAN ABBS from
Limerick to New York.
7 March, 1850.

John Slattery
Mary Cahill
Thomas Carroll
Mary   "
John   "
Biddy   "
Hanah Hayes
Johanna Morrissey
Mick Sheehan
Catherine Sheehan
Mary Brazil
Michael Brazil
Patrick Bourke
Mary Begley
Patrick Hassett
Eliza Healey
Mary Quade
Betty Farrell
Catherine O'Dea
Honor Hogan
William Jackson
Ellen Purcell
Thomas   "
Abby Nulty
Anne Johnson
Edward Quirk
Patrick Forrestal
Johanna Gleeson
John Darcy

EMIGRANT PASSENGER LISTS TO AMERICA

List of Passengers from Co. Roscommon to New York via Liverpool on Ship ROSCIUS, 19. September, 1847. Age given after the name.

John Carlon or Carlin	30
Honor "	40
Bridget "	18
Ellen "	9
Mary "	7
Patrick Colgan	36
Mary "	40
Michael "	19
Patrick "	8
Anne "	7
Bridget "	12
Margaret "	16
Terence Connor	50
Mary "	35
Thomas "	20
Mary "	11
Patrick Croghan	28
John "	24
Margaret "	26
Martin Donlan or Donnellan	32
Hugh McDermott	50
Eliza "	48
Bernard "	28
Hugh "	12
James "	26
John "	24
William "	18
Anne "	25
Bessy "	20
Ellen "	13
Rosanna "	14
Susan "	22
Catherine Mullera, Mullerea or Mulere	30
Patrick Narry or Neary	40
Mary "	28
Bridget "	1
Richard Padian	32
Mary "	30
James "	9
William "	12
Bridget "	10
Maria "	6
James Reynolds	28
Bridget "	60
John "	24
Joseph "	22
Thomas "	40
Bridget "	14
Catherine "	2
James Stuart	63
Ellen "	60
George "	20
Ellen "	18
Patrick Stuart or Stewart	18
Catherine "	25

List of Passengers from Co. Roscommon to New York via Liverpool on Ship CREOLE, 18 October, 1847.

William Brennan or Brannon	70
Andrew "	20
Daniel "	24
Gilbert "	7
Roger "	28
William "	26
Jane "	18
John Carrington	14
Ellen Costello	55
John Costello	8
Bridget "	16
Mary "	18
Mary Deffely or Deffley	60
George Deffely or Deffely	26
James "	20
Patrick "	60
Mary "	55
Bridget "	14
Patrick Donlon	28
Anne "	27
Patrick Donlan	60
Edward "	25
John "	36
Patrick "	27
William "	16
Margaret "	14
Garret Fallon	32
Eliza "	26
Bridget "	20
Thomas Fallon	33
Anne "	32
Martin "	5
Ellen "	8
Mary "	1
Patrick "	16
Bridget "	25
Thomas Fallon	43
Mary "	18
James Hanly or Hanley	30
Susan "	30
John "	7
Peter "	5
Thomas Hanly or Hanley	60
Mary "	50
Darby "	16
Edward "	18
Michael "	13
Patrick "	24
Honor "	22
Mary "	19
Michael McCormick	19
Honor "	17
Margaret "	19
Sally "	16
John Magan	34
Patrick Magan	22
Anne "	28
Ellen "	26
Catherine "	24
John Maguire	30
Mary "	30
Patrick "	5
Mary "	3
James Mullera	50
Bridget "	50
Denis "	12
Anne "	9
Bridget "	10
Mary Neary	35
James "	3
Anne "	7
John "	16
Bridget "	14
Catherine Neary	24
Catherine Quinn	30
George Stuart	40
Bridget "	32
Charles "	6
John "	4
Mary "	10
John Stuart	21
William Stuart	47
Bridget "	43
Charles "	14
Michael "	12
William "	8
Eliza "	10

List of Passengers from Co. Roscommon to New York via Liverpool on Ship METOKA, 26 September, 1847.

Patrick Colgan	
Anne "	40
Bernard "	8
Michael "	4
William "	1
Anne "	12
Betty "	6
Betty Colgan	6
Mary "	15
Patrick Finne or Finn	35
Margaret "	24
Michael "	22
Bridget "	20
Margaret "	9
Michael Gallagher	24
Margaret "	20
James Hanly or Hanley	64
Betty "	54
James "	14
John "	18
Martin "	22
Patrick "	20
Roger "	12
Mary "	17
Catherine McCormack or McCormick	55
Patrick "	22
Peter "	15
Anne "	9
Ellen "	30
Edward McCormick	40
Margaret "	32
Edward "	4
James "	1
Thomas "	8
Anne "	14
Catherine "	6
Mary "	18
Mary McCormick or McCormack	26
Anne "	20
Bridget "	24
Mary McDermott	44
John "	13
Thomas "	15
Bridget "	11
Ellen "	20
Mary "	17
Patrick McDonnell	24
John Moran	56
Winifred Moran	44
Francis "	7
John "	15
Catherine "	10
James Mullera or Mulera	22
Thomas "	20
Bernard O'Neal or O'Neill	45
Betty "	40
Bernard "	13
John "	16
Anne "	20
Thomas Reynolds	33
Mary "	30
Andrew "	5
James "	8
John "	6
Thomas "	2
Mary "	infant
Andrew "	27
Bridget "	60
Honor Winters or Winter	60
Thomas "	30
Honor "	18
Margaret "	24
Catherine "	1
John Wynne or Winn	52
Patrick "	22
Mary "	13

List of Passengers from Co. Roscommon to New York via Liverpool on Ship CHANNING, 13 March, 1848.

William Cline	58
Margaret Colgan	66
Thomas Costello	46
Mary "	54
Martin "	12
Michael "	14
Pat "	17
Thomas "	6
Anne "	16
Pat Farrell	55
Mary "	50
William Farrell	18
Bridget "	14
Mary "	16
Francis Fox	35
Mary "	33
Francis "	4
Pat "	7
Thomas "	26
Catherine Fox	16
Bernard Gill	30
Michael Hoare	35
Mary "	30
James "	5
John "	7
Thomas "	2
Bridget "	8
Mary "	11
James Kelly	45
Mary "	40
Edward "	18
James "	16
John "	2
Anne "	12
Catherine Kelly	14
Eliza "	10
Ellen "	7
Mary "	20
Pat McCormick	32
Catherine McCormick	28
Michael "	4
Pat "	6
Anne "	8
Mary "	20
Andrew McDonnell	18
Anne "	22
Ellen "	16
Michael McDonnell	50
Michael "	21
Catherine McDonnell	24
Mary "	18
John McGann or McGanne	24
Atty "	19
Luke "	20
Anne "	26
Mary "	15
John "	1
Mary McGann or McGanne	40
James "	18
John "	5
Thomas "	8
Anne "	1
Bridget "	10
Eliza "	14
Thomas McManus	29
James "	20
Thomas McManus	24
Andrew "	21
Pat "	23
Mary "	18
Mary Madden	46
Thomas Madden	13
Catherine Madden	16
Anne Mullera	25
Pat "	29
John Mullera	35
Sarah "	30
Francis "	6
James "	4
John "	8
Patrick "	12
Thomas "	10
Pat "	25
Thomas Mullera	36
Mary "	30
Thomas "	6
Anne "	2
Bridget "	55
Bartholomew or Bartley Narry	45
Michael "	26
William "	36
Michael Reynolds	9
Bridget Stewart	35
James "	17
Michael "	,5
Bridget8 "	14
Francis Stewart	'56
Anne "	50
John "	30

Bridget Wynne	30
Michael Wynne	60
Bell "	55
James "	16
Catherine "	13
Mary "	18

List of Passengers from Co. Roscommon to New York via Liverpool on Ship PROGRESS, 25 April, 1848.

Luke Caveney	46
Mary "	40
Edward "	12
Luke "	10
Patrick "	17
Thomas "	15
Anne "	7
Catherine Caveney	1
Mary "	19
James Connor	45
Honor "	44
Martin "	22
John Connor	37
Catherine Connor	27
Pat Kelly	40
Eliza "	36
Thomas "	12
William Kelly	8
Anne "	10
Bridget "	1
Maria "	14

List of Passengers from Galway to Quebec on Ship SEA BIRD, 15 June, 1848.

Michael Brien, Byrne or Bryne	22
Anne Bryne	20
Anne Carney	20
John Carty or McCarthy	60
Bridget "	55
Edward "	12
Martin "	15
Peter "	10
Thomas "	14
Mary "	25
Peggy "	21
Ann "	2
John Casey	16
Pat "	15
Michael Coffey	20
Bridget Conway	42
Pat "	16
Mary "	12
James Conway	27
Margaret or Mary Conway	24
Thomas Conway	7
Pat "	2
Margaret "	3
Bridget Cosgrave	50
James "	13
John "	26
Michael "	16
Pat "	7
Peter "	29
Thomas "	20
Anne "	18
Margaret "	17
Mary "	10
James Cosgrave	41
Mary "	37
Pat "	6
Thomas "	3
William "	2½
Catherine "	2
Maria "	8
Anne "	12
Bridget "	22
John Cosgrave	24
Francis "	20
Ann8 "	34
James "	1
John "	4
Thomas "	11
Bridget "	12

Julia Cosgrave	22
Pat Cosgrave	35
Mary "	32
John "	4
Bridget "	3
Thomas Cosgrave	38
Hannah "	23
Hannah "	1½
Peter Craughwell	40
Winifred "	36
John "	4
Patrick "	6
Bridget "	14
Catherine "	18
Ellen "	11
Kitty "	20
Mary "	16
Rose "	13
Thomas Craughwell	20
Pat "	15
Honoria "	18
Mary "	16
Thomas Daw or Dawe	32
Bridget "	28
Pat "	2
Biddy "	4
Mary Ann "	½
James "	20
John "	18
Anne "	20
Mary "	16
Pat Kennedy	28
Anne "	24
Bridget "	24
Catherine Kennedy	19
Pat "	10
Pat (John) Kennedy	48
Mary "	40
John "	16
Thomas "	6
Ann "	14
Biddy "	16
Bridget "	20
Catherine "	18
Hannah "	12
Mary "	10
Peggy "	4
Anthony Kilcannon	17
Bridget Killalea	35
John "	8
Mark "	1
Margaret "	7
Mary "	11
Bridget Killalea	16
Darby Killalea	46
Margaret "	44
John "	15
Bridget "	9
Mary "	16
John Killalea	19
Mathias Killalea	45
Sally "	40
Lawrence "	8
Mathias "	10
Michael "	19
Thomas "	14
Peggy "	16
Patrick Killalea	42
Patrick "	17
Henry Dempsey	50
Catherine "	47
Henry "	4
John "	13
Michael "	10
Patrick "	21
Anne "	13
Catherine "	1½
Margaret "	18
Mary "	15
John Dempsey	57
Bridget "	55
John "	30
Biddy "	30
Ann "	5
Catherine Dempsey	1
Margaret "	6
Michael Dempsey	32
Catherine "	31
Pat "	5
Bridget "	8
Bryan Dolan	17

John Dolan	15
Thomas Dolan	15
Catherine Donnellan, Donolan or Donlon	55
John "	26
Pat "	20
Thomas "	30
Bridget "	17
Catherine "	33
Thomas Dooley	1
Mary Dowd	20
Mary Egan	20
Nicholas Flannery or Flanary	40
Nancy "	38
John "	½
Michael "	12
Pat "	13
Catherine "	8
Ellen "	5
Margaret "	7
Mary "	10
Winifred "	4
John Foster	20
Michael Golden	24
Hannah "	24
Thomas "	1
Mary "	3
Margaret Gormally	37
Mary Gormally or Gormley	36
John "	13
Thady "	4
Bridget "	11
Catherine "	9
Denis Grady or Gready	30
John "	21
Honoria "	20
Mary Gready	18
Thomas Guinnessy	22
Bridget "	20
Judy Hambury or Hansbury	23
Michael Horan	38
Anne "	34
Michael "	6
Thomas "	2
Catherine "	4
Eliza "	16
Catherine Jennings	19
Bryan Kelly	21
Ellen C. Rafferty	22
John Rafferty	50
Mary Ann Rafferty	50
John "	15
Pat "	18
Bridget "	24
Catherine "	20
Mary Ann "	22
Mary Rafferty	40
John Jun. Rafferty	20
Pat "	16
Thomas "	12
Catherine "	15
Mary Spencer	13
Anne White	16
John 'Black' White	50
Bridget "	41
John "	16
Martin "	12
Michael "	6
Pat "	14
Biddy "	15
Jane "	3
Mary "	20
Nancy "	18
Pat White	26
Biddy Loftus	40
John "	15
Michael "	15
Thomas "	6
Biddy "	9
Ellen "	3
Mary "	22
Mary Ann "	16
Bridget Lynskey	25
Michael Lynskey	50
Judy "	40
John "	16
Thomas "	21
Catherine "	10

Mary Lynskey	12
Timothy Lynskey	40
Richard Manly	48
Bridget "	40
James "	9
John "	12
Richard "	3
Bridget "	16
Ellen "	18
Mary "	14
John Morrissey	40
Hannah "	33
Pat "	3
Bridget "	2
Catherine "	4
Ellen "	11
Maria "	10
Thomas (Roger) Morrissey	37
Peggy "	36
John "	12
Bridget "	6
Mary "	8
Mary Mullen or Mullin	45
John "	14
Catherine Naughton	26

List of Passengers from Galway to Quebec on Ship NORTHUMBERLAND, 17 August, 1849.

Mary Byrne	20
Michael Byrne or Birne	41
Bridget "	38
John "	8
Michael "	11
Timothy "	4
Ellen "	18
Pat Byrne	15
Bridget Byrne	26
Thomas Byrne	21
Ellen "	20
Mary "	19
Thomas Carroll	31
Bridget "	23
John "	22
Michael "	24
Bridget "	15
Mary Ann "	18
Ann Rafferty	20
Mary "	½
Owen Carty	22
Catherine Carty	20
John Conway	31
Biddy "	20
Catherine Conway	36
Mary "	25
Mary Ann "	41
Ellen Cosgrave	24
William "	21
Ellen "	19
Michael Craughwell or Croghell	20
Ann "	22
Ellen "	16
Nancy Craughwell	41
Pat "	20
Margaret "	17
Peggy Kennedy	40
John "	15
Thomas "	7
Margaret Curley	30
Biddy "	5
John Kelly (Sen.)	52
Barney "	21
John Kelly (Jnr.)	24
Michael Kelly	18
Thomas "	19
Ann "	17
Bridget "	8
Mary "	11
Margaret Kelly	35
Catherine "	9
Margaret "	7
Mary Connolly	18
Mary Kennedy	24
Thomas Kennedy	30
Biddy "	20
Honoria "	18

Peggy Kennedy	17
Ellen "	3
Kennedy	33
Daniel Kennedy	18
Michael "	17
Pat "	12
Ann "	15
Bridget "	9
Catherine "	9
Mary Ann "	6
Abegail Killalea	27
Biddy "	25
Catherine "	20
Ellen "	17
Catherine Killalea	45
Ann "	20
Catherine "	7
Margaret "	15
Bridget Egan	51
John "	18
Michael "	10
Pat "	14
Michael Glynn	55
Julia "	53
Michael "	21
Pat "	16
Timothy "	8
Bridget "	26
Margaret "	19
Mary "	24
Peggy "	23
Leonard	
Peter Grady or Gready	31
Mary "	27
Thomas "	½
Catherine 8 "	2
Thomas Grady or Gready	41
Catherine "	36
John "	14
Michael "	3 mths.
Pat "	6
Thomas "	2
Ann "	11
Bridget "	4
John Guinnessy	27
Hanora "	25
John "	2
Thomas "	3 mths.
Pat "	55
Mary "	51
James "	20
Malachy "	16
Pat "	13
Ann "	14
Catherine Guinness	3
Catherine Hanbury, Hambury or Hamberry	36
Michael Hart	36
Pat "	2
Mary "	8
Catherine Hart	32
James "	23
John "	1
Michael "	17
Thomas "	16
Catherine "	14
Catherine Kelly	21
Ellen Rafferty	24
Catherine "	15
Mary "	20
Bridget White	36
John "	6
Pat "	16
Bridget "	8
Margaret "	10
Mary "	16
Bridget White	39
Ann "	14
Catherine "	6
Mary "	15
Sally "	19
Michael White	21
Margaret "	22
Thomas White	26
Honor or Harriet White	28
Michael "	6
Bridget "	3
Margaret "	7
John Looby, Luby or Lubey	15

Margaret or Mary Lynskey	61
Mary "	20
Thomas McLoughlin	37
Ellen "	35
Bridget "	4
Catherine "	1
Anthony Manahan or Monaghan	20
Pat Mannion	38
Peggy "	40
John "	17
Malachy "	10
Pat "	13
Thomas "	8
Mary "	5

List of Passengers from Cork via Liverpool to New York on board COLUMBUS, 7 September, 1849.

John Casey	56
Michael Casey	13
Bab or Barbara Casey	19
Johanna "	18
Rosean "	16
David Connell	45
Margaret "	35
Dan "	15
Jerry "	10
John "	13
Pat "	3
Eileen "	½
Johanna "	8
Margaret "	9
Mary "	5
Patrick Connell	50
Ellen "	44
Dan "	16
John "	13
Philip "	19
Johanna "	4
Judy "	15
Margaret "	7
Mary "	22
John Cremin	28
Kitty "	25
Timothy "	3 mths.
Daniel Daly	50
Margaret Daly	50
John "	26
Bessy "	25
Judy "	20
Margaret "	19
Denis (Daniel) Danihy	40
Johanna "	40
Con "	15
Dan "	17
Denis "	7
Matt "	5
Michael "	13
Mary "	19
Mary "	13
Denis (Matt) Danihy	60
Johanna "	50
Daniel "	19
Denis "	7
John "	17
Matt "	21
Michael "	11
Tade "	3
Bridget "	15
Eileen "	10
Mary "	23
Tim Danihy	40
Mary "	42
Con "	3
Dan "	13
Michael "	8
Tade "	5
Nelly "	10
Daniel Fenigan	55
Johanna "	48
Johanna "	20
Judy "	7
Kitty "	10
Mary "	22
John Foley or Fowley	52
Eileen "	50

Dan Foley or Fowley	18
John " "	21
Pat " "	16
Eileen "	28
Johanna" "	11
Julea " "	8
Mary " "	24
John Galvin	32
Margaret Galvin	30
Patrick "	2
Tade "	4
Biddy "	6
Tade "	30
Margaret Keeffe or O'Keeffe	50
Eugene "	17
Jeane "	13
Johanna "	21
Nano "	23
Daniel Kelleher	69
Dan "	29
Kitty "	26
Tade "	2
Kitty "	3
Mary "	21
John "	36
Connor or Daniel Leary	55
Ellen Leary	50
Jerry "	11
John "	18
Eileen "	16
Johanna "	20
Mary "	13
Peggy "	5
Matthew Leary	50
Mary "	45
Dan "	6
Darby "	18
John "	16
Matt "	1
Pat "	13
Johanna "	4
Judy "	20
Denis McAuliffe	28
Michael "	22
Robert "	17
Johanna "	24
Margaret McCarthy	22
John Sullivan	35
Ellen "	30
John "	½
Mary "	25

List of passengers from Galway to New York on ship BARK CARACTACUS 4 May, 1849

James Morgan, labourer	24
James Lawless, do.	50
Rose Lawless, spinster	41
John Keely, labourer	33
Judy Murphy, spinster	40
Biddy Murphy, do.	21
Peter Higgins, labourer	30
Martin King, do.	21
Honor Fury, spinster	25
Michael Morris, carpenter	
Thomas Murphy, labourer	19
Margaret Cahill, child	14
Honor " do.	11
Patrick Tynan, mason	41
Peter Scully, labourer	19
John Tracey, do.	21
Thomas Donoghue, do.	18
Thomas Killen, do.	20
Dudley Ridge, do.	21
Sabina Dolan, spinster	17
John Burke, child	5
Mary Kelly, spinster	18
Catherine Kelly, do.	16
Judy Burke, spinster	30
John Cunniff, labourer	45
John Fagan, "	25
Biddy Connors, spinster	19
Conor Brodie, labourer	27
John Burke, do.	27
James Nolan, labourer	22
James Shaughnessy,	18

List of passengers from Belfast to New York on ship Emma Pearl, 4, May, 1849

Andrew McClelland, labourer	60
Sarah " do.	55
Margaret " spinster	27
Richard " labourer	23
Mary McKnight, spinster	60
William McKnight,	22
Elizabeth "	21
Mary " infant	
Thomas Clegg, labourer	35
Sarah "	21
David " infant	
Thomas Boyd	28
Margaret Boyd	26
John Rogan	24
Rose Rogan	25
Patrick Bannon	56
Mary "	40
Cecily "	19
James "	17
Mary "	9
Betty "	7
Anne "	3
Catherine " 10 months	
Daniel Comb	21
John McComb	26
John Moreland	29
Eliza "	29
Thomas " infant	
William Bryen	25
Catherine Bryen	25
Margaret "	3
Eliza " infant	
Francy Wallace	26
John Fox	26
Bernard Lally	24
Bridget "	24
Henry Hollan, labourer	40
Eliza "	35
Sarah "	12
Rachel Hogg, spinster	17
John Donaghy	38
William Donaghy	3
John " infant	
Daniel McDonald	21
Bernard McNally	20
Biddy Canavan	16
William Boyle	20
James Hamilton	20
Nancy McDonald	20
Isabella Anderson	34
Robert "	14
Rebecca "	7
William "	5
John Donley	24
Jane "	22
Thomas Maguire	25
Mary Maguire	17

LIST of passengers from NEWRY, Ireland, to New York on Ship JAMES 10 May, 1849

Michael Vallely, labourer	30
Margaret " wife	28
James McKeon, labourer	20
Sally McKenna, servant	20
Margaret O'Neill do.	23
Susan " do.	19
John Hanvey, labourer	18
Pat " do.	15
Bridget Hanvey, servant	11
Jane McNally, do.	19
Hugh McGeogh, labourer	21
Jane McCartin, servant	19
Bridget Quin, "	17
Mary Fanning, "	23
Mary McGrory, "	18
William Dongan, shoemaker	30
Jane " wife	25
Anne McDermott, servant	24
Roger White, labourer	20

Passengers on Ship
MARCHIONESS OF BUTE
from Newry to New
York, 15 May, 1850.

Rosanna Halligan
Eliza   "
James Wilson
Samuel Todd
Edward Cassidy
Patrick   "
John Quinn
Peter Connor
James McShane
Rose Garvey
Christy Garvey
William Kennedy
Jane Hamilton
James Devlin
Patrick McDonnell
Alice Cassidy
Margaret Sinclair
Alice Simms
Thomas McBride
Stephen Sloan
Betty Managhan
Margaret Toal
John Hanratty
Michael Donaghy
Alice McVeigh
Ann Collins
Francis Stephens
Bridget Delan
James Wright
Catharine Dunlop

Passengers on Ship
INFANTRY from
Liverpool to New
York, 29 July,
1850.

Biddy Doyle
Patrick Doyle
John   "
Kitty   "
Michael Walsh
Ellen   "
Thomas McCartney
James Rooney
William Carberry
Mary Curley
Thomas Plunkett
Sara Dunn
Patrick Byrne
Bridget McGee
Alice Cullan
Ann Kinlan
Patrick Riley
Patrick Haley
Patrick Lanagan
Michael Doran
Philip Ready
Daniel Heaney
Ann Ashley
Ann McCuskin
Thomas Dawson
Philip   "
Sarah Franklin
William Stewart
June Whyte
Biddy McGlone
Thomas Kearney
William Carroll
Daniel Meehan

List of Passengers
on Ship ADAM CARR
from Glasgow to New
York, 2 September,
1850.

William Glendinning
Catherine   "
Richard Henderson
Ellen   "
John Stewart
Robert Davis
Mary Ann Shearer

John Shearer
Thomas Foster
Michael McNally
Daniel Fitzpatrick
Dennis Dee
James Laden
Michael Donhay
Ann   "
Elizabeth Banks
Thomas Miller
James Dowdall
David Meagan
William Phillips
James Scott
Robert Maxwell
Jane Breen
Margaret Robinson
William Robertson
Rose McGraw
Peter McGuire
John Downey
Conn Connor
Hugh McLaughlin
Ellen McCue
Margaret White

List of Passengers
on Ship ISAAC WRIGHT
from Liverpool to
New York,
1 November, 1850.

Mary Scanlon
Patrick Scanlon
Francis McManus
Bridget Eagan
Julia Dailey
Mary Coffey
Elizabeth Connell
Daniel Sullivan
John Finegan
Bella Hughes
John Smithwick
Johanna Higgins
Martin Gleeson
Ann Haligan
Catherine Thornton
Pat Pender
James Lapan
John Cahill
P. Garvey
James Degan
Patrick Kirby
Judy Quigley
Mary Blake
Maria Ellis
Mary Devane
Thomas Hanley
Malachy Collins
Ann Flaherty
Margaret Usher
John Monaghan
Thomas Sheady
Eliza Reardon

List of Passengers
on Ship COLONIAL
from Liverpool
to New York,
23 January, 1851.

John Grady
Michael Cargan
Thomas Martin
James Bruton
Michael Earley
Edward Shilley
John Fagan
Margaret Foley
Patrick Watson
James Carey
Mary Mackham
John Cotter
James Flemming
Eliza Kernan
Bridget Bransfield
Catherine Callahan
John Donlan
Catherine Hopkins

Michael Whelan
Ann Mullins
Ellen Luby
Edward Butler
Maria Fox
Ellen Coffee
Jane Miller
Mary Arnold
John Drew
James Haggerty
Michael Ahern
Catherine Rogers
Margaret Slattery
Dennis Graham
Owen Cosgrave

List of Passengers
on Ship WILLIAM
from Westport to
New York, 30 April,
1851.

Hugh Bones
Honor   "
John Salmon
Bridget Brogan
Ann   "
Michael Gannon
Mary Malley
James Coleman
Nancy Handers
Martin Flannery
Philip Gibbons
Patrick Heraghty
Winny Garravan
Maria McEneely
Honor Joyce
John Loftus
Honor Kerigan
Elizabeth Murtagh
Ellen Scully
Frank Quin
Patrick Durkan
Michael Beckett
Edward Gough
Ann Short
Daniel Murdock
Mary Cain
Patrick McNally
John Timlin
Patrick Magan
Honor Langan
Patrick Gibbons
James Gill

Passengers on Ship
VICTORIA from
Limerick to New
York, 23 August,
1851.

John Fitzgibbon
Connor Ward
Margreth Griffin
Mary Nolan
Ellen Murray
Peter Sweeney
Mathias Nester
Bridget Fury
Thomas Kildeay
John Tierney
Margaret Conway
Mary Tracy
Martin Rooney
Thomas Noon
Catharine Burt
Bridget Finn
Hanna Hayes
John Morris
James Matthews
Bridget Mullin
Catharine Forde
Mary Brady
Bridget Lynch
Patrick Deigan
Catharine Commans
Bridget Carr
Martin Shanahan
Patrick Conneally

Margareth Joyce
Susan McMan
Anthony Puniard

List of Passengers
on Ship NATHANIEL
G. WEEKS from
London to New York,
1 November, 1851.

John Driscole
Ellen Ager
Amos Hinckley
James Wright
Patrick Roach
Patrick O'Connor
William O'Brien
William Taylor
John Tucker
Soloman Cohen
Catherine Hickey
John Cunningham
George Caxon
John Roan
Enorah Dowling
Ellen Sullivan
Michael Regan
Mary Buckley
Ellen Donoghue
William Buckman
Timothy Carron
William Altyn
John Brown
Louis Cohen
Samuel Henry
Aaron Moses
Joseph Ellis
Michael Redman
Caroline Wilmore
Catherine Hurley
Edward Evershed
John Ireland
Ellen Dillon

List of Passengers
on Ship RODERICK
DHU from Liverpool
to New York,
6 January, 1852.

Matt Douglas
Tipperary
John Maher
Killkelly
Judith Maher
Mick Mullin
Mayho
James Cunningham
Roscommon
Pat O'Neil
Limerick
John Cummin
Limerick
Mick Hardman
Galway
Alice Barry
Tipperary
Ellen Neilson
Co. Clare
Joseph Russell
Co. Clare
Laurence Millvihili
Co. Clare
James Murphy
Co. Mayo
William Byrne
Wicklow
Catherine Connor
Oxford
Alice Carlin
Tyrone
Sarah Carlin
Tyrone
Ann Riley
Mayo
Mary Leslie
Donegal
Margaret Cassidy
Tyrone

Dennis Mahony
Kerry
Catherine Delany
Kilkenny
Ellen Slevin
Tyrone
Pat Healey
Furghmenagh
Mick Redman
Furghmenagh
Pat Murphy
Wexford
Robert Elliot
Furmannah
Dennis Carroll
Co. Kerry
Bridget Bennett
Roscommon

List of Passengers
on Ship ODESSA from
Dublin to New York,
2 April, 1852.

Michael Kenney
Jno. Archer
Jno. Wilson
William Lennox
Edward Collins
John Ford
Patrick Duffy
Charles Hurley
William Dalton
James Daly
Edward Gibney
Patrick Gallagher
John Kelly
James Bulger
William Moffatt
Thomas Hinly
Margaret Rowe
John Plunkett
Charles Long
Ann Cooleghan
James Markey
Ann Rogers
James Kavanagh
Bridget Lynch
Owen Hammond
Mary Flynn
Bridget Darby
Charles Egan
William Norris
James Corrigan

List of Passengers
on Ship RAJAH from
Liverpool and Tralee
to New York, 2 September,
1852.

J. Maloney
M. Connor
B. Griffin
M. Moriarty
J. Boyle
J. Hanihan
W. Kerby
P. Egan
C. Carroll
D. Callahan
J. Quirk
M. Sheahan
E. Jefcott
M. Brusnan
D. Keating
C. Lucy
E. Plowman
J. Lovett
M. Lean
E. Devine
D. Whelan
E. Barrett
D. Hurlehy
J. Morris
B. Corbett
M. Driscoll
M. Cahilan
M. Sears

List of Passengers
on Ship MARCHIONESS
OF CLYDESDALE from
Glasgow (passengers
embarked at Greenock)
to New York,
6 December, 1852.

Mary Taggart
Hugh Flinn
Hugh Gallacher
Robert Quigley
Ellen Sweeney
John Mullan
Martha Richard
John Carr
Margaret Livingstone
George Kelly
Joseph Docherty
Jane Devlin
Rebecca Young
James Mowbray
Patrick O'Hara
Michael McSwegon
John Simpson
John Marshall
James Mehan
William Armstrong
Charles McHugh
Stephen McIntyre
Thomas Moore
Mary Kane
John Feeney
James McIlver
Samuel McDermott
Mary Johnstone
Margaret Rourke
Patrick McGroharty
Isabella McDaid
Sally McAvana

List of Passengers
on Ship COLUMBIA from
Liverpool to New
York, 3 March, 1853.

William Welsh
Laurence Quinlan
Hugh Higgins
Michael Evans
Catherine Gibbons
Patrick Scales
James Dillon
Pat Brown
Catherine Garity
Susan Blacker
Alexander Gamble
Daniel Lunney
Laurence Martin
Thomas Whelan
Laurence Ward
Edward Fitzpatrick
James Tyrrol
Henry Blake
William Green
James Power
Michael Summers
Oliver Bower
Patrick Laurence
Henry Cooper
Patrick Coffey
John Mortimer
Bessey Gaffney
Ann Oates

List of Passengers
on Ship PRINCETON
from Liverpool to
New York, 18 July,
1853.

Ellen Grany
Co. Kerry
John Connor
Co. Kerry
Mary Dunlevy
Co. Kerry
Mary Welsh
Co. Kerry
Mary Sullivan

Co. Kerry
Philip Brady
Fermanaugh
Margaret Brady
Fermanaugh
Peter Gavican
Roscommon
Ann Cunningham
Roscommon
Kitty Radir
Clare
Johanna Welsw
Limerick
Johanna Calligan
Cork
Ann Cullum
Longford
Margaret McDavatt
Tyrone
Bridget Tiernan
Leitrim
Patrick Gaynor
Leitrim
Catherine Butler
Tipperary
Ellen Dower
Tipperary
Julia Tobin
Limerick
Mary Brown
Roscommon
John Ward
Galway
Catherine Murray
Galway
Margaret Norton
Galway
Catherine Tierney
Galway
Mary Higgin
Queens
Rosana Quin
Queens
Mary Callaghan
Armaugh
Michael Manly
Mayo
Julia Tynan
Queens
Betsy Dargan
Westmeath
Mary Mahoney
Cork

Passengers on Ship
TELEGRAPH from
Liverpool and
Tralee to New York,
25 October, 1853.

Bridget Fitzgerald
Jeremiah Foreham
Patrick Casey
Patrick Higgins
David Ready
Mathew Moriarty
Catherine Dalton
Catherine Courteray
Mary Keating
William Joy
Peggy Joy
Mary Spillane
Daniel Dowd
Francis Abott
Kate Conway
Mary Rice
Maurice Burns
Daniel Flynn
Catherine Flaherty
Maurice Cuonihan
Denis Barton
William Shanahan
Denis Quill
Catherine Stack
Honora Cusack
William Costello
Johanna Scanlon
Thomas Evans
May Day
Robert Baker

Passengers on Ship
HERMAN ROOSEN from
Dublin to New York,
23 January, 1854.

Patrick Smith
John Ryan
Mary Woods
Michael Conlan
Laurence Rutledge
John Keogh
Peter Noonan
Mark Scott
James Dean
Judith Dunn
Ann Neale
Bridget Morrison
John Redmond
James Masterson
Ellen Walker
Bridget Keeffe
Bridget Lynch
John Keyne
Eliza Wallengood
John Dwyer
Thomas Atkinson
Anne Heusen
Patrick Magee
Bridget Darling
Mary McGuinness
Gabriel Warner
Rosa Thompson
Richard Monks
Ann Roe
Margaret Sheridan
Mary Farrelly
Ellen Malone

Passengers on Ship
STAR OF THE WEST
from Liverpool to
New York, 3 April
1854.

Anne Horan
Patrick Nowlan
Patrick Delany
James Litton
John Mockler
Martin Carroll
John Bushell
Bessy Cosgrove
James Cleary
Joseph Newton
Philip Grimes
David Thomas
James Stone
William Glass
Thomas Carmody
Catherine Dolphin
Michael Rooney
Mary Seymour
John Nagle
James Cawley
Andrew Dudley
Michael Finn
James Gash
Bridget Behan
Abraham Cooke
Margaret Coughlin
Julia Crowley
John Devaney
Andrew Heffernan

Passengers on Ship
WILLIAM TAPSCOTT
from Liverpool to
New York, 14 August,
1854.

James Lane
Mary Madden
James Boyle
Patrick Boyle
Mary Kane
Alice Murray
Pat Gilmartine
Thomas McCord
Ellen Hagan

Mary Wall
Ellen Quigley
Mary Cox
Mary Hiney
Peter Gilroy
Brid Sheehan
Thomas Burns
David Lynch
John Clinton
Hugh Morris
Mary Fountain
Margaret Gannon
Mary Broderick
John Donlan
Kerry
Jno. Casey
Kerry
Pat Loughrea
Kerry
Michael McCanary
Kerry
Catherine Curley
Kerry
Pat Healey
Kerry
Jeremiah Sullivan
Kerry
Thomas Connolly
Kerry

List of Passengers
on Ship WEBSTER
from Liverpool to
New York, 20 November,
1854.

Peggy Barrett
Alexander Chambers
Michael Havey
Edward Brothers
William Ward
Margaret Devine
Mary McGowan
James Baines
Thomas Mulhall
Ellen Rourke
Barney Donnelly
Richard Savage
James Tighe
Mary McGarry
Ellen Mulligan
Margaret Coddingham
Anne Coffey
Judy Collins
Ellen Higgins
Bridget McEvoy
James Beardsley
Johanna Hanlon
Maria Clay
Mary Slattery
Margaret McInerny
Honora Norton
Margaret Cussack
Catharine Bowers

List of Passengers
on Ship NEW WORLD
from Liverpool to
New York, 19 March,
1855.

Bernard Cain
Catherine Connell
Charles Cooney
Edward Fay
John Hyland
Pat Keenan
Catherine Gregan
Ann Healy
James Chamberlain
Hamelton Smith
Mary Birmingham
Michael O'Keefe
Hannah Glenn
Margaret Cassidy
Mary Lockart
Thomas Burke
Delia Rush
Richard Cullen

Stephen Eason
Fanny Frain
Matt Farrell
James Lyons
Mary Curly
Jno. Sweeny
Michael Corcoran
Michael O'Hara
Connell Duggan

Passengers on Ship
KATHERINE from Belfast
co New York, 1 June, 1855.

William Boyd
William Ross
James Bell
James Lowrey
William Knowles
Samuel Taylor
Susanna Rodgers
William McCartney
John Caughey
George Andrews
Margaret McComb
Jane Jameson
Amelia Palmer
Robert Nisbett
John Harper
Henry Rowane
Alexander McGlade
Sarah Carson
William Redment
David Maxwell
Hugh Flinn
John Johnstone
Catherine Smith
Ellen McGee
Mary McFurson
William Williamson

Passengers on Ship WEBSTER
from Liverpool to New York,
3 September, 1855.

Terence McGarraty
Ann Pickering
John Shorten
Ann Corrigan
Jane Faulkener
Ann Welsh
Christian Durgan
Henry Maher
John Leahey
Ellen Delaney
Margaret Cox
Catharine Gilmore
Patrick Nolan
Edward Hughes
William Dryden
William Caughlan
Hugh Sinclair
Matilda Brown
Barbara Doyle
David Gillespie
Agnes Devlin
William Farley
Joshua Oldroyd
John Heffron
Eliza Brophy
Winny Ford
Catharine Harrington

1826	Maii Continuatio	1826
Margaritta Donoghue	Ego R. J. Mahony B. Margtam filia legtm. Johannis Donoghue & Johanna Leahy Caths de Cnia drom Kerry	Sylvestrus Donoghue Catharina Donoghue
Stephanus Fughrue	Idem B. Stephanum filiu legtm. Johannis Fughrue & Alena Falvey Caths de Kilville	Maria Leahie
Carolus Pz Brosnihan	Idem B. Carolum filiu legtm. Michaeli Brosnihan & Maria Kissane Caths de Brinlathnoine	Johannes Kissane Maria Nagle
Patricius Casy	Idem B. Patricium filiu legtm. Mauricii Casey & Catharina Cotter Caths de Rien	Brient Brien Margta Cotter
Margaretta Kerrisk	Idem B. Margtam filiu legtm. Davidi Kerrisk & Maria Sullivan Caths de L. Kissiviglen	Danielus Kerrisk Margta Hanran
Thomas Leyne	Idem B. Thomam filiu legtm. Patricii Leyne & Honora Kissane Caths Killarnia	Demetrius Kissane Margaretta Sullivan
Thomas Robert	Idem B. Thomam filiu legtm. Thomas Robert & Juliana Browin Caths de Killarnia	Robertus Robert Margta Quinn
Maria Connell	Ego R. E. Sullivanie B. Mariam filiu legtm. Gulielmi Connell & Alicia Fleming Caths Killarnia	Cornelius Sullivan Margta Connell

Detail showing record of baptisms from early 19th century Irish Parish Register.

Irish Parish Registers

One of the surest ways of tracing an ancestor rooted in the ordinary stock of Ireland is through parish registers because parents invariably saw to it that their children were baptised into one or other of the christian churches. Exactly when such events began to be recorded and whether such records as were made survive to the present day are, of course, matters of considerable interest to the family historian. The age of church records will understandably vary from parish to parish but as a general rule registers of the relatively better off town and city parishes will be found to be appreciably older than those of rural parishes. Cities like Galway and Waterford for example have parish books (Roman Catholic) extending back to about the year 1680 while on the other hand the registers of many Mayo and Donegal parishes with entries only from the year 1850 are far too late to be of any great assistance to the family researcher. It is, however, well to remember that even in country areas where a literary tradition existed nurtured by a bardic or classical school local parish records will surprisingly often be extant to about 1770.

Record keeping at parish level in the eighteenth and nineteenth century in Ireland was not an easy matter for local clergy because of widespread illiteracy among congregations. Moreover, the penal laws enacted after the Treaty of Limerick in 1691 which for catholics and presbyterians virtually proscribed public worship were not finally removed from the statute book until the Emancipation Act of 1829. In many areas people were too poor to afford a chapel or house of worship in which circumstances the priest would journey on horseback from house to house performing baptisms later returning to his home and entering the names of the newly baptised in his register.

A typical baptismal entry will specify the exact date of baptism, the name of the child, the names of the parents including very often the maiden name of the mother – this latter especially so in the case of catholic records – the names of the sponsors and sometimes the street or townland address of the father. A marriage entry will indicate the date of the wedding together with the names of the contracting parties and witnesses. In addition one occasionally finds in parish books items such as the names of subscribers to a chapel building fund, a list of men, horses and materials for building a chapel, parish building accounts, census of parishioners, parish history notes, minutes of famine relief committees, lists of persons receiving famine relief, lists of marriage dispensations, not overlooking the hastily penned note to the effect that 'Fr. John has gone to take the spa water at Mallow for a week'.

Even the unexpected can be met with in a parish book. Love, loyalty and the law could be said to be the ingredients of a human story underlying the following note found in a county Kilkenny parish register illustrating religious disabilities in early nineteenth century Ireland:

> 'Rev. John Fitzpatrick told me that he married Thomas Behal and Frances Fitzgerald ... in the presence of Major Thomas Fitzgerald and Sara Fitzgerald on the 15th Nov. 1807 — but, that fearing the penalty of the law, the bride being a Protestant, he had not registered the marriage in the parish book — this memorandum is therefore to supply the place of said register. November 11th, 1835. W. Hart, R.C.C.'.

Established Church records parish for parish are much older than say Catholic or Presbyterian church records. A canon of the Irish Church in 1634 required that 'in every parish church or chapel within this realm shall be provided one parchment book at the charge of the parish wherein shall be written the day and the year of every christening and burial'. Consequently, quite a number of Irish Church books reach back in date to about the middle of the seventeenth century, for example, the registers of Christ Church, Cork begin 1643, those of Templemore (Derry) in 1642, Lisburn 1639, St. Michan's, Dublin 1636, Harristown, Co. Kildare 1666 and St. John, Cashel 1668.

One of the side effects of Disestablishment was that parish registers of the Church of Ireland prior to 1870 were declared public records coming under the jurisdiction of the Master of the Rolls who promptly decided that country churches and rectories were not adequate to house so important a collection of records and duly commanded that the registers be sent to the Public Record Office in Dublin for safe keeping. Subsequent events were to prove him wrong for almost a thousand parish books perished in the fire which destroyed that storehouse of Irish civilisation on June 28, 1922. Fortunately many rectors were wiser in their generation and had transcript copies made of their books before parting with them thus to some extent mitigating the loss of the original registers. Many more protested that they were in a position to provide for the safety of their registers at local level and having satisfied the authorities in this regard were allowed to retain their books.

Due to the close union between church and state following the Act of Supremacy of Henry VIII in 1534, Established Church records were used much as a census might today for the information of central government, with the onus on clergy to keep records of dissenters, non-conformists and other undesirables in the eyes of the authorities. Whatever theological differences may have divided them in life, protestants, catholics, presbyterians, methodists, baptists and huguenots frequently found common ground in death in the parish graveyard and so were duly entered in the burial registers of the Established Church. Some thirty of the oldest parish books of the Established Church are of course in print thanks to the efforts of the Parish Register Society in the early years of the present century.

Presbyterian church records as a body are extant from the early years of the nineteenth century. Some forty older books referring mainly to the eighteenth century have been deposited in the archives of the Presbyterian Historical Society in Belfast.

The custodian of the registers of a parish is the local Parish Priest (Catholic), Rector (Church of Ireland) or Minister (Presbyterian) without whose permission in writing authorities in central archives will not allow one to inspect copies of registers they may have in their possession.

Below will be found listings of parishes and congregations, county by county, relating to the three main christian denominations in Ireland. The date appearing after each parish represents the earliest year for which baptismal registers are known to be extant for that parish. As a general rule, marriage registers will be found to be more or less coeval with baptismal registers. In addition Church of Ireland books frequently contain many excellent early burial registers.

Finally, since many of our parishes grew up around the sites of old monasteries and abbeys and were named after townlands in which such foundations occurred the name of an adjacent market town or post town is appended after the name of lesser known parishes for ease of location.

ROMAN CATHOLIC CHURCH REGISTERS

Co. Antrim

Ahoghill	1853
Antrim	1874
Armoy	1848
Ballintoy	187
Ballyclare	1869
Ballymacarrett	1841
Ballymoney &	
Derrykeighan	1853
Belfast (various city parishes)	
St. Malachy	1858
St. Peter	1866
St. Patrick	1875
St. Mary	1867
St. Joseph	1872
Braid	
(Ballymena)	1825
Carnlough	1869
Carrickfergus	1828
Culfeightrin	
(Ballycastle)	1825
Cushendall	1838
Cushendun	1862
Derryaghy	1855
Duneane	
(Toomebridge)	1834
Dunloy	
(Cloughmills)	1840
Glenavy &	
Killead	1849
Glenarm	1825
Greencastle	1854
Kirkinriola	
(Ballymena)	1848
Larne	1821
Loughuile	1845
Portglenone	1864
Portrush	1844
Ramoan	
(Ballycastle)	1838
Randalstown	1825
Rasharkin	1848
Tickmacrevan	
(Glenarm)	1825

Co. Armagh

Aghagallon & Ballinderry	
(Lurgan)	1828
Armagh	1796
Ballymacnab	
(Armagh)	1844
Ballymore & Mullaghbrac	
(Tandragee)	1843
Creggan	
(Crossmaglen)	1796
Derrynoose	
(Keady)	1835
Drumcree	
(Portadown)	1844
Forkhill	1845
Killeavy	
(Bessbrook)	1835

Kilmore	
(Rich Hill)	1845
Loughgall	1835
Loughgilly	1849
Seagoe	1836
Shankill	
(Lurgan)	1822
Tynan	1822

Co. Carlow

Bagenalstown	1820
Ballon	1785
Borris	1782
Carlow	1774
Clonegall	1833
Clonmore	1819
Hacketstown	1820
Leighlinbridge	1783
Myshall	1822
St. Mullins	1796
Tinryland	1813
Tullow	1763

Co. Cavan

Annagelliffe & Urney	
(Cavan)	1812
Annagh	
(Belturbet)	1855
Ballintemple	1862
Castlerahan	
(Ballyjamesduff)	1752
Castletera	1862
Crosserlough	1843
Denn	1856
Drumgoon	1829
Drumlane	1836
Drumlumman	
North	1859
Glangevlin	
(Swanlinbar)	1835
Kilbride &	
Mountnugent	1832
Killann	
(Bailieboro')	1835
Killinkere	
(Virginia)	1766
Killeshandra	1835
Kilmore	1859
Kilsherdany	
(Coothill)	1803
Kinawley	
(Swanlinbar)	1835
Kingscourt	1838
Knockbride	1835
Laragh	1860
Lavey	1866
Lurgan	
(Virginia)	1755
Templeport	1836

Co. Clare

Ballina	1832

Ballyvaughan	1854
Broadford	1844
Carron	1853
O'Callaghan's Mills	1835
Carrigaholt	1853
Clareabbey	1853
Clondegad	1846
Clonrush	1846
Corofin	1819
Cratloe	1802
Crusheen	1860
Doonass & Trugh	1851
Doora & Kilraghtis	1821
Dysart	1845
Ennis	1841
Ennistymon	1870
Feakle Lr.	1860
Inagh	1850
Inch & Kilmaley	1828
Kilballyowen	1878
Kildysart	1829
Kilfarboy	1831
Kilfenora	1836
Kilfidane	1868
Kilkee	1869
Kilkeedy	1833
Killaloe	1825
Killanena	1842
Killard	1855
Killimer	1859
Kilmacduane	1854
Kilmihil	1849
Kilmurry-Ibrickane	1839
Kilmurry-M'Mahon	1840
Kilnoe &	
Tuamgraney	1832
Kilrush	1827
Liscannor	1843
Lisdoonvarna	1854
Newmarket	1828
New Quay	1847
Ogonnelloe	1832
Parteen	1847
Quin	1816
Scariff & Moynoe	1852
Sixmilebridge	1828
Tulla	1819

Co. Cork

Aghabulloge	1856
Aghada	1815
Aghinagh	1848
Annakissy	1806
Ardfield & Rathbarry	1801
Aughadown	1822
Ballincollig	1820
Ballinhassig	1821
Ballyclogh	1807
Ballyhea	1809
Ballymacoda &	
Lady's Bridge	1835
Ballyvourney	1825
Bandon	1794

Bantry	1819
Blackrock	1810
Blarney	1791
Boherbue	1833
Bonane	1846
Barryroe	1804
Buttevant	1814
Caheragh	1818
Carrigaline	1826
Carrigtwohill	1817
Castlemagner	1832
Castlelyons	1791
Castletownroche	1811
Charleville	1774
Clondrohid	1807
Clonmeen	1847
Clonthead &	
Ballingeary	1836
Cloyne	1791
Cobh	1812
Conna	1834
Cork	
St. Finbarr	1756
St. Patrick	1831
St. Peter & Paul	1766
St. Mary	1748
Courceys	1819
Castletownbere	1819
Castlehaven	1842
Clonakilty &	
Darrara	1809
Donaghmore	1803
Doneraile	1815
Douglas	1812
Drimoleague	1817
Dromtariffe	1832
Dunmanway	1818
Enniskeane &	
Desertserges	1813
Eyeries	1843
Fermoy	1828
Freemount	1827
Glanmire	1806
Glanworth &	
Ballindangan	1836
Glounthane	1829
Goleen	1827
Grenagh	1840
Imogeela	1835
Inniscarra	1814
Innishannon	1825
Iveleary	1816
Kanturk	1822
Kilbehenny	1800
Kilbritain	1811
Kildorrery	1824
Killeigh	1829
Kilmichael	1819
Kilnamartyra	1803
Kilmurry	1786
Kilworth	1829
Kilmeen &	
Castleventry	1821

Co. Cork (Cont/d.)

Kinsale	1808
Liscarrol	1812
Lisgoold	1807
Macroom	1803
Mallow	1757
Midleton	1819
Millstreet	1853
Mitchelstown	1792
Monkstown	1795
Mourne Abbey	1829
Muintervara	1820
Murragh	1834
Newmarket	1821
Ovens	1816
Passage	1795
Rath & Islands	1818
Rathcormac	1792
Rathmore	1837
Roscarberry & Lissevard	1814
Schull	1827
Shandrum	1829
Skibbereen	1827
Timoleague & Cloghagh	1842
Tracton Abbey	1802
Watergrasshill	1836
Youghal	1803

Co. Derry

Ballinderry	1826
Ballynascreen	1825
Ballyscullion (Bellaghy)	1844
Banagher	1848
Coleraine	1843
Cumber Upr. (Claudy)	1863
Desertmartin	1848
Drumehose (Limavady)	1855
Dungiven	1847
Errigal	1846
Faughanvale	1860
Glendermot (Waterside, Derry)	1864
Kilrea	1846
Magilligan	1855
Maghera	1841
Magherafelt	1834
Moneymore	1832
Templemore (Derry City)	1823
Termoneeny	1837

Co. Donegal

All Saints, Raymorky & Taughboyne (St. Johnston)	1843
Annagry	1868
Ardara	1869
Aughnish & Aghaninshin (Ramelton)	1873
Castlemacaward & Templecrone (Dungloe)	1876
Clonvaddog (Fanad)	1847
Clondahorky	1877
Conwal & Leck (Letterkenny)	1853
Drumhome	1866
Glencolumkille	1880
Gweedore	1868
Iniskeel (Glenties)	1866
Inver	1861
Kilcar	1848
Killybegs & Killaghtee	1845
Killygarvan & Tullyfern	1868
Killymard	1874
Kilbarron (Ballyshannon)	1854
Kilmacrenan	1862
Kilteevogue	1855
Mevagh (Carrigart)	1871
Raphoe	1876
Stranorlar	1860
Termon & Gartan	1862
Tullabegley E., Raymunterdoney & Tory	1868
Burt, Inch & Fahan	1859
Clonca (Malin)	1856
Clonleigh (Lifford)	1773
Clonmany	1852
Culdaff	1838
Desertegny & Lower Fahan (Buncrana)	1864
Donagh (Carndonagh)	1847
Donaghmore	1857
Iskaheen & Moville Upper	1858
Moville Lower	1847

Co. Down

Aghaderg (Loughbrickland)	1816
Annaclone	1834
Ardkeen	1828
Ballygalget (Portaferry)	1828
Ballynahinch	1827
Banbridge	1843
Ballyphilip	1843
Bangor	1855
Bright (Ardglass)	1856
Clonallon (Warrenpoint)	1826
Clonduff (Hilltown)	1850
Donaghmore	1835
Dromara	1844
Dromore	1823
Drumaroad (Castlewellan)	1853
Drumbo	
Drumgath (Rathfriland)	1841
Drumgooland Upr.	1827
Drumgooland Lr.	1832
Downpatrick	1851
Dunsford	1848
Kilbroney (Rostrevor)	1808
Kilclief & Strangford	1866
Kilcoo (Rathfriland)	1832
Kilkeel	1839
Loughinisland	1806
Maghera & Bryansford (Newcastle)	1845
Magheralin	1815
Moira	1815
Mourne	1842
Newcastle	1845
Newry	1818
Newtownards, Comber & Donaghadee	1864
Saintfield (Downpatrick)	1865
Saul & Ballee	1844
Tullylish	1833
Tyrella & Dundrum	1854

Co. Dublin

Balbriggan	1816
Baldoyle	1784
Balrothery	1816
Blanchardstown	1774
Booterstown	1796
Clondalkin	1778
Donabate	1760

Dublin City

St. Agatha (North William Street)	1852
St. Andrew (Westland Row)	1741
St. Audeon (High Street)	1778
St. Catherine (Meath Street)	1740
St. James (James Street)	1752
St. Lawrence O'Toole (Seville Place)	1853
St. Mary (Pro-Cathedral, Marlborough Street)	1734
St. Michael & John (Lower Exchange Street)	1742
St. Michan (Halston Street)	1725
St. Nicholas of Myra (Francis Street)	1742
St. Paul (Arran Quay)	1731
Dun Laoire	1773
Finglas	1788
Garristown	1857
Howth	1784
Lucan	1818
Lusk	1757
Palmerstown	1798
Rathfarnham	1818
Rolestown	1857
Saggart	1857
Sandyford	1857
Skerries	1751
Swords	1763

Co. Fermanagh

Aghavea	1862
Aughalurcher (Lisnaskea)	1835
Carn (Belleek)	1851
Cleenish	1835
Culmaine	1836
Devenish	1853
Enniskillen	1838
Galloon	1853
Inishmacsaint	1848
Irvinestown	1846
Roslea	1862
Tempo	1845

Co. Galway

Abbeyknockmoy	1834
Addergoole & Liskeevey	1858
Annaghdown	1834
Aran Islands	1872
Athenry	1858
Ahascragh	1840
Ardrahan	1839
Abbeygormican & Killoran	1859
Aughrim & Kilconnell	1828
Ballymacward & Clonkeenkerrill	1841
Ballinakill	1839
Bullaun, Grange & Killaan	1827
Beagh	1855
Ballinakill	1869
Boyounagh	1838
Creagh & Kilclooney (Ballinasloe)	1820
Clonfert, Donanaghta & Meelick	1829
Clontuskert	1827
Claregalway	1849
Castlegar	1827
Duniry & Kilnelahan	1849
Donaghpatrick & Kilcoona	1844
Dunmore	1833
Fahy & Kilquain	1836
Fohenagh & Kilgerrill	1827
Galway - St. Nicholas	1690

Co. Galway (Cont/d.)

Kilconickny, Kilconieran	
& Lickerrig	1831
Kilcooley & Leitrim	1815
Killalaghten &	
Kilrickhill	1853
Killimorbologue &	
Tiranascragh	1831
Killimordaly &	
Kiltullagh	1830
Kilmalinoge &	
Lickmolassy	
(Portumna)	1830
Kilnadeema &	
Kilteskill	
(Loughrea)	1836
Kiltomer & Oghill	1834
Killian & Killeroran	
(Ballygar)	1804
Kilcummin	
(Oughterard)	1809
Killannin	1875
Kilcameen &	
Ballynacourty	1855
Kinvarra	1831
Kilbeacanty	1854
Kilchreest	1855
Kilcolgan, Dromacoo	
& Killeenavara	1854
Kilcornan	1854
Killora &	
Killogilleen	1847
Kilmacduagh &	
Kiltartan	1848
Kilthomas	1854
Kilkerrin &	
Clonberne	1855
Killascobe	1807
Killeen (Carraroe)	1853
Killererin	1851
Kilmoylan &	
Cummer	1813
Loughrea	1827
Lettermore	1848
Lackagh	1842
Moycullen	1786
Moylough &	
Mountbellew	1848
Moyrus	1853
Oranmore	1833
Omey &	
Ballindoon	1838
Rahoon	1819
Roundstone	1872
Salthill	1840
Spiddal	1861
Tynagh	1809
Tuam	1790
Woodford	1821

Co. Kerry

Abbeydorney	1835
Annascaul	1829
Ardfert	1819
Ballybunion	1831
Ballyferriter	1807
Ballyheigue	1840
Ballylongford	1823
Ballymacelligott	1868
Boherbue	1833
Bonane &	
Glengarriff	1846
Brosna	1868
Cahirciveen	1846
Cahirdaniel	1831
Castlegregory	1828
Castleisland	1823
Castlemaine	1804
Causeway	1782
Dingle	1825
Dromod	1850
Duagh	1819
Firies	1830
Fossa	1857
Glenbeigh	1834
Glenflesk	1821
Kenmare	1819
Kilcummin	1821
Kilgarvan	1818
Killarney	1792
Killeentierna	1801
Killorglin	1886
Knocknagoshel	1850
Listowel	1802
Lixnaw	1810
Milltown	1825
Moyvane	1855
Prior	1832
Rathmore	1827
Sneem	1845
Spa	1866
Tarbert	1859
Tralee	1772
Tuogh	1844
Tuosist	1844
Valentia	1825

Co. Kildare

Allen	1820
Athy	1779
Ballymore Eustace	1779
Balyna (Johnstown)	1818
Caragh (Downings)	1849
Carbury	1821
Castledermot	1789
Celbridge	1857
Clane	1785
Clonbullogue	1819
Kilcock	1771
Kilcullen	1777
Kildare	1815
Kill	1840
Maynooth	1814
Monasterevin	1819
Naas	1813
Narraghmore	1827
Newbridge	1786
Suncroft	1805

Co. Kilkenny

Aghaviller	1847
Ballyhale	1823
Ballyregget	1856
Callan	1821
Castlecomer	1812
Clara	1835
Clough	1858
Conahy	1832
Danesfort	1819
Dunnemaggan	1821
Durrow	1789
Freshford	1773
Galmory	1861
Glenmore	1831
Gowran	1809
Graignenamanagh	1818
Inistiogue	1810
Johnstown	1814
Kilmacow	1858
Lisdowney	1817
Mooncoin	1779
Muckalee	1801
Mullinavat	1843
Paulstown	1828
Rosbercon	1817
St. Canice's	
(Kilkenny)	1768
St. John's	
(Kilkenny)	1809
St. Mary's	
(Kilkenny)	1754
St. Patrick's	
(Kilkenny)	1800
Slieverue	1766
Templeorum	1803
Thomastown	1782
Tullaherin	1782
Tulleroan	1843
Urlingford	1805
Windgap	1822

Co. Laois

Abbeyleix	1824
Aghaboe	1795
Arles	1821
Ballinakill	1794
Ballyadams	1820
Ballyfin	1824
Borris-in-Ossory	1840
Camross (Mountrath)	1816
Castletown	1772
Clonaslee	1849
Durrow	1789
Mountmellick	1814
Mountrath	1823
Portarlington	1820
Portlaoise	1826
Raheen	1819
Rathdowney	1763
Rosenallis	1765
Stradbally	1820

Co. Leitrim

Annaduff	1849
Aughavas	1825
Ballinamore	1869
Ballymeehan	
(Rossinver)	1851
Carrigallen	1829
Clooneclare	
(Manorhamilton)	1853
Drumlease	
(Dromahaire)	1859
Drumreilly	1867
Fenagh	1825
Glenade	1867
Gortletheragh	1830
Inishmagrath	
(Drumkeeran)	1854
Killargue	1852
Killasnet	1852
Killenummery &	
Killerny	1828
Kiltoghert	1826
Kiltubbrid	1841
Kinlough	1835
Mohill-Manachain	1836

Co. Limerick

Abbeyfeale	1856
Adare	1832
Ardagh	1845
Ardpatrick	1861
Askeaton	1829
Athea	1830
Ballingarry	1825
Ballybricken	1800
Ballygran &	
Colman's well	1841
Ballylanders	1847
Banogue	1861
Bruff	1808
Bulgaden &	
Ballinvana	1812
Caherconlish	1841
Cappagh	1841
Cappamore	1845
Castleconnell	1850
Charleville	1774
Coolcappa	1833
Croagh	1836
Croom	1770
Donaghmore	1830
Doon	1824
Dromin	1817
Drumcollogher	1830
Effin	1843
Emly	1810
Fedamore	1806
Feenagh	1854
Freemount	1835
Galbally	1810
Glenroe	1853
Glin	1851
Hospital	1810
Kilbenny	1824
Kildimo	1846
Kilfinane	1832
Killeedy	1840
Kilmallock	1837
Kilteely	1815
Knockaderry	1838
Knockaney	1808

Co. Limerick (Cont/d.)

Knocklong	1809
Loughill	1855
Mahoonagh	1812
Manistir	1845
Monagea	1777
Mungret	1844
Murroe & Boher	1814
Newcastle West	1815
Cola & Solohead	1809
Pallesgreen	1811
Parteen	1847
Patrick'swell	1801
Rathkeale	1811
Rockhill	1842
St. John's (Limerick)	1788
St. Mary's (Limerick)	1745
St. Michael's (Limerick)	1776
St. Munchin's (Limerick)	1764
St. Patrick's (Limerick)	1812
Shanagolden	1824
Stonehall	1825
Templeglantine	1864
Tournafulla	1867

Co. Longford

Abbeylara	1854
Ardagh & Moydow	1793
Carrickedmond	1825
Cashel	1850
Clonbroney	1849
Clonguish	1829
Columcille (Dring)	1845
Drumlish	1834
Granard	1779
Kilcommuck	1859
Kilglass & Rathreagh	1855
Killashee	1826
Killoe (Drumlish)	1826
Mostrim	1838
Rathcline (Lanesboro')	1850
Scrabby & Columcille East (Cloonagh)	1833
Shrule (Ballymahon)	1820

Co. Louth

Ardee	1763
Carlingford	1811
Clogherhead	1744
Collon	1789
Darver	1787
Dundalk	1790
Dunleer	1772
Faughart	1851
Kilkerley	1752
Kilsaran	1809

Lordship & Ballymascanlan	1838
Louth	1833
Mellifont	1821
Monasterboice	1814
St. Mary's (Drogheda)	1835
St. Peter's (Drogheda)	1744
Tallanstown	1817
Termonfeckin	1823
Togher	1791

Co. Mayo

Attymass	1875
Addergoole	1840
Ardagh	1870
Aughaval (Westport)	1823
Achill	1867
Aghamore	1864
Aglish, Ballyheane & Breaghwy (Castlebar)	1824
Aghagower (Westport)	1828
Bohola	1857
Backs (Rathduff)	1848
Ballycastle	1864
Ballysokeary	1843
Belmullet	1841
Balla & Manulla	1837
Ballinrobe	1843
Ballyovey	1869
Bekan (Claremorris)	1832
Burriscarra & Ballintubber (Claremorris)	1839
Burrishoole (Newport)	1870
Ballyhaunis	1851
Crossmolina	1831
Clare Island	1851
Cong & Neale	1870
Crossboyne & Tagheen	1862
Clonbur	1853
Islandeady (Castlebar)	1839
Kilconduff & Meelick (Swinford)	1850
Kilgarvan (Ballina)	1844
Killasser (Swinford)	1847
Kilbeagh (Charlestown)	1845
Killedan	1834
Kilmovee	1854
Kilshalvey	1842
Kilfian	1826
Killala	1852
Kilmoremoy (Ballina)	1823

Kiltane (Bangor-Erris)	1860
Keelogues	1847
Kilcolman (Claremorris)	1835
Kilcommon & Robeen	1857
Kilgeever (Louisburg)	1850
Kilmaine	1854
Kilmeena	1858
Knock	1868
Kilbride	1853
Lackan	1852
Mayo & Roslee	1841
Templemore	1872
Toomore (Foxford)	1833
Turlough (Castlebar)	1847

Co. Meath

Ardcath	1795
Athboy	1794
Ballinabrackey	1826
Ballivor & Kildalkey	1837
Beauparc (Yellow Furze)	1815
Blacklion	1815
Bohermeen (Navan)	1805
Carnaross	1806
Castletown (Navan)	1805
Clonmellon	1759
Curraha (Ashbourne)	1823
Drumconrath	1811
Duleek	1852
Dunboyne	1787
Dunderry	1837
Dunshaughlin	1789
Johnstown	1839
Kells	1791
Kilbride	1802
Kilmainham & Moybologue	1869
Kilcloon (Dunboyne)	1836
Kilbeg (Kells)	1817
Kilmessan & Dunsany	1742
Kilskyre (Ballinlough)	1784
Lobinstown (Navan)	1823
Longwood	1829
Moynalty	1811
Navan	1782
Nobber	1754
Oldcastle	1789
Oristown (Kells)	1757
Rathkenny	1784
Ratoath & Ashbourne	1781

Rosnaree & Donore	1840
Skyrne	1841
Slane	1851
Stamullen	1831
Summerhill	1812
Trim	1829

Co. Monaghan

Aghabog	1856
Aughmullen	1841
Clontibret	1861
Clones	1848
Donagh (Grasslough)	1836
Donaghmoyne	1852
Drumully (Scotshouse)	1845
Drumsnat & Kilmore	1836
Ematris (Rockcorry)	1848
Errigal Trough (Emyvale)	1835
Killevan (Newbliss)	1850
Monaghan	1835
Maghaire Rois	1836
Magheracloone (Carrickmacross)	1836
Muckno (Castleblaney)	1835
Tullycorbet (Ballybay)	1862
Tydavnet	1835

Co. Offaly

Birr	1838
Clara	1821
Clonmacnoise	1826
Daingean	1795
Dunkerrin	1820
Edenderry	1820
Eglish	1809
Gallen & Reynagh (Banagher)	1811
Kilcormac	1821
Killeigh (Geashill)	1844
Killina (Rahan)	1810
Kinnetty	1833
Lemanaghan (Ferbane)	1821
Lusmagh	1850
Rhode	1829
Seirkieran	1830
Shinrone	1842
Tisaran & Fuithre (Ferbane)	1819
Tullamore	1809

Co. Roscommon

Ardcarne	1843
Athleague & Fuerty	1808
Aughrim & Kilmore	1816
Ballintober, Ballymoe	1831

Co. Roscommon (Cont/d.)

Boyle & Kilbryan	1793
Castlemore & Kilcolman	1851
Cloontuskert, Kilgeffin	1865
Dysert & Tissara	1850
Elphin & Creeve	1808
Glinsk & Kilbegnet	1836
Kilbride	1835
Kilcorkey & Frenchpark	1845
Kilglass & Rooskey	1865
Kilkeevan (Castlerea)	1804
Killukin	1811
Kilnamanagh & Estersnow	1853
Kiltoom	1835
Kiltrustan, Lissonuffy & Cloonfinlough (Strokestown)	1830
Loughglynn	1817
Ogulla & Baslick	1865
Oran	1845
Roscommon & Kilteevan	1820
St. John's (Knockcroghery)	1841
Tibohine	1833

Co. Sligo

Aghanagh (Ballinafad)	1803
Ahamlish (Cliffoney)	1796
Ballisodare & Kilvarnet	1842
Cloonacool	1859
Curry	1867
Drumcliffe	1841
Drumrat	1843
Easky	1864
Emlefad & Kilmorgan	1824
Geevagh	1851
Kilfree & Killaraght	1844
Killoran	1846
Kilmacteigue	1845
Kilshalvey, Kilturra & Cloonoghill	1842
Riverstown	1803
Skreen & Dromard	1848
Sligo, Coolera, Calry, Rosses Point & St. Mary's	1858
Templeboy	1815
Tumore	1833

Co. Tipperary

Annacarty	1821
Ardfinnan	1809
Ballinahinch	1839
Ballingarry	1814
Ballylooby	1809
Ballyneale	1839
Ballyporeen	1817
Bansha & Kilmoyler	1820
Boherlahan & Dualla	1830
Borrisokane	1821
Borrisoleigh	1814
Burgess & Youghal	1828
Cahir	1809
Carrick-on-Suir	1784
Cashel	1793
Castletownarrha	1820
Clerihan	1852
Clogheen	1778
Cloghprior & Monsea	1835
Clonmel	1790
Clonoulty	1804
Cloughjordan	1833
Cappawhite	1815
Drangan	1811
Drom & Inch	1827
Dunkerrin	1820
Emly	1810
Fethard & Killusty	1806
Golden	1833
Gortnahoe	1805
Holycross	1835
Kilbarron	1827
Kilcommon	1813
Killenaule	1743
Kilsheelan	1836
Knockavilla	1834
Lattin & Cullen	1846
Loughmore	1798
Moycarky	1793
Mullinahone	1820
Nenagh	1792
Newcastle	1846
New Inn	1820
Newport	1795
Oola & Solohead	1809
Powerstown	1808
Roscrea	1810
Silvermines	1840
Templemore	1807
Templetuohy	1809
Thurles	1795
Toomevara	1831
Tipperary	1793
Upperchurch	1829

Co. Tyrone

Aghaloo	1846
Ardboe	1827
Ardstraw (Cappagh)	1846
Artrea	1832
Ballinderry (Cookstown)	1826
Ballyclog	1822
Beragh	1832
Bodoney	1850
Camus (Strabane)	1773
Cappagh	1846
Clogher	1856
Clonfeacle (Moy)	1814
Clonoe (Coalisland)	1810
Desertcreat	1827
Donaghcavey (Fintona)	1857
Donaghedy	1855
Donaghenry (Coalisland)	1822
Donaghmore	1837
Dromore	1855
Drumglass (Dungannon)	1821
Drumragh (Omagh)	1846
Eglish (Dungannon)	1862
Errigal Keeran (Ballygawley)	1847
Kildress	1835
Kileeshil (Tullyallen)	1845
Kilskerry (Trillick)	1840
Leckpatrick (Strabane)	1863
Lissan (Cookstown)	1832
Longfield	1846
Pomeroy	1837
Termonamongan	1863
Termonmaguirk (Carrickmore)	1834
Urney	

Co. Waterford

Abbeyside	1828
Aglish	1837
Ardmore	1823
Ballyduff	1805
Cappoquin	1810
Carrickbeg	1842
Clashmore	1811
Dungarvan	1787
Dunhill	1829
Kilgobnet	1848
Kill	1831
Killea	1780
Kilrossanty	1822
Kilsheelan	1840
Knockanore	1833
Lismore	1820
Modelligo	1846
Newcastle	1846
Portlaw	1809
Ring	1813
St. John's (Waterford)	1759
St. Patrick's (Waterford)	1731
St. Peter & Paul's	1737
Tallow	1797
Touraneena	1851
Tramore	1798
Trinity Within (Waterford)	1729
Trinity Without (Waterford)	1752

Co. Westmeath

Ballinacargy	1837
Ballymore	1824
Castlepollard	1763
Castletown	1829
Churchtown	1816
Clara	1821
Clonmellion	1785
Collinstown	1807
Delvin	1785
Drumraney	1834
Kilbeggan	1818
Kilbride	1832
Kilkenny West	1829
Killucan	1821
Kinnegad	1827
Lemanaghan & Ballynahowen	1821
Milltown	1781
Moate & Colry	1823
Moyvore	1831
Mullingar	1737
Multyfarnham	1824
Rathaspick & Russagh	1822
Rochfortbridge	1823
St. Mary's (Athlone)	1813
Streete	1820
Taghmon	1781
Tubber	1821
Tullamore	1801
Turbotstown	1819

Co. Wexford

Adamstown	1807
Ballindaggin	1841
Ballygarrett	1828
Ballyoughter	1810
Bennow	1832
Blackwater	1815
Bree	1837
Bunclody	1834
Castlebridge	1832
Clongen	1847
Cloughbawn	1816
Craanford	1853
Crossebeg	1856
Cushinstown	1759
Davidstown	1805
Enniscorthy	1794
Ferns	1819
Glynn	1817
Gorey	1847
Kilanieran	1852
Killaveny	1800
Kilmore	1752
Kilrush	1842
Lady's-Island	1773
Litter	1789
Marshallstown	1854
Mayglass	1843
Monageer	1838
New Ross	1789

Co. Wexford (Cont/d.)

		Taghmon	1801	Ashford	1864	Kilbride &		
		Tagoat	1853	Avoca	1791	Barnderrig	1835	
Oulart	1837	Tintern	1827	Baltinglass	1807	Kilquade	1826	
Oylegate	1804	Templetown	1792	Blessington	1852	Rathdrum	1795	
Piercestown	1839	Wexford	1671	Bray:		Rathvilly	1797	
Ramsgrange	1835			Bray Town	1800	Valleymount	1810	
Rathengan	1803	**Co. Wicklow**		Dunlavin	1815	Tinahealy	1835	
Rathnure	1846			Enniskerry	1825	Wicklow	1747	
Suttons	1824	Arklow	1809	Glendalough	1807			

CHURCH OF IRELAND REGISTERS

Co. Antrim		Co. Carlow		(Ballyconnell)	1797
		Lisburn (Blaris)	1639		
Aghalee	1782	Magheragall		**Co. Clare**	
Ahoghill		(Lisburn)	1772	Aghade (Carlow)	1740
(Ballymena)	1811	Muckamore		Aghold	1700	Ennis	1805
Antrim	1700	(Antrim)	1847	Barragh		Killaloe	1679
Ballinderry	1805	Skerry	1805	(Enniscorthy)	1831	Kilnasoolagh	
Ballintoy		Stoneyford	1845	Carlow	1744	(Newmarket)	1731
(Ballycastle)	1712	Templecorran	1848	Dunleckney	1791	Kilrush	1773
Ballyclug	1841	Templepatrick	1827	Fenagh (Carlow)	1809	Ogonnilloe	
Ballymacarrett	1827	Whitehouse		Hacketstown	—	(Scariff)	1807
Ballymena	1815	(Belfast)	1840	Killeshir (Carlow)	1824	
Ballymoney	1807			Kiltennell		**Co. Cork**	
Ballynure	1812	**Co. Armagh**		(New Ross)	1837	Abbeymahon	
Ballysillan	1856	Aghavilly (Armagh)	1844	Myshall	1814	(Timoleague)	1827
Belfast		Annaghmore		Painestown (Carlow)	1833	Abbeystrewry	
Christ Church	1868	(Loughgall)	1856	Rathvilly	1826	(Skibbereen)	1778
Mariner's	1745	Ardmore	1822	Tullow	1696	Aghabullog	
St. Anne		Armagh	1750	Urglin (Carlow)	1710	(Coachford)	1808
(Shankill)	1819	Ballymore				Aghada (Cloyne)	1815
St. George	1853	(Tandragee)	1783	**Co. Cavan**		Ardfield	
St. John	1853	Ballymoyer		Annagelliffe (Cavan)	1804	(Clonakilty)	1835
St. Mark		(Whitecross)	1820	Annagh (Belturbet)	1801	Ballyclough	
(see Ballysillan)		Camlough (Newry)	1832	Ashfield (Cootehill)	1821	(Mallow)	1795
St. Mary	1867	Creggan		Bailieborough	1744	Ballydehob (Skull)	1826
St. Matthew	1846	(Crossmaglen)	1808	Ballymachugh	1816	Ballyhay	
Trinity	1844	Derrynoose		Billis (Virginia)	1840	(Charleville)	1728
Upper Falls	1855	(Armagh)	1710	Castleterra		Ballyhooly	
Carnamoney	1789	Drumbanagher		(Ballyhaise)	1800	(Mallow)	1788
Carrickfergus	1740	(Newry)	1838	Cavan	1842	Ballymartyl	
Craigs (Belfast)	1839	Drumcree		Cloverhill	1861	(Ballinhassig)	1785
Derryaghey		(Portadown)	1780	Drumgoon		Ballymodan	
(Lisburn)	1696	Eglish (Moy)	1803	(Cootehill)	1802	(Bandon)	1695
Derrykeighan	1802	Grange (Armagh)	1780	Drung	1785	Ballymoney	
Drummaul		Keady	1780	Kildallon		(Ballineen)	1805
(Randalstown)	1823	Kilcluney		(Ballyconnell)	1856	Berehaven	1787
Dunluce		(Markethill)	1832	Kildrumferton		Blackrock	
(Bushmills)	1809	Killylea	1845	(Kilnelack)	1801	(st. Michael)	1828
Dunseverick		Loughgall	1706	Killeshandra	1735	Brigown	
(Bushmills)	1832	Loughgilly		Killsherdaney		(Mitchelstown)	1775
Finvoy		(Markethill)	1804	(Cootehill)	1810	Buttevant	1757
(Ballymoney)	1811	Milltown		Killoughter		Carrigaline	1723
Glenarm	1788	(Magheramoy)	1840	(Redhills)	1827	Carrigamleary	
Glenary	1707	Mullavilly		Kilmore (Cavan)	1702	(Mallow)	1779
Glynn (Larne)	1838	(Tandragee)	1821	Knockbride		Carrig Park	1779
Inver (Larne)	1806	Newtownhamilton	1823	(Bailieborough)	1825	Carrigtwohill	1779
Lambeg	1810	Sankill	1681	Lurgan (Virginia)	1831	Castlemagner	1810
Layde		Tartaraghan		Quivy (Belturbet)	1854	Castletownroche	1728
(Cushendall)	1826	(Loughgall)	1824	Swanlinbar	1798	Churchtown	
		Tynan	1686	Tomregan		(Mallow)	1806

Co. Cork (Cont/d.)

Clenore (Mallow)	1813
Clonfert (Newmarket)	1771
Clonmeen (Mallow)	1764
Cloyne	1708
Cork	
Christ Church	1643
St. Luke	1837
St. Nicholas	1721
St. Anne	1772
St. Finbarr	1752
Corbeg	1836
Desertserges (Bandon)	1837
Doneraile	1730
Douglas (Cork)	1792
Drishane	1792
Dromdaleague	1812
Dromtariff (Millstreet)	1825
Fanlobbus (Dunmanway)	1855
Farrihy (Kildorrery)	1765
Fermoy	1801
Garrane (Middleton)	1856
Glanworth	1805
Inniscarra (Cork)	1820
Innishannon	1693
Kanturk	1818
Kilbolane (Kanturk)	1779
Kilbrogan (Bandon)	1752
Kilcummer (Fermoy)	1856
Killanully (Carrigaline)	1831
Killowen (Bandon)	1833
Kilmeen (Clonakilty)	1806
Kilworth	1766
Knocavilly (Bandon)	1837
Liscarrol	1805
Lisgould (Middleton)	1847
Lislee (Bandon)	1809
Litter (Fermoy)	1811
Macroom	1727
Magourney (Coachford)	1757
Mallow	1776
Marmulland (Passage West)	1801
Middleton	1810
Monanimy (Mallow)	1812
Monkstown	1842
Mourne Abbey (Mallow)	1807
Murragh (Bandon)	1754
Nathlash (Kildorrery)	1844

Nohoval (Kinsale)	1785
Queenstown (Cobh)	1761
Rahan (Mallow)	1773
Rathcooney (Glanmire)	1749
Rincurran (Kinsale)	1793
Rushbrook	1806
Templemartin (Bandon)	1806
Timoleague	1823
Tullylease	1850
Wallstown (Doneraile)	1829
Youghal	1665

Co. Derry

Ballinderry (Moneymore)	1802
Ballyeglish (Moneymore)	1868
Ballynascreen	1808
Banagher (Derry)	1839
Castledawson	1744
Clooney	1867
Coleraine	1769
Cumber (Clady)	1804
Desartlyn (Moneymore)	1797
Desartmartin	1797
Drumachose (Limavady)	1728
Dungiven	1778
Glendermot	1810
Kilcronaghan (Tubbermore)	1749
Killowen (Coleraine)	1824
Kilrea	1801
Learmount (Derry)	1832
Londonderry	1642
Maghera	1785
Magherafelt	1718
Tamlaght (Portglenone)	1858
Tamlaghard (Magilligan)	1747
Tamlaghfinlagan	1796
Termoneeny (Castledawson)	1821
Woods Chapel	1800

Co. Donegal

Ardara	1829
Burt	1802
Clondevaddock (Ramelton)	1794
Donegal	1803
Drumholm (Ballintra)	1691
Fahan (Buncrana)	1761
Finner	1815
Glencolumbkille	1827

Inniskeel (Ardara)	1826
Inver	1805
Kilbarrow (Ballyshannon)	1785
Kilcar (Killybegs)	1819
Killaghtee (Glenties)	1810
Killybegs	1789
Kilteevogue (Stranorlar)	1818
Moville	1814
Muff	1803
Raphoe	1831
Stranorlar	1821
Taughboyne (Derry)	1819
Templecarn	1825
Tullyaughnish (Ramelton)	1798

Co. Down

Aghaderg (Loughbrickland)	1814
Annalong (Castlewellan)	1842
Ardkeen	1746
Ballee (Downpatrick)	1792
Ballyculter (Strangford)	1777
Ballyhalbert (Kircubbin)	1852
Ballyphilip (Portaferry)	1745
Ballywalter (Newtownards)	1844
Bangor	1803
Clonduff (Hilltown)	1782
Comber	1683
Donaghadee	1778
Donaghcloney	1834
Downpatrick	1750
Drumballyroney (Rathfriland)	1831
Drumbeg (Lisburn)	1823
Drumbo (Lisburn)	1791
Drumgooland	1779
Dundonald (Belfast)	1811
Gilford	1869
Hillsborough	1777
Holywood	1806
Inch (Downpatrick)	1767
Innishargy	1783
Kilbroney (Rostrevor)	1814
Kilcoo	1786
Killaney	1858
Killinchy	1819
Kilmood (Killinchy)	1822
Kilmore	1820
Knockbreda (Belfast)	1784

Knocknamuckley (Gilford)	1838
Loughlin Island (Clough)	1760
Magheralin	1692
Moira	1845
Moyntags (Lurgan)	1822
Newcastle	1823
Newry	1822
Saintfield	1724
Seagoe	1672
Seapatrick (Banbridge)	1802
Tullylish (Banbridge)	1820
Tyrella (Clough)	1839
Warrenpoint	1825

Co. Dublin

Balbriggan	1838
Blackrock	1855
Castleknock	1709
Chapelizod	1812
Clondalkin	1728
Clonsilla	1830
Donabate	1811
Donnybrook	1712
Holmpatrick	1779
Howth	1804
Irishtown (Sandymount)	1812
Killesk	1829
Kilmainham	1857
Kilsallaghan	1818
Kilternan	1817
Kingstown (Dun Laoghaire)	1843
Lusk	1809
Malahide	1822
Monkstown	1680
Newcastle	1773
Santry	1753
Swords	1705
Taney (Dundrum)	1835
Whitechurch (Terenure)	1825

For Dublin City parishes see page 55.

Co. Fermanagh

Aghadrumsee (Clones)	1821
Aghalurcher (Lisnaskea)	1788
Aghaveagh (Lisnaskea)	1815
Belleek	1822
Bohoe (Enniskillen)	1840
Clabby (Fivemiletown)	1862
Coolaghty (Kesh)	1835
Derryvullan (Enniskillen)	1803

Co. Fermanagh (Cont/d.)

Devenish	
(Ballyshannon)	1800
Drumkeeran (Kesh)	1801
Galloon	1798
Innishmacsaint	1813
Killesher	
(Enniskillen)	1798
Kinawley	1761
Lisnaskea	1804
Mullaghafad	
(Scotstown)	1836
Magheracross	1800
Magheraculmoney	
(Kesh)	1767
Maguiresbridge	1840
Tempo	1836
Trory	
(Enniskillen)	1779

Co. Galway

Ahascragh	1775
Ardrahan	1804
Aughrim	1814
Ballinacourty	
(Oranmore)	1838
Ballinakill	
(Clifden)	1852
Ballinakill	
(Portumna)	1766
Creagh	
(Ballinasloe)	1823
Galway	
St. Nicholas	1782
Inniscaltra	
(Mountshannon)	1851
Kilcolgan	1847
Kilcummin	
(Oughterard)	1812
Killannin	
(Headford)	1844
Loughrea	1747
Moylough	
(Mountbellew)	1821
Moyrus	
(Roundstone)	1841
Omey (Clifden)	1831
Tuam	1808

Co. Kerry

Aghadoe	
(Killarney)	1842
Ballymacelligot	1817
Ballynacourty	
(Kilflynn)	1803
Ballyseedy	
(Tralee)	1830
Castleisland	1835
Dingle	1707
Dromod (Prior)	1827
Kenmare	1799
Kilcolman	
(Killorglin)	1802
Kilgarvan	1811
Kilnaughton (Tarbert)	1793
Liselton	1840
Listowel	1790
Tralee	1771
Valentia	1826

Co. Kildare

Athy	1669
Ballymore-Eustace	1838
Ballysax	1830
Carbery	1814
Celbridge	1777
Clane	1802
Clonsast	
(Celbridge)	1805
Harristown	
(Athy)	1666
Kilcullen	1778
Kildare	
St. Bridget	1801
Kill	1814
Lackagh	
(Monastereven)	1830
Naas	1679
Straffan (Naas)	1838
Timolin	
(Baltinglass)	1812

Co. Kilkenny

Blackrath	
(Kilkenny)	1810
Castlecomer	1799
Clonmore	1817
Fertagh	
(Johnstown)	1797
Fiddown	
(Pilltown)	1686
Gallskill	
(Pilltown)	1753
Graig	1827
Grangesylvae	
(Gowran)	1850
Innistiogue	1797
Kilbeacon	
(Pilltown)	1813
Kilcollum	1817
Kilkenny	
St. Canice	1789
St. Mary	1729
Kilmacow	1792
Kilmanagh (Callan)	1784
Kilmoganny	
(Knocktopher	1782
Macully (Pilltown)	1817

Co. Leitrim

Drumlease	
(Dromahaire)	1828
Kiltoghert	
(Carrick-on-Shannon)	1810
Manorhamilton	1816
Outragh (Ballinamore)	1833

Co. Leix (Queen's)

Abbeyleix	1781
Ballyfin	1821
Castletown	1802
Clonenagh	
(Mountrath)	1749
Coolbanagher	1802
Durrow	1731
Killeban	1802
Lea	
(Portarlington)	1801
Maryborough	
(Portlaoise)	1793
Mountmellick	1840
Offerlane	
(Borris-in-Ossory)	1807
Oregan	
(Rosenallis)	1801
Portarlington	1694
Rathdowney	1756
Rathsaran	
(Rathdowney)	1810
Stradbally	1772
Timahoe	1845

Co. Limerick

Abington	1811
Adare	1804
Ardcanny	
(Pallaskenry)	1802
Ballingarry	1785
Bruff	1850
Cahernarry	
(Nr. Limerick)	1857
Cappamore	1858
Doon	1804
Fedamore	1840
Kildimo	1809
Kilfergus (Foynes)	1812
Kilfinane	1804
Kilflyn	
(Ardpatrick)	1813
Kilkeedy	
(Mungret)	1799
Kilmoylan	1812
Limerick	
St. John	1697
St. Mary	1726
St. Michael	1801
St. Munchin	1700
Rathkeale	1746
Rathronan (Ardagh)	1818
Shanagolden	1803
Tullybrackey (Bruff)	1820

Co. Longford

Ardagh	1811
Clonbroney	1821
Clongesh	1820
Forgney	
(Ballymahon)	1803
Granard	1820
Kilcommick	
(Ballymahon)	1795
Killashee (Lanesboro')	1771
Mostrim	
(Edgeworthstown)	1801
Moydow	1794
Street	1801
Shrule	1821
Templemichael	
(Longford)	1795

Co. Louth

Ardee	1735
Charlestown	1822
Collon	1790
Drogheda	
St. Peter	1654
St. Mary	1811
Dundalk	1729
Jonesborough	1812
Mellifont	1812
Tullyallen	1812

Co. Mayo

Achill	1854
Aghagower	
(Westport)	1825
Ballincholla	
(The Neale)	1831
Ballysakeery	
(Ballina)	1802
Cong	1811
Crossmolina	1768
Dugort	1838
Killala	1757
Kilmainemore	
(Ballinrobe)	1744
Kilmoremoy	
(Ballinahaglish)	1801
Knappagh	
(Westport)	1855
Turlough	
(Castlebar)	1821
Westport	1801

Co. Monaghan

Ballybay	1813
Carrickmacross	1796
Castleblaney	1810
Clones	1682
Currin	
(Rockcorry)	1810
Donagh	
(Glasslough)	1796
Emyvale (Trough)	1809
Killarney	
(Carrickmacross)	1825
Killeevan (Clones)	1811
Kilmore	1796
Magheracloone	1806
Monaghan	1802
Newbliss	1841
Tedavnet	
(Scotstown)	1822
Tyholland	
(Monaghan)	1806

Co. Meath

see page 145

Co. Offaly (King's)

Ballyboy	
(Frankford)	1796
Birr	1772
Castlejordan	
(Edenderry)	1823
Cloneyhork	
(Portarlington)	1824
Clonmacnoise	1824
Durrow	1816
Ettagh (Roscrea)	1825
Ferbane	1819
Gallen (Cloghan)	1842
Geashill	1713
Kilbride	
(Tullamore)	1811
Killeigh	
(Tullamore)	1808
Kinnitty	1800
Monasteroris	
(Edenderry)	1698
Shinrone	1741
Templeharry	
(Shinrone)	1800

Co. Roscommon

Ardcarna (Boyle)	1820
Boyle	1793
Bumlin	
(Strokestown)	1811
Croghan	
(Boyle)	1862
Estersrow	
(Boyle)	1800
Kilbryan	
(Boyle)	1852
Kilglass	
(Rooskey)	1823
Kilkeevan	
(Castlerea)	1748
Kiltoom	
(Athlone)	1797
Kiltullagh	
(Castlerea)	1822

Co. Sligo

Ballysumaghan	
(Collooney)	1828
Drumcliff	1805
Easkey	1822
Emlafad	
(Ballymote)	1831
Kilmactranny	
(Boyle)	1816
Knocknarea	
(Sligo)	1842
Lissadell	1836
Sligo	
St. John	1802

Co. Tipperary

Aghnameadle	
(Moneygall)	1834
Ballingarry	
(Cashel)	1816

Ballintemple	
(Golden)	1805
Borrisnafarney	
(Roscrea)	1827
Cahir	1801
Carrick-on-Suir	1803
Cashel	1668
Clonmel	1766
Clonoulty	
(Cashel)	1817
Cloughjordan	1827
Cullen	
(Tipperary)	1770
Dunkerrin	1800
Fethard	1804
Holycross	1784
Innislonagh	
(Clonmel)	1801
Mealiffe	
(Thurles)	1791
Modreeny	1827
Newport	1782
Shanrahan	
(Clogheen)	1793
Templemichael	
(Carrick-on-Suir)	1791
Terry Glass	
(Borrisokane)	1809
Tipperary	1779
Toem (Cashel)	1802
Tullamelan	
(Clonmel)	1823

Co. Tyrone

Arboe	
(Cookstown)	1773
Ardtrea	
(Cookstown)	1811
Badoney (Gortin)	1818
Ballyclog	
(Stewartstown)	1818
Brackaville	1836
Caledon	1791
Camus	1803
Cappagh	1758
Carnteel	
(Aughnacloy)	1805
Clonfeacle	
(Dungannon)	1763
Derg (Castlederg)	1807
Derrylorgan	
(Cookstown)	1796
Desertcreat	
(Cookstown)	1812
Donagheady	
(Strabane)	1754
Donaghenry	
(Dungannon)	1734
Donaghmore	
(Castlefin)	1748
Drumglass	
(Dungannon)	1664
Drumrath	
(Omagh)	1800
Edenderry	
(Omagh)	1841

Errigal	
(Garvagh)	1812
Findonagh	
(Donacavey)	1777
Fivemiletown	1804
Kildress	
(Cookstown)	1749
Killyman	
(Dungannon)	1741
Kilskerry	
(Enniskillen)	1772
Lissan	
(Cookstown)	1753
Sixmilecross	1836
Termonmongan	
(Castlederg)	1812
Tullyniskin	
(Dungannon)	1794
Urney (Strabane)	1813

Co. Waterford

Cappoquin	1844
Dungarvan	1741
Innislonagh	1800
Killea	
(Dunmore)	1816
Kilmeadon	1683
Killrosantry	1838
Kilwatermoy	1860
Kill (Passage)	1730
Lismore	1693
Macully	1817
Portlaw	1741
Tallow	1772
Templemichael	1801
Waterford	
St. Olave's	1658
St. Patrick's	1723

Co. Westmeath

Abbeyshrule	1821
Athlone	
St. Mary	1746
Delvin	1817
Kilbixy	
(Ballinacargy)	1843
Kilkenny	
(Ballymore)	1783
Killucan	1700
Mayne	
(Castlepollard)	1808
Willbrooke	
(Athlone)	1756

Co. Wexford

Ardamine	
(Gorey)	1807
Ballycanew	1733
Ballycarney	
(Ferns)	1835
Carnew	1749
Clonegal	1792
Clonmore	1828
Enniscorthy	1798
Ferns	1775
Gorey	1801

Inch (New Ross)	1726
Killanne	1771
Killegney	
(Enniscorthy)	1800
Killeney	1788
Killinick	
(Wexford)	1804
Killurin	1816
Kilmallog	
(Wexford)	1813
Kilnehue	
(Gorey)	1817
Kilpipe (Arklow)	1828
Kiltennell	
(Gorey)	1806
Leskinfere	
(Gorey)	1802
Mulrankin	1768
Newtownbarry	
(Bunclody)	1779
Owenduff	
(Taghmon)	1752
Rathaspick	1844
Rossdroit	
(Enniscorthy)	1802
Tacumshane	
(Rosslare)	1832
Templescobin	
(Enniscorthy)	1802
Tomhaggard	
(Rosslare)	1809
Toombe (Ferns)	1770
Wexford	1674

Co. Wicklow

Ballinaclash	
(Rathdrum)	1839
Ballintemple	
(Arklow)	1823
Ballynure	
(Dunlavin)	1807
Blessington	1695
Bray	1666
Castlemacadam	
(Ovoca)	1720
Crosspatrick	
(Tinahely)	1830
Delgany	1666
Dunlavin	1697
Glenealy	1825
Kilcommon	
(Hacketstown)	1814
Killiskey	
(Ashford)	1818
Mullinacuff	
(Tinahely)	1838
Newcastle	1698
Ovoca	1720
Powerscourt	1677
Preban	
(Tinahely)	1827
Rathdrum	1706
Shillelagh	1833
Stratford	
(Baltinglass)	1812
Wicklow	1655

PRESBYTERIAN REGISTERS

†In Presbyterian Historical Society's Archives, Belfast.

Co. Antrim

†Antrim	1674
Armoy	1842
Ballycarny	1832
Ballycastle	1829
Ballyeaston (Ballyclare)	1821
Ballylinney (Ballyclare)	1837
Ballymena	1825
Ballymoney	1817
Ballynure	1819
Ballywillan (Portrush)	1816
Ballymacarrett (Belfast)	1837
Ballysillan	1839
Belfast	
Fisherwick Place	1810
†Rosemary St.	1722
Broadmills (Lisburn)	1824
Broughshane	1830
Buckal	1841
†Carnmoney	1708
Carrickfergus	1823
Castlereagh	1807
+Cliftonville	1825
Cloughwater	1852
Connor (Ballymena)	1819
Crumlin	1839
Cullybackey	1812
†Dongore (Templepatrick)	1806
†Drumbo (Lisburn)	1764
†Dundonald (Belfast)	1678
Dundron (Belfast)	1829
Finvoy (Ballymoney)	1843
Gilnahurk (Belfast)	1797
Glenarn	1850
Glenwherry (Ballymena)	1845
Grange (Toomebridge)	1824
Kilraught (Ballymorey)	1836
Larne	1824
Loughmourne	1848
†Lylehill (Templepatrick)	1832
Masside	1843
Portrush	1843
Raloo (Larne)	1840
Randalstown	1837
Rasharkin	1834
Templepatrick	1831
Tobberleigh	1831

Co. Armagh

Ahorey (Loughgall)	1838
†Armagh	1707
Bessbrook	1854
Cladymore	1848
Clare (Tandragee)	1838
Cremore	1831
Donacloney (Lurgan)	1798
Gilford	1843
Keady	1819
Kingsmills (Whitecross)	1842
Knappagh	1842
Lislooney	1836
Loughgall	1842
Lurgan	1746
Markethill	1821
†Mountnorris	1804
Newmills (Portadown)	1838
Newtownhamilton	1823
Portadown	1822
Poyntzpass	1850
Richhill	1856
Tandragee	1835
Tullyallen	1795
Vinecash (Portadown)	1838

Co. Cavan

Bailieborough	1852
Ballyjamesduff	1845
Bellasis	1845
Cavan	1851
Cootehill	1828
†Killeshandra	1743

Co. Cork

Bandon	1842
Cork	1832
Cobh (Queenstown)	1847

Co. Derry

†Ballykelly	1699
Banagher (Derry)	1834
Boveedy (Kilrea)	1841
Castledawson	1835
†Coleraine	1842
Crossgar (Coleraine)	1839
†Cumber (Claudy)	1827
Derrymore (Limavady)	1825
Derry	1815
Draperstown	1837
Drumachose	

(Limavady)	1838
Dunboe (Coleraine)	1843
Dungiven	1835
†Faughanvale (Eglinton)	1819
Garvagh	1795
Gortnassy (Derry)	1839
†Killaigh (Coleraine)	1805
Kilrea	1825
Lecompher (Moneymore)	1825
Limavady	1832
Maghera	1843
†Magherafelt	1703
Magilligan	1814
Moneymore	1827
Portstewart	1829

Co. Donegal

Ballindrait	1819
Ballyshannon	1836
Buncrana	1836
Burt	1834
Carnone (Raphoe)	1834
†Carrigart	1844
Convoy	1822
Donegal	1825
Donoughmore (Castlefin)	1844
Knowhead (Muff)	1826
Letterkenny	1841
Monreagh (Derry)	1845
Moville	1834
Newtowncunning- ham	1830
Ramelton	1808
Raphoe	1829
St. Johnston	1838
Trentagh (Kilmacrennan)	1836

Co. Down

Anaghlone (Banbridge)	1839
Anahilt (Hillsborough)	1780
Annalong	1840
Ardaragh (Newry)	1804
Balltdown (Banbridge)	1809
Ballygilbert	1841
Ballygraney (Bangor)	1838
Ballynahinch	1841
Ballyroney (Banbridge)	1831
Ballywalter	1824
†Banbridge	1756
Bangor	1833

Carrowdore (Greyabbey)	1843
Clarkesbridge (Newry)	1833
Clonduff (Banbridge)	1842
Clough (Downpatrick)	1836
Cloughey	1844
Comber	1847
Conligh (Newtownards)	1845
Donaghadee	1822
Downpatrick	1827
Dromara	1823
Dromore	1834
Drumbanagher (Derry)	1832
Drumgooland	1833
Drumlee (Banbridge)	1826
Edengrove (Ballynahinch)	1829
Glastry	1728
Groomsport	1841
Hillsborough	1832
Kilkeel	1842
Killinchy	1835
†Killyleagh	1693
Kilmore (Crossgar)	1833
†Kirkcubbin	1785
Leitrim (Banbridge)	1837
Lissera (Crossgar)	1809
Loughagherry (Hillsborough)	1801
Loughbrickland	1842
Magherally (Banbridge)	1837
Millisle	1773
Mourne (Kilkeel)	1840
Newry	1829
Newtownards	1833
†Portaferry	1699
Raffrey (Crossgar)	1843
Rathfriland	1804
Rostrevor	1851
Saintfield	1831
†Scarva	1807
Seaforde	1826
Strangford	1846
Tullylish (Gilford)	1813
Warrenpoint	1832

Co. Dublin

Abbey (Abbey St.)	1777
Ormond Quay	1787
Clontarf	1836

144

Co. Fermanagh

Enniskillen	1837
Lisbellaw	1849
Pettigo	1844

Co. Galway

Galway	1831

Co. Kerry

Tralee	1840

Co. Laois (Queens)

†Mountmellick	1849

Co. Leitrim

Carrigallen	1844

Co. Limerick

Limerick	1829

Co. Longford

Tully (Edgeworthstown)	1844

Co. Louth

Corvally (Dundalk)	1840
Dundalk	1819

Co. Mayo

Dromore (Ballina)	1849

Co. Monaghan

Ballyalbany	1802
Ballybay	1833
Ballyhobridge (Clones)	1846
Broomfield (Castleblaney)	1841
†Cahans (Ballybay)	1752
Castleblaney	1832
Clones	1856
Clontibret	1825
Corlea	1835
Derryvalley (Ballybay)	1816
Drumkeen (Newbliss)	1856
†Frankford (Castleblaney)	1820
†Glennan (Glasslough)	1805
Middletown (Glasslough)	1829
Monaghan	1824
Newbliss	1856
Scotstown	1856
Stonebridge (Newbliss)	1821

Co. Tyrone

Albany (Stewartstown)	1838

Ardstraw	1837
Aughataire (Fivemiletown)	1836
Aughnacloy	1843
Ballygawley	1843
Ballygorey (Cookstown)	1834
Ballynahatty (Omagh)	1843
Ballyreagh (Ballygawley)	1843
Brigh (Stewartstown)	1836
Carland (Castlecaulfield)	1759
Castlederg	1823
Cleggan (Cookstown)	1848
Clenanees (Castlecaulfield)	1840
Clogher	1819
Coagh	1839
Cookstown	1836
Donaghheady (Strabane)	1838
Drumguin	1845
Dungannon	1790
Edenderry (Omagh)	1845
Eglish (Dungannon)	1839
Fintona	1836
Gillygooly (Omagh)	1848

Gortin	1843
Leckpatrick (Strabane)	1838
Minterburn (Caledon)	1829
Moy	1851
Newmills (Dungannon)	1850
Omagh	1821
Orritor (Cookstown)	1831
Pomeroy	1841
Sandholey (Cookstown)	1844
Strabane	1828
Urney (Sion Mills)	1837

Co. Waterford

Waterford	1770

Co. Wexford

Wexford	1844

Co. Wicklow

Bray	1836

CHURCH OF IRELAND REGISTERS (continued)

Co. Meath

Athboy	1736
Ballymaglasson (Dunshaughlin)	1800
Clonard	1792
Drumconrath	1785
Dunshaughlin	1800

Kells	1773
Killochonagan (Trim)	1853
Kilmore (Kilcock)	1800
Knockmark (Dunshaughlin)	1825
Nobber	1828

Oldcastle	1814
Rathbeggan (Dunboyne)	1821
Rathcore (Enfield)	1810
Syddan (Navan)	1720
Trim	1836